S0-BMV-081

The Parables

Understanding the Stories Jesus Told

SIMON J. KISTEMAKER

Baker Books

A Division of Baker Book House Co
Grand Rapids, Michigan 49516

Copyright 1980 by Baker Book House Company

Published by Baker Books
a division of Baker Book House Company
P.O. Box 6287, Grand Rapids, MI 49516-6287

New paperback edition published 2002

Previously published under the title *The Parables of Jesus*

Second printing, November 2002

Printed in the United States of America

All rights reserved. No part of this publication may be reproduced, stored in a retrieval system, or transmitted in any form or by any means—for example, electronic, photocopy, recording—without the prior written permission of the publisher. The only exception is brief quotations in printed reviews.

Library of Congress Cataloging-in-Publication Data

Kistemaker, Simon.
    [Parables of Jesus]
    The parables : understanding the stories Jesus told / Simon J. Kistemaker.
       p.   cm.
    Originally published : The parables of Jesus, ©1980.
    Includes bibliographical references and index.
    ISBN 0-8010-6391-4 (pbk.)
    1. Jesus Christ—Parables. I. Title.
BT375.3 .K57 2002
226.8′06—dc21   2001056683

Unless otherwise indicated, Scripture is taken from the HOLY BIBLE, NEW INTERNATIONAL VERSION®. NIV®. Copyright © 1973, 1978, 1984 by International Bible Society. Used by permission of Zondervan Publishing House. All rights reserved.

For current information about all releases from Baker Book House, visit our web site:
http://www.bakerbooks.com

The Parables

Contents

Preface

Few are the books written from an evangelical perspective covering all the parables and most of the parabolic sayings. In this book I have tried to meet the need of pastors and students of the Bible who wish to consult an evangelical book comprising all the parables of Jesus and the majority of the parabolic sayings recorded in the Synoptic Gospels.

This book is aimed at the level of theologically trained pastors. But because technical details have been relegated to endnotes, the text itself is user-friendly to any serious student of the Bible. The book features a select bibliography that directs the readers to appropriate sources should they wish to pursue a topic further.

Many people have helped to make this book a reality. I wish to express my thanks and appreciation to Reformed Theological Seminary for granting me a sabbatical leave. I thank the staff of the Tyndale House Library (Cambridge, England), the University of Cambridge Library, and Reformed Theological Seminary Library. I also express my gratitude to the editorial staff at Baker Book House for their insight, interest, and assistance.

Introduction

Newspapers often put a cartoon in a prominent place on the editorial page. With a few simple lines, the artist sketches a caricature of the political, social, or economic situation we face. By means of a drawing, he conveys a striking message even an editor cannot match in eloquence.

Jesus drew verbal pictures of the world around him by telling parables. By teaching in parables he depicted what was happening in real life. That is, he told a story, taken from daily life, using an accepted, familiar setting, to teach a new lesson. That lesson quite often came at the end of the story and had an impact that required time for absorption and assimilation. When we hear a parable, we nod in agreement because the story is true to life and readily understood. Although the application of the parable may be heard, it is not always grasped. We see the story unfold before our eyes, but we do not perceive the significance of it.[1] The truth remains hidden until our eyes are opened and we see clearly. Then the new lesson of the parable becomes meaningful. It is as Jesus told his disciples, "The secret of the kingdom of God has been given to you. But to those on the outside everything is said in parables" (Mark 4:11).

FORMS

The word *parable* in the New Testament has a broad connotation, including parable forms that are generally divided into three categories.[2] They are the true parables, story parables, and illustrations.

1. The true parables. These use an illustration from daily life within reach of anyone who hears the parable. Everyone acknowledges the truth conveyed; there is no basis for any objection or criticism. Everyone has seen seed growing by itself (Mark 4:26–29); yeast at work in a

batch of dough (Matt. 13:33); children playing games in the marketplace (Matt. 11:16–19; Luke 7:31, 32); a sheep wandering away from the flock (Matt. 18:12–14); and a woman losing a coin in her house (Luke 15:8–10). These and many other parables start with self-evident truths portraying either nature or human life. They are usually related in the present tense.

2. Story parables. Differing from a true parable, the story parable does not rely on an obvious truth or generally accepted custom. The true parable is told in the present tense as fact; the story parable, on the other hand, refers to a particular event that happened in the past—usually the experience of one person. It is the experience of the farmer who sowed wheat but eventually learned that his enemy had sown weeds on that same plot of ground (Matt. 13:24–30). It is the story of the rich man whose manager had wasted his possessions (Luke 16:1–9). It is the account of the judge who, because of the repeated plea of a widow, administered justice (Luke 18:1–8). The historicity of these stories is not at stake, because not the fact but the truth conveyed is significant.

3. Illustrations. Illustrative stories appearing in the Gospel of Luke are usually categorized as example stories. They include the parable of the good Samaritan (Luke 10:30–37); the parable of the rich fool (Luke 12:16–21); the parable of the rich man and Lazarus (Luke 16:19–31); and the parable of the Pharisee and the tax collector (Luke 18:9–14). These illustrations differ from the story parables in design. Whereas the story parable is an analogy, illustrations exhibit examples to be either imitated or avoided. They focus directly on the character and the conduct of an individual; the story parable does this only indirectly.

Classifying parables is not always a simple matter. Some parables display characteristics of two groups—the true parable and the story parable—and may be grouped with either one. Also, the Gospels contain numerous parabolic sayings. It is often difficult to determine precisely which saying of Jesus constitutes a true parable and which is a parabolic saying. Jesus' teaching on the yeast (Luke 13:20, 21) is classified as a true parable, but his longer message on the salt (Luke 14:34, 35) is called a parabolic saying. Moreover, some sayings of Jesus are introduced as parables. For instance, "He also told them this parable: 'Can a blind man lead a blind man? Will they not both fall into a pit?'" (Luke 6:39).

How does a parable differ from an allegory? John Bunyan's *Pilgrim's Progress* is an allegorical presentation of a Christian's journey through life. The names and circumstances in the book are substitutes for reality. Every fact, feature, and name is symbolic, and must be translated point by point into real life in order to be properly understood. A parable, on the other hand, is true to life and generally teaches only one basic truth. In his parables, Jesus used many metaphors, such as a king, servants, and virgins, but these are not removed from reality. They never relate a world of fantasy or fiction. They are stories and examples from the world in which Jesus lived, and they are told in order to convey a spiritual truth by means of a single point of comparison. The details of the story are supportive of the message the parable conveys. They should not be given a point-by-point analysis and interpreted as an allegory, for then they lose their significance.

COMPOSITION

Although it is generally true that a parable teaches only one basic lesson, this rule should not be pressed too far. Some of Jesus' parables are complex in composition. The sower parable is comprised of four parts, and each part calls for an interpretation. Likewise, the wedding banquet parable is not a single story but has an additional section about a guest without the proper wedding clothes. And the conclusion of the tenants parable switches from the vineyard imagery to that of the building trade. In view of this, the exegete is wise not to strive for a one-point interpretation of complex parables.

While reading the parables of Jesus, one wonders why many details have been left out that would be expected as part of the stories. For example, in the story of the friend who knocks at his neighbor's door in the middle of the night to ask for three loaves of bread, the neighbor's wife is not mentioned. In the parable of the prodigal son, the father is a leading character, but not a word is said about the mother. The parable of the ten virgins introduces the bridegroom, but completely ignores the bride. These details, however, are not relevant to the general composition of the parables, especially if we understand the literary device of *triads* that Jesus often used in his parables. In the parable of the friend at midnight, there are three characters: the traveler, the friend, and the neighbor. The prodigal son parable also contains three persons: the father, the younger son, and the older brother. And in the story of the ten virgins there are three elements: the five wise virgins, the five foolish virgins, and the bridegroom.[3]

Moreover, in Jesus' parables it is not the beginning of the story but the end that is important. The accent falls on the last person that is mentioned, the last deed, or the last saying. The so-called end-stress in the parable is a deliberate design in its composition.[4] It was not the priest or the Levite who alleviated the wounded man's pain but the Samaritan. Even though the servant who gained five additional talents and the servant who presented two more talents to his master received praise and commendation, it was the servant's deed of burying his one talent in the ground that brought him scorn and condemnation. And in the parable of the landowner, who throughout the day kept hiring men to work in his vineyard and at six o'clock heard complaints from some of the workers, it is the landowner's reply that is most significant: "Friend, I am not being unfair to you. . . . Or are you envious because I am generous?" (Matt. 20:13, 15).

The art of composing and telling parables demonstrated by Jesus finds no parallel in literature. But close to the parables of Jesus are those of the ancient rabbis of the first and second centuries in the Christian era. Rabbinic parables are usually introduced by a stock formula: "A parable: To what is it like?" Also, in some parables the literary devices of the triad and the end-stress are used. For example:

> A parable: To what is this like? To a man who was travelling on the road when he encountered a wolf and escaped from it, and he went along relating the affair of the wolf. He then encountered a lion and escaped from it, and went along relating the affair of the lion. He then encountered a snake and escaped from it, whereupon he forgot the two previous incidents and went along relating the affair of the snake. So with Israel: the latter troubles make them forget the earlier ones.[5]

However, the similarity between Jesus' parables and those of the rabbis is only formal. Rabbinic parables normally are introduced to explain or elucidate the Law, verses of Scripture, or a doctrine. They are not used for teaching new truths, as is the case with the parables of Jesus. By means of his parables Jesus explained the great themes of his teaching: the kingdom of heaven; the love, grace, and mercy of God; the rule and return of the Son of God; and the being and destiny of mortals.[6] Although rabbinic parables fail to teach anything beyond an application of the Law, Jesus' parables are part of God's revelation. In his parables Jesus reveals new truths, for he was commissioned by God to make known God's will and Word (John 3:34). The parables of Jesus, therefore, are God's revelation; rabbinic parables are not.

PURPOSE

The parables show that Jesus was fully acquainted with human life in its multiple ways and means. He was knowledgeable in farming, sowing seed, detecting weeds, and reaping a harvest. He was at home in the vineyard, knew the times of reaping fruit from vine and fig tree, and was aware of the wages paid for a day's work. Not only was he familiar with the workaday world of the farmer, the fisherman, the builder, and the merchant, but he moved with equal ease among the managers of estates, the ministers of finance at a royal court, the judge in a court of law, the Pharisees, and the tax collectors. He understood Lazarus's poverty, yet he was invited to dine with the rich. His parables portray the lives of men, women, and children, the poor and the rich, the outcast and the exalted. Because of his acquaintance with the broad expanse of human life, he was able to minister to people of all social strata. He spoke the language of the people and taught them at their own level. Jesus used parables to make his message accessible to the people, to teach the crowds the Word of God, to call his listeners to repentance and faith, to challenge the believers to put words into deeds, and to admonish his followers to watchfulness.

Jesus taught the parables to communicate the message of salvation in a clear and simple manner. His audience could readily understand the story of the prodigal son, the two debtors, the great supper, and the Pharisee and tax collector. In the parables, they met Jesus as the Christ, who taught with authority the message of God's redemptive love.

From the Gospel accounts, however, it appears that the interpretation of the parables took place in the private circle of the disciples. Jesus told them, "The secret of the kingdom of God has been given to you. But to those on the outside everything is said in parables so that,

> 'they may be ever seeing but never perceiving,
> and ever hearing but never understanding;
> otherwise they might turn and be forgiven!'"

> Mark 4:11, 12

Does this mean that Jesus, who was sent by God to proclaim redemption to fallen, sinful human beings, hides this message in the form of incomprehensible parables? Are parables some kind of riddles understood only by those who are initiated?

The words of Mark 4:11, 12 need to be understood in the broader context in which the writer places them.[7] In the preceding chapter Mark relates that Jesus encountered blatant unbelief and direct opposition. He was accused of being possessed by Beelzebub and of driving out demons by the prince of demons (Mark 3:22). The contrast Jesus presents, therefore, is one between believers and unbelievers, between followers and opponents, between receivers and rejecters of God's revelation. Those who do the will of God receive the message of the parables, for they belong to the family of Jesus (Mark 3:35). Those who seek to destroy Jesus (Mark 3:6) have hardened their hearts to the knowledge of salvation. It is a matter of faith and unbelief. Believers hear the parables, and receive them in faith and understanding, even though full comprehension may come only gradually. Unbelievers reject the parables because they are alien to their thinking.[8] They refuse to perceive and understand God's truth. Thus, because of their blind eyes and deaf ears, they deprive themselves of the salvation Jesus proclaims, and they bring upon themselves God's judgment.

That the disciples of Jesus at first did not fully understand the parable of the sower is not surprising (Mark 4:13). The teaching of the parable perplexed Jesus' immediate followers because they had not yet seen the significance of his person and ministry in relation to God's truth revealed in the parable. Only by faith were they able to see the truth to which the parables bore witness.[9] Jesus provided a comprehensive interpretation for the parable of the sower and the parable of the wheat and weeds. (In others he at times added clarification in a conclusion.) The disciples were given insight into the relationship between the events Jesus depicted in the parable of the sower and the kingdom of heaven inaugurated in the person of Jesus, the Messiah.[10]

INTERPRETATION

In the early church, the church fathers began to look for various hidden meanings concerning the coming of Jesus in the Old Testament Scriptures. As a natural consequence of this trend, the Fathers began to find hidden meanings in the parables of Jesus. Perhaps they were influenced by Jewish apologetics in substituting the simplicity of Scripture for subtle speculations. In any event, the result was allegorical interpretations of the parables. Thus from the time of the church fathers until the middle of the nineteenth century, most exegetes interpreted the parables allegorically.

Origen, for instance, believed that the parable of the ten virgins was filled with hidden symbols. The virgins, said Origen, are all the people who have received the Word of God. The wise believe and live a righteous life; the foolish believe but fail to act. The five lamps of the wise represent the five natural senses, which are all trimmed by proper use. The five lamps of the foolish fail to give light and move out into the night of the world. The oil is the teaching of the Word, and the sellers of oil are the teachers. The price they ask for the oil is perseverance. Midnight is the time of reckless neglect. The great cry that is heard comes from the angels who awaken all people. And the bridegroom is Christ who comes to meet his bride, the church. So Origen interpreted the parable.

For commentators in the nineteenth century it was still customary to identify the individual details of a parable. In the parable of the ten virgins, the burning lamp represented good works, and the oil corresponded to the believer's faith. Others saw oil as a symbolic representation of the Holy Spirit.

Yet not all interpreters of the parables took the allegorical path. In the time of the Reformation, Martin Luther tried to change the direction of interpreting Scripture. He preferred a method of biblical exegesis that included a consideration of the historical setting and the grammatical structure of a parable. John Calvin was even more direct. He avoided allegorical interpretations of a parable altogether and instead sought to establish the main point of its teaching. When he had ascertained the meaning of a parable, he did not trouble himself with its details. In his opinion, the details had nothing to do with what Jesus intended to teach with the parable.

During the second half of the nineteenth century, C. E. van Koetsveld, a Dutch scholar, gave further impetus to the approach initiated by the Reformers. He pointed out that the extravagant allegorical interpretations of the parables given by numerous commentators obscured rather than clarified the teaching of Jesus.[11] To interpret a parable properly, the exegete must grasp its basic meaning and distinguish between what is essential and what is not. Van Koetsveld was succeeded in his approach to the parables by the German theologian A. Jülicher, who observed that although the term *parable* is used frequently by the evangelists, the word *allegory* never occurs in their Gospel accounts. Succinctly put, an allegory is a series of symbols that need to be interpreted, while a parable is a single simile that has only one point of reference.[12] To be complete, however, we admit that some parables feature allegorical elements, but these must be seen as exceptions and not the rule.[13] For instance, the parable of the lost son intimates that the father is God, the older son represents Pharisees and teachers of the Law, and the younger son typifies tax collectors and prostitutes. The parable only serves the purpose of comparing one individual with another; it is not true allegory in which each detail is equal to something that differs entirely from the intent of the text.[14] In the New Testament we encounter elements of allegory but never a full-fledged allegorical parable. Without a doubt, Jesus' parables depict real-life incidents that communicate irrefutable truth. Details in these parables call up analogies that challenge the reader and the hearer to fill in appropriate comparisons.[15] Anyone interpreting the parables should know the one basic point a parable conveys, understand the central message Jesus is teaching, and fittingly apply the parable to the life of the people in an audience.[16]

By the end of the nineteenth century, the allegorical shackles that had bound the exegesis of the parables were broken and a new era in parable research emerged.[17] Whereas Jülicher saw Jesus as a teacher of moral principles, C. H. Dodd viewed him as a dynamic historical person who with his teaching brought about a crisis period. Said Dodd, "The task of the interpreter of the parables is to find out, if he can, the setting of a parable in the situation contemplated by the Gospels."[18] Jesus taught that the kingdom of God, the Son of man, judgment, and blessedness had entered the historical setting of the day. For Jesus, according to Dodd, the kingdom meant the rule of God exemplified in his own ministry. Therefore, the parables Jesus taught must be understood to have a direct bearing upon the actual situation of God's rule on earth.

J. Jeremias continued the work of Dodd. He, too, wished to discover the parabolic teachings that go back to Jesus himself. However, Jeremias set out to trace the historical development of the parables, which he believed occurred in two stages. The first stage pertains to the actual situation of Jesus' ministry, and the second is a reflection of the way the parables were put to use in the early Christian church. The task Jeremias gave himself was the recovery of the original form of the parables in order to hear the voice of Jesus.[19] With his intimate knowledge of the land, culture, customs, people, and languages of Israel, Jeremias was able to amass a wealth of information that makes his work one of the most influential books on the parables.

Nevertheless, the question may be asked whether the original form can be separated from the historical context without succumbing to a fair amount of guesswork. On the other hand, one can also take the text of the parables and accept it as a true presentation of Jesus' teaching. That is, the biblical text the evangelists have given us may reflect the historical contexts in which the parables were originally taught. We have to depend on the text we have received, and we do well to leave the parables and their historical settings intact. This does call for a measure of trust—namely, that the evangelists in recording the parables understood Jesus' intention for teaching the parables in the settings they describe.[20] At the time the parables were recorded, eyewitnesses and ministers of the Word handed down the oral tradition of the words and deeds of Jesus (Luke 1:1, 2). Because of the link with eyewitnesses, we may be confident that the contexts in which the parables are placed refer to the times, places, and circumstances in which Jesus originally taught them.

In recent times, representatives of the new hermeneutic school have increasingly moved the parables away from their historical setting to a broadly based literary emphasis within an existential structure.[21] That is, these scholars treat the parables as existential literature, remove them from their historical moorings, and replace their original meaning with a contemporary message. They deny that the meaning of a parable finds its origin in the life and ministry of Jesus;[22] they are not interested in its source and setting but rather in its literary form and existential interpretation.[23] They see the parables as layer upon layer of interpretations of what Jesus originally said. Because they teach that the early church created the substance of the parables, the modern reader has to peal away layers of accretions to determine the authenticity and historicity of the words Jesus spoke.[24]

For these scholars the literary structure of the parable is important because it leads modern people to a moment of decision: they must either accept or reject the challenge the parables place before them.

That the parables call a person to action is readily agreed; in the application of the good Samaritan parable the expert in the Law who questioned Jesus is told, "Go and do likewise" (Luke 10:37). However, the existentialist in his interpretation of the parable capitalizes on the imperative mood and disregards the indicative mood in which the parable is presented. He separates the words of Jesus from their cultural setting and thereby deprives them of the power and authority Jesus has given them.

Moreover, by treating the parables as literary structures separated from their original settings, the existentialist must provide them with a new setting. Thus he places the parables in a contemporary context. But this method can hardly be called exegesis, for an existential philosophy has been drawn into the biblical text. This is eisegesis, not exegesis. Unfortunately, the ordinary Christian who seeks guidance in his or her understanding of the parables by the representatives of the new hermeneutic school must first seek training in existential philosophy, neoliberal theology, and the literary jargon of structuralism before he or she is able to benefit from their insights.

PRINCIPLES

Interpreting the parables does not call for a thorough training in theology and philosophy, but it does imply that the exegete adhere to some basic principles of interpretation. These principles in brief are related to the history, grammar, and theology of the biblical text. Wherever possible, the interpreter ought to make a study of the historical setting of the parable, including a detailed analysis of the religious, social, political, and geographical circumstances revealed in the parable. For instance, the setting of the good Samaritan parable demands some familiarity with the religious instruction of the clergy of the day. The expert in the Law, coming to Jesus asking what he had to do to inherit eternal life, touched off the conversation that led to the story of the good Samaritan.

With respect to the parable of the good Samaritan, the exegete should familiarize himself with the origin, status, and religion of the Samaritans; the functions, office, and residence of the priest and Levite; the topography of the area between Jerusalem and Jericho; and the Jewish concept of neighborliness. By taking note of the historical context of the parable, the interpreter sees the reason Jesus taught this story and he learns the objective lesson Jesus sought to convey in the parable.[25]

Second, the exegete must pay close attention to the literary and grammatical structure of the parable. The moods and tenses that an evangelist employs as he relates the parables are most significant, for they shed light on the main teaching of the story. Word studies in their biblical context as well as in extracanonical writings are an essential part of the process of interpreting a parable. Thus, a study of the word *neighbor* in the context of the command "Love your neighbor as yourself," as given in the Old and New Testaments, proves to be a rewarding exercise. Also, the interpreter needs to look at the introduction and conclusion of a parable; these may contain a literary device such as a rhetorical question, an exhortation, or a command. The parable of the good Samaritan concludes with the pointed command, "Go and do likewise" (Luke 10:37). The expert in the Law who had asked Jesus about inheriting eternal life became inescapably involved in fulfilling the command to love his neighbor as himself. Introductions, and especially conclusions, contain the leads that aid the interpreter in finding the main points of parables.

Third, the main point of a given parable should be checked theologically against the teaching of Jesus and the rest of Scripture.[26] When the basic teaching of a parable has been fully explored and is correctly understood, the unity of Scripture will come to expression and the proper meaning of the passage can be advanced in all its simplicity and lucidity.

Last, but not least, the interpreter of the parable must translate its meaning in terms relevant to the needs of today. The task is to apply the central teaching of a parable to the life situation of the person listening to the interpretation. In the parable of the good Samaritan, the command to love one's neighbor becomes meaningful when the person who has been robbed and is bleeding along the Jericho road is no longer only a figure out of the ancient past. Instead, the neighbor who claims our love is the person who is a homeless, dispossessed refugee. He meets us on the Jericho road of the daily newspaper and the TV report on the evening news.

CLASSIFICATION

The parables of Jesus can be grouped and classified in various ways. Those of the sower, the seed growing secretly, the wheat and the weeds, the barren fig tree, and the budding fig tree are all nature parables. A number of parables Jesus told have to do with work and wages. Some of these are the parables of the workers in the vineyard, the tenant, and the shrewd manager. Other parables feature the theme of weddings, and festive or solemn occasions. These include the parables of the children playing in the marketplace, the ten virgins, the great supper, and the wedding banquet. And still others show the general motif of the lost and found. They include the parables of the lost sheep, the lost coin, and the lost son.

It is not always certain, however, how a parable ought to be categorized. Is the parable of the fishnet a nature parable, or should it be listed with the ones on work and wages? And where does the parable of the good Samaritan fit? It is easy to see that categorizing the parables may be somewhat arbitrary and, in some instances, forced.

The Synoptic Gospels present parables with parallels in two or often three of the Gospels and also parables that are peculiar to an individual evangelist. Whereas Mark has only one parable unique to his Gospel (the seed growing secretly), Matthew and Luke contain quite a few. In my presentation of the parables, I have followed the sequence of the Gospels by first discussing those of Matthew, with the one peculiar to Mark taken up in the order of the parables of the sower and the wheat and weeds, and then the ones presented in the Gospel of Luke. In the parables that have parallels, I have adopted almost uniformly the sequence of Matthew, Mark, and Luke. This procedure has been employed to help the reader who wishes to consult a survey of the Synoptic parallels, for example, K. Aland's *Synopsis of the Four Gospels.*[27]

In this study of the parables, references to Greek and Hebrew words are infrequent. When they do appear, they are given in a transliterated form and a translation is provided. The English Bible used is the New International Version (with permission from the Executive Committee). For the benefit of the reader, the NIV text is printed in full at the beginning of each parable. Those parables that have parallels in the three Synoptic Gospels are given in the sequence of Matthew, Mark, and Luke. A total of forty parables and parabolic sayings are discussed in this book. All the major parables are listed, as well as the greater part of the parabolic sayings. Of course, a selection had to be made concerning these sayings, so that the parable of salt is included but that of the light omit-

ted.[28] Only the parabolic sayings of the Synoptic Gospels have been stud-
ied, not those of the Gospel of John.

The literature on the parables is voluminous—an unending stream
of books and articles. Hardly any parable has been neglected by recent
scholars. New insights from studies in Jewish culture and law have been
most valuable in gaining a better understanding of Jesus' teaching. The
aim of this book is to present the pastor and serious Bible student with
adequate and contemporary coverage of the writings on the parables
without getting lost in all the details. The notes and the selected bibliography will aid the theologian who wishes to more intensively pursue
the study of Jesus' parables. By way of the bibliographical material and
the index, he or she will gain access to the literature available on the
parables of Jesus.

1 Salt

Matthew 5:13

[13]"You are the salt of the earth. But if the salt loses its saltiness, how can it be made salty again? It is no longer good for anything, except to be thrown out and trampled by men."

Mark 9:50

[50]"Salt is good, but if it loses its saltiness, how can you make it salty again? Have salt in yourselves, and be at peace with each other."

Luke 14:34, 35

[34]"Salt is good, but if it loses its saltiness, how can it be made salty again? [35]It is fit neither for the soil nor for the manure pile; it is thrown out.

"He who has ears to hear, let him hear."

Salt has been used throughout history for preserving and flavoring food. It is one of the basic necessities of life. Its use is universal and its supplies seemingly inexhaustible. But beside beneficial qualities, salt has destructive powers as well. It can turn fertile soil into barren wasteland.[1] The area around the Dead Sea is a case in point.

In modern times we find it unthinkable that salt can lose its saltiness. Sodium chloride (the chemical name for common table salt) is a stable compound. It is free of any impurities. In ancient Israel, however, salt was obtained by evaporating water from the Dead Sea. That water contains various substances other than salt. Evaporation produces salt crystals as well as chlorides of potassium and magnesium. Because salt crystals are the first to form in the evaporation process they can be collected, thus providing relatively pure salt. If the evaporated salt is not separated, however, and if in time the salt crystals attract moisture, dissolve, and leach out, the residue loses its saltiness and becomes useless.[2]

21

What can you do with saltless salt? It is good for nothing. A farmer does not want these chemicals on his land because in their crude state they harm plants. To throw the residue on a manure pile does not help either, for every so often the manure is gathered and spread over the land as fertilizer. The only thing that can be done with saltless salt is to throw it outside where people can trample it underfoot.[3] If salt loses its basic property of being salty,[4] it cannot be made salty again.

In the Sermon on the Mount, Jesus addresses the crowds together with his disciples and says, "You are the salt of the earth." As salt has the characteristic of checking deterioration, so Christians should be a moral influence in the society in which they live. By their words and deeds they should arrest spiritual and moral corruption. And just as salt is invisible (for example, in bread) but nevertheless a potent agent, so Christians are not always seen but individually and collectively they permeate society and constitute a restraining force in a perverse and depraved world.

"Have salt in yourselves, and be at peace with each other," says Jesus (Mark 9:50). He exhorts his followers to use their spiritual resources to promote peace,[5] first at home and then abroad. For if Christians are unable to live at peace among themselves, they have lost their effectiveness in the world. Many people may never read the Bible, yet they constantly watch those who do. In the early Christian church, the eloquent Chrysostom once said that if Christians lived the life that is expected of them, unbelief would disappear.

2 Two Builders

Matthew 7:24–27

[24]"Therefore everyone who hears these words of mine and puts them into practice is like a wise man who built his house on the rock. [25]The rain came down, the streams rose, and the winds blew and beat against that house; yet it did not fall, because it had its foundation on the rock. [26]But everyone who hears these words of mine and does not put them into practice is like a foolish man who built his house on sand. [27]The rain came down, the streams rose, and the winds blew and beat against that house, and it fell with a great crash."

Luke 6:47–49

[47]"I will show you what he is like who comes to me and hears my words and puts them into practice. [48]He is like a man building a house, who dug down deep and laid the foundation on rock. When a flood came, the torrent struck that house but could not shake it, because it was well built. [49]But the one who hears my words and does not put them into practice is like a man who built a house on the ground without a foundation. The moment the torrent struck that house, it collapsed and its destruction was complete."

Jesus often witnessed the sudden downpour of a cloudburst that caused the dry creek beds to turn into violent streams. Such scenes are common in Israel, where the weather can quickly change and at times drastically alter the landscape.

Rural houses in Jesus' day were generally built of hardened mud. Thieves were able to dig through the walls of such houses (Matt. 6:19). Four men dug through the roof of the house where Jesus was teaching in order to let down their paralyzed friend (Mark 2:3, 4). For builders it was good business practice to build away from possible watercourses, even though these gullies might remain dry for years in succession.[1]

The wise builder selects a site on a rock. Then he will not need to worry about a torrential rain, the sudden rising of a watercourse that can sweep a house away, and the battering winds that will beat against the house. A house built upon rock has a foundation that lasts.

A foolish builder constructs his house as though he is pitching a tent. It does not occur to him that a house should be built as a permanent structure. He builds his house upon sand, perhaps because of easy access to water in a nearby creek. As long as the weather is steady and the sky remains blue, the occupants of the house have nothing to fear. When with little warning the weather changes, the clouds gather, the rain descends, the streams rise, and winds blow, however, then that house comes down with a great crash.

The evangelists Matthew and Luke word the parable differently. To some degree the variations may be explained with reference to the audiences the evangelists addressed. Matthew wrote for a Jewish reader living in Israel, while Luke brought the gospel to the Hellenist residing in Asia Minor and other parts of the Mediterranean world. To a Jew acquainted with the building techniques prevalent in ancient Israel, the parable of the two builders written by Matthew was self-explanatory. Luke, however, did not write for people living in Galilee or Judea. He had to address the Greek and Hellenist. Thus Luke substituted building procedures that differed from those in Israel.[2] The builder digs down deep and lays the foundation of the house on rock, Luke writes. Beside the difference in the construction of a dwelling, Luke had to take geographical and climatological changes into consideration. Whereas Matthew wrote about the falling rain, the rising streams, and the blowing winds, Luke referred to the flood that came and the torrent that struck. Matthew spoke of building on sand, Luke of building on ground. These differences in detail do not alter the meaning of the parable. The builder uses foresight in constructing a house on a permanent foundation.

A person who hears Jesus' words and puts them into practice is like the wise builder. It is foolish to hear the words of Jesus and not obey them. Such a person may be compared to a builder who builds his house on the sand or ground without a foundation.

This parable echoes the words of the prophet Ezekiel. He describes a flimsy wall that is built, rain that comes down in torrents, hailstones that come hurtling down, and violent winds that burst forth. As a result, the wall collapses (Ezek. 13:10–16).

At the conclusion of the Sermon on the Mount (Matthew 5–7) or the sermon on the level place (Luke 6), Jesus wanted his audience to be not merely hearers but also doers of the word he had spoken. Merely listening to Jesus' words is insufficient. The believer must take Jesus at his word and build his house of faith on him alone. Jesus is the foundation upon whom the wise man builds. In the words of Paul, "By the grace God has given me, I laid a foundation as an expert builder, and someone else is building on it. But each one should be careful how he builds. For no one can lay any foundation other than the one already laid, which is Jesus Christ" (1 Cor. 3:10, 11).

Whoever is wise listens seriously and directs his or her life in accordance with Jesus' words. Whoever listens to Jesus but does not put his words into practice comes to utter ruin. Such a listener has not taken time to dig and to lay a foundation. His or her house is ready in record time and is temporarily adequate for his or her needs, but when adversity strikes in the whirlwind of life, the house that does not have Jesus as its foundation collapses and is completely destroyed.

This parable indirectly calls attention to God's judgment, which everyone, the wise as well as the foolish builder, must face. The wise man who has built his house of faith on Jesus is able to withstand the storms of life. He stands secure, overcomes, and triumphs. In the Beatitudes, Jesus calls the poor, the meek, and the downtrodden *blessed*. In the parable, those people who have built upon the Rock demonstrate a quiet fortitude in everything they do. They hear the word of Jesus and they practice it. Because of this, they will never come to ruin. They believe in Jesus and obey his word.

3 Children in the Marketplace

> **Matthew 11:16–19**
>
> [16]"To what can I compare this generation? They are like children sitting in the marketplaces and calling out to others:
>
> > [17]"'We played the flute for you,
> > and you did not dance;
> > we sang a dirge,
> > and you did not mourn.'
>
> [18]"For John came neither eating nor drinking, and they say, 'He has a demon.' [19]The Son of Man came eating and drinking, and they say, 'Here is a glutton and a drunkard, a friend of tax collectors and "sinners"'. But wisdom is proved right by her actions."
>
> **Luke 7:31–35**
>
> [31]"To what, then, can I compare the people of this generation? What are they like? [32]They are like children sitting in the marketplace and calling out to each other:
>
> > "'We played the flute for you,
> > and you did not dance;
> > we sang a dirge,
> > and you did not mourn.'
>
> [33]"For John the Baptist came neither eating bread nor drinking wine, and you say, 'He has a demon.' [34]The Son of Man came eating and drinking, and you say, 'Here is a glutton and a drunkard, a friend of tax collectors and "sinners."' [35]But wisdom is proved right by all her children."

Jesus told a delightful parable of children playing in the marketplace. He took the scene directly from daily life, a familiar sight of children making up their own plays and acting them out. The little drama could very well have unfolded as follows.

Several boys and girls were playing together in the marketplace, most likely when it was not in use. Some of the children wanted to play a wedding. Beside the bride and groom, a flute player was needed, as were a number of children to dance at the wedding. Although bride and groom were ready and one of the children provided the wedding music on his flute, the rest of the children refused to dance. They were not interested in playing a wedding.

Next, some of the children wanted to act out a funeral. One of them had to play the dead person, while others sang a dirge. The rest had to mourn—but they refused. They had no desire to be part of that funeral game. The children who had planned the games sat down and called out to the others:

> We played the flute for you,
> and you did not dance;
> We sang a dirge,
> and you did not mourn.

APPLICATION

According to Matthew's Gospel, the children sitting in the market-place call out to others, their playmates. In the Gospel of Luke, the children are calling out to each other. In Matthew's presentation one group of children is creative and suggests two different games to another group.[1] Luke's account gives the impression that one group of children wanted to play a happy game, while the other group decided on a sad one. Neither group desired to follow the suggestion of the other. It may also be that the taunts made by only the one group have been recorded,[2] and that the use of "each other" should not be pressed unduly.

But how is the parable applied? Basically, there are two ways of applying the scene that Jesus described. First, the children who suggest the wedding and the funeral games represent Jesus and John the Baptist, respectively. The children who refuse to participate in these games are the Jews. John came to them and struck a dirgelike note, but they were in no mood to listen to him. To get rid of John they said he was possessed. Jesus, however, came and brought joy and happiness in numerous ways; the Jews sneered at him because he entered the homes of moral and social outcasts, where he ate and drank with them.

The second interpretation is the reverse of the first. That is, the children who suggest the glad and sad games of wedding and funeral are the Jews who want John to be merry and Jesus to mourn. When neither lives up to their expectations, they complain. They say to John, "We played the flute for you, and you did not dance." And they say to Jesus, "We sang a dirge, and you did not mourn."[3]

Of the two, the second explanation is more plausible. First, it establishes a definite link between "the people of this generation" (Luke 7:31) and the children who make the reproaches. The Jews are displeased with both John the Baptist and Jesus, just as the children are with their playmates. Second, it places the complaints of the children applied to John and Jesus in chronological order.[4] John came as an ascetic who lived on locusts and wild honey—eating bread and drinking wine was not for him—and the Jews accused him of being demon-possessed. Jesus, by contrast, ate bread and drank wine, and they branded him a glutton and drunkard, a friend of tax collectors and "sinners." God had sent his messengers in the persons of John and Jesus, but their contemporaries did nothing but find fault with them.

PARALLELS

The games the children wanted to play and their subsequent reproaches find an echo in the Book of Ecclesiastes, which has a section of poetry that observes there is a time for everything. There is "a time to weep and a time to laugh, a time to mourn and a time to dance" (Eccles. 3:4), says the Preacher.

The taunt that the Jews hurled at Jesus, however, was by no means harmless name-calling. They accused him of being a glutton and a drunkard. This was the description of an unruly son who, according to the Mosaic Law, ought to be stoned to death (Deut. 21:20, 21). Jesus' association with social and moral outcasts, who were regarded as apostates by the religious leaders, was considered reprehensible. Because of his association, the Jews felt that he himself was to be regarded as an apostate.[5]

In rabbinic literature, a striking parallel appears. Although it is difficult to ascertain when this parallel was written and where it originated in oral form, the wording itself is interesting:

> Jeremiah spoke right up to the Holy One, blessed be He: Thou didst bring it about that the curly-haired Elijah rose to act in their behalf, and they laughed at him saying: "Behold how he curls his locks!" and sneeringly called him "the curly-haired fellow." And when Thou didst bring it about that Elisha rose to act in their behalf, they said derisively to him: "Go up, thou baldhead; go up, thou baldhead."[6]

CONCLUSION

The culmination of this parable differs in the two Gospel accounts. Matthew's and Luke's accounts vary in the concluding phrase, "But wisdom is proved right by her actions" (Matt. 11:19), and "But wisdom is proved right by all her children" (Luke 7:35). The suggestion has been made that the difference in wording may go back to an Aramaic expression that in translation was misunderstood.[7] Whatever the cause may be, the meaning that the words convey does not vary. Wisdom represents God's wisdom; it may even be a circumlocution for God himself. According to Matthew, the divine works of Jesus (Matt. 11:5) are proof of God's wisdom. In Luke's Gospel, God's children are a testimony to the veracity of his wisdom. For example, tax collectors and immoral women rejected as outcasts by religious people of their day saw in John the Baptist and in Jesus the wisdom of God revealed. Both John and Jesus proclaimed the message of redemption to them—John in all austerity at the Jordan (Luke 3:12, 13) and Jesus in table-fellowship in their homes (Luke 5:30).

4 Sower

Matthew 13:1–9

¹That same day Jesus went out of the house and sat by the lake. ²Such large crowds gathered around him that he got into a boat and sat in it, while all the people stood on the shore. ³Then he told them many things in parables, saying: "A farmer went out to sow his seed. ⁴As he was scattering the seed, some fell along the path, and the birds came and ate it up. ⁵Some fell on rocky places, where it did not have much soil. It sprang up quickly because the soil was shallow. ⁶But when the sun came up, the plants were scorched, and they withered because they had no root. ⁷Other seed fell among thorns, which grew up and choked the plants. ⁸Still other seed fell on good soil, where it produced a crop—a hundred, sixty or thirty times what was sown. ⁹He who has ears, let him hear."

Mark 4:1–9

¹ Again Jesus began to teach by the lake. The crowd that gathered around him was so large that he got into a boat and sat in it out on the lake, while all the people were along the shore at the water's edge. ²He taught them many things by parables, and in his teaching said: ³"Listen! A farmer went out to sow his seed. ⁴ As he was scattering the seed, some fell along the path, and the birds came and ate it up. ⁵Some fell on rocky places, where it did not have much soil. It sprang up quickly, because the soil was shallow. ⁶But when the sun came up, the plants were scorched, and they withered because they had no root. ⁷Other seed fell among thorns, which grew up and choked the plants, so that they did not bear grain. ⁸Still other seed fell on good soil. It came up, grew and produced a crop, multiplying thirty, sixty, or even a hundred times."

⁹Then Jesus said, "He who has ears to hear, let him hear."

Luke 8:4–8

⁴While a large crowd was gathering and people were coming to Jesus from town after town, he told this parable: ⁵"A farmer went out to sow his seed. As he was scattering the seed, some fell along the path; it was trampled on, and the birds of the air ate it up. ⁶Some fell on rock, and when it came up, the plants withered

because they had no moisture. [7]Other seed fell among thorns, which grew up with it and choked the plants. [8]Still other seed fell on good soil. It came up and yielded a crop, a hundred times more than was sown."

When he said this, he called out, "He who has ears to hear, let him hear."

SETTING

In our industrialized society, agriculture has become obsessed with food production. Farming is not merely a way of life; on the contrary, it has become a way to make a living. Modern technology has been fully applied to farming methods, so that the farmer is a technician of sorts—an expert in applying fertilizers, herbicides, and insecticides—and a businessman who knows the cost of production, the value of his product, and the marketing schedule.

When Jesus taught the parable of the sower to his Galilean audience, they literally saw the farmer sowing his seed in the nearby fields in the month of October. Of course, the evangelists do not tell us when Jesus taught the parable. It may very well have been at the time when the sower went out to sow. The crowds (according to Matthew, large crowds) had come to the beach on the northwestern edge of the Lake of Galilee. They may have numbered in the thousands. To address such a multitude Jesus used a floating pulpit, sitting down in a boat most likely pushed away from the shore.[1] Thus the surface of the water deflected his voice, which on a quiet day could reach the audience seated or standing on the beach. These natural surroundings were far more effective than a modern public address system.

Jesus did not have to explain the activities of the farmer. Perhaps in the distance they could see the farmer at work, sowing kernels of wheat or barley. They may even have skirted his field on the way to the beach. In the agricultural society of the day, many in the audience were farmers or had worked on a farm.

Farming was relatively simple in Jesus' day. Although the parable does not say anything about farming methods, from the Old Testament (Isa. 28:24, 25; Jer. 4:3; Hosea 10:11, 12) and from rabbinic sources we learn that at the end of a long and hot summer the farmer would go to his field, and sow wheat or barley on top of the hard ground. He would plow the field to cover the seed, and wait for the winter rain to come to germinate the kernels.[2]

The farmer in Jesus' parable took his supply of grain to the field in a bag slung around his neck and shoulders. The bag hung in front of him, and with rhythmic steps he cast the seed in strips across the field. He was not concerned about the relatively few kernels that landed on the path bordering the field, or about the seed that fell in the shallow soil where the limestone was jutting out of the earth, or about the wheat that dropped among the thorn plants that would come to life in the spring of the year and choke out the growing wheat. For the farmer it was all in a day's work.

In bygone eras, the area where Jesus taught the parable had been covered by dust from the frequent eruptions of a volcanic range. Wherever the dust settled heavily on the limestone, there the land was particularly fertile while leaving other places barren. In a particular field one may find rich soil, gravelly soil, and rocky protrusions.[3]

The description is commonplace and accurate. The farmer could not prevent some kernels from falling on the hard path. Sooner or later the birds would take care of them. Some birds would even come to pick up the seeds that were sown on the field. That was all part of farming in that day. Also, the farmer could do next to nothing about the limestone cropping up here and there. Such was the lay of the land. Moreover, he had tried to eliminate the thorny weeds by digging up the roots of these obstinate plants. Yet they seemed to have a way of coming back.

The farmer looked forward to harvest time when he would bring in the crop. An average yield in those days could be less than tenfold.[4] Should he get returns of thirtyfold, or still more favorably sixtyfold, he would have a bumper crop. Very occasionally he might harvest a hundredfold (Gen. 26:12). In short, the farmer did not notice the wheat kernels he lost at the time of sowing. He put his hope in the future and with anticipation waited for the time of harvest.

No one in Jesus' audience would have taken issue with him. The climax of the story may have surprised his listeners; instead of a normal crop of a tenfold yield, Jesus talked of a return of up to a hundredfold. The point of the story, therefore, is an abundant harvest.

DESIGN

The parable of the sower is one of the few parables found in all three Synoptic Gospels. When the individual writers incorporated Jesus' story of the farmer sowing and harvesting his crop, they addressed their own audiences. Matthew, Mark, and Luke obviously placed the parable in the context of their respective Gospels to show the point of Jesus' teaching.

In Matthew's Gospel, chapter 13 is preceded by an account of the healing ministry of Jesus (chapters 8 and 9). At the conclusion of this section, Matthew records that Jesus was teaching in the synagogues, preaching the good news of the kingdom, and healing every kind of disease and sickness (9:35). Then he looked at the crowds, and because they lacked spiritual guidance he had compassion on them. He compared them to sheep without a shepherd. "Then he said to his disciples, 'The harvest is plentiful but the workers are few. Ask the Lord of the harvest, therefore, to send out workers into his harvest field'" (9:37, 38).

In chapter 10 Matthew records the sending out of the twelve disciples, commissioned to go to the lost sheep of Israel. But Jesus warned the disciples of rebuff, persecution, and death. They would meet opposition, endure hatred, and face loss of life. Matthew depicts the same theme in the next two chapters. The crowds had followed John the Baptist, but the people said he had a demon. And of Jesus they said he was a glutton and a drunkard, a friend of tax collectors and "sinners" (11:19). The people in Chorazin, Bethsaida, and Capernaum refused to repent and believe his words. It seemed as if Jesus had been plowing on shallow ground, and the seed he had sown had failed to produce a crop. Yet, in spite of the misunderstanding of John the Baptist (11:3), the unbelief of the Galileans (11:21, 23), and the enmity of the religious leaders (12:2, 24, 38), the kingdom of God had come and continued its advance. Those people who do the will of God are part and parcel of that kingdom. They are Jesus' brother, sister, and mother (12:50).

At this point, Matthew introduces the parable of the sower. The structural redaction of the Gospel account reveals the skillful hand of a literary architect.[5] The evangelist has set the stage for the parable of the sower. The object is to alert his readers to the unexpected harvest gathered in God's kingdom.

Mark, on the other hand, seems to stress the teaching ministry of Jesus along the shores of the Galilean Lake. He begins the passage by saying, "Again Jesus began to teach by the lake" (4:1). Whereas Matthew omits the reference to Jesus seated in the boat "on the lake," Mark refers to the lake at least three times in that introductory verse. He informs his readers that once more Jesus met a large crowd at the water's edge (see 2:13 and 3:7). Mark inserts three of the four parables (the sower, the growing seed, and the mustard seed) in his Gospel at this point in the narrative to indicate the place of teaching, the audience Jesus faced, and the purpose of the parables.

The writer of the third Gospel sets forth an abbreviated version of the parable of the sower, but places it within the context of acceptance and rejection. Jesus' words and deeds found ready acceptance among the common people, tax collectors, immoral women, and others (7:29, 37; 8:1–3), but he met stiff opposition from the Pharisees and experts in the Law (7:30, 39). Luke's version of the parable differs little from that of

Matthew and Mark, even though it is much shorter and shows a change in vocabulary here and there. "These changes show that Luke or oral tradition felt quite free to modify details in the wording of the story, something which modern preachers regularly do when they are recounting the parables."[6]

INTERPRETATION

Matthew 13:18–23

[18]"Listen then to what the parable of the sower means: [19]When anyone hears the message about the kingdom and does not understand it, the evil one comes and snatches away what was sown in his heart. This is the seed sown along the path. [20]The one who received the seed that fell on rocky places is the man who hears the word and at once receives it with joy. [21]But since he has no root, he lasts only a short time. When trouble or persecution comes because of the word, he quickly falls away. [22]The one who received the seed that fell among the thorns is the man who hears the word, but the worries of this life and the deceitfulness of wealth choke it, making it unfruitful. [23]But the one who received the seed that fell on good soil is the man who hears the word and understands it. He produces a crop, yielding a hundred, sixty or thirty times what was sown."

Mark 4:13–20

[13]Then Jesus said to them, "Don't you understand this parable? How then will you understand any parable? [14]The farmer sows the word. [15]Some people are like seed along the path, where the word is sown. As soon as they hear it, Satan comes and takes away the word that was sown in them. [16]Others, like seed sown on rocky places, hear the word and at once receive it with joy. [17]But since they have no root, they last only a short time. When trouble or persecution comes because of the word, they quickly fall away. [18]Still others, like seed sown among thorns, hear the word; [19]but the worries of this life, the deceitfulness of wealth and the desires for other things come in and choke the word, making it unfruitful. [20]Others, like seed sown on good soil, hear the word, accept it, and produce a crop—thirty, sixty or even a hundred times what was sown."

Luke 8:11–15

[11]"This is the meaning of the parable: The seed is the word of God. [12]Those along the path are the ones who hear, and then the devil comes and takes away the word from their hearts, so that they may not believe and be saved. [13]Those on the rock are the ones who receive the word with joy when they hear it, but they have no root. They believe for a while, but in the time of testing they fall away. [14]The seed that fell among thorns stands for those who hear, but as they go on their way they are choked by life's worries, riches and pleasures, and they do not mature. [15]But the seed on good soil stands for those with a noble and good heart, who hear the word, retain it, and by persevering produce a crop."

The parable of the sower is one of the few parables Jesus explains to his disciples and others with them. We would not have expected that the parable needs explanation, but in fact it needs an application in order to be understood spiritually. The initial question of the disciples, "Why do you speak to the people in parables?" receives an answer that is not readily understandable. Jesus replies, "The knowledge of the secrets of the kingdom of heaven has been given to you, but not to them. Whoever has will be given more, and he will have an abundance. Whoever does not have, even what he has will be taken from him. This is why I speak to them in parables: 'Though seeing, they do not see; though hearing, they do not hear or understand'" (Matt. 13:11–13).

We note that the disciples ask why Jesus speaks to *the people* in parables, and that he answers why he speaks to *them* in parables. Mark makes the distinction of the "us" and "them" even more pronounced by reporting "But to those on the outside everything is said in parables" (4:11).

What, precisely, does Jesus mean by the phrase "the secrets of the kingdom"? If Jesus is the Great Teacher (Rabbi), we might expect him to teach spiritual truths in simple language. It would be difficult to believe that Jesus, by adopting a certain mode of speech, intended to conceal his teaching from the crowd. And yet he speaks of the mysteries of the kingdom.

The Qumran documents refer to the role of the Teacher of Righteousness commissioned to reveal divine mysteries. Moreover, the Teacher would instruct his disciples in the revelation he received from God.[7] Jesus brought divine revelation by teaching his disciples the secrets of the kingdom of heaven. Others who were not part of the broader circle of Jesus' disciples (that is, those on the outside) did not have the understanding of the kingdom that the immediate followers of Jesus had.[8]

Jesus indirectly refers to the spiritual birth requisite for entering the kingdom of God (John 3:3, 5). In other words, the ability as well as the privilege of discerning the secrets of the kingdom had been given to the disciples. To those on the outside, this privilege was not given.[9]

The crowds addressed by Jesus are referred to as "them." This in itself is not surprising in view of the woes Jesus had pronounced on the unrepentant cities of Chorazin, Bethsaida, and Capernaum (Matt. 11:20–24). The elders, scribes, Pharisees, and the priestly hierarchy constantly opposed Jesus. Matthew seems to have employed a simple term for the Jewish crowd surrounding Jesus—they are "them."[10]

However, the secrets of the kingdom are not to be hidden forever. Mark adds the following words to Jesus' explanation of the parable of the sower: "For whatever is hidden is meant to be disclosed, and whatever is concealed is meant to be brought out into the open" (4:22).[11] The truth Jesus proclaims by means of parables is given to those who see and understand.

Matthew, by contrast, says that the one who has will be given more, resulting in abundance, but the one who does not have will have to give up even what he has (13:12). Writing for the Jews, Matthew implies that those Jews who have not been given spiritual perception and who reject the words of Jesus have to give up their understanding of the Old Testament teachings on the kingdom of God. Without a spiritual understanding of these teachings, the Old Testament oracles become meaningless. Thus, although they (the Jews) see, they do not see; although they hear, they do not hear and understand (Matt. 13:13).

All evangelists quote the words of Isaiah 6:9, 10—

> In them is fulfilled the prophecy of Isaiah:
>   "You will be ever hearing but never understanding;
>   you will be ever seeing but never perceiving.
>   For this people's heart has become calloused;
>   they hardly hear with their ears,
>   and they have closed their eyes.
>   Otherwise they might see with their eyes,
>   hear with their ears,
>   understand with their hearts
>   and turn, and I would heal them."
>
>   Matthew 13:14, 15

And all three Synoptic evangelists seem to employ the Isaianic quotation to express the reason why people who have hardened their hearts will lose even their spiritual heritage.[12] Other commentators interpret the use of Isaiah 6:9, 10 as an explanation or warning concerning the results of a hardened heart.[13]

Of the three Synoptic evangelists, Mark provides the fullest account of Jesus' interpretation of the parable.[14] He includes a word of rebuke from the lips of Jesus: "Don't you understand this parable?" (4:13). By implication, Mark indicates that the parable of the sower is unique. Perhaps it receives special significance because Jesus provides an explanation for the parable. But the words of rebuke also indicate that the disciples, whose hearts were enlightened, should have understood the basic meaning of the parable.

Matthew's account is more precise in its composition. It is Matthew who gives a title to this parable: the parable of the sower. And it is the Gospel of Matthew that sets a pedagogical tone with a uniformity of style and with reverberating symmetrical phrases.

But before we move on to the interpretation of the parable itself, we should note that the imagery Jesus used in the parable of the sower is also portrayed in 2 Esdras 9:30–33:

> And you said, "Hear me, Israel, listen to my words, you descendants of Jacob: this is my law, which I am sowing among you to bear fruit and to bring you everlasting glory." But our fathers, though they received your law, did not observe it; they disobeyed its commandments. Not that the fruit of the law perished—that was impossible, for it was yours; rather those who received it perished, because they failed to keep safe the seed that had been sown in them.[15]

In Jesus' day the verb *to sow* could be employed metaphorically, meaning "to teach." We may assume that this was the manner of speech in the local synagogues. Jesus' formulation and interpretation of the parable of the sower blends in very well with the speech pattern of the day.

What is striking in the interpretation of the parable is the *absence* of a number of factors. Foremost is the figure of the sower. Although he is mentioned only by way of introduction in the parable, in the interpretation his presence, although assumed, is not explained. Instead, the emphasis falls on the seed that is sown. Luke calls the seed "the word of God"; Mark calls it merely "the word." And Matthew, in view of the quotation from Isaiah, says by implication, "When anyone hears the message about the kingdom and does not understand it, the evil one comes and snatches away what was sown in his heart. This is the seed sown along the path" (13:19). Although we would have expected some reference to rain, which obviously would increase the yield, nothing is said about it (see, for example, Deut. 11:14, 17).[16] No mention is made of the hard work of plowing the field, although clearly that had to be part of the process. God's provision of rain and man's working in the field have no bearing on the construction and interpretation of the parable.

The emphasis of the parable is the farmer's ups and downs in growing a crop.[17] He may lose his crop, in this case three times, but in the end reap an abundant harvest. In the same way, missionaries, evangelists, and pastors are keenly aware of hardened hearts, hostile responses, and dismal failures among their hearers. But convinced of the innate power of God's Word, they continue to preach and, consequently, expect an astonishing harvest. The parable assures gospel preachers and teachers of growing success in spite of the fact that some of their hearers reject the message of salvation.

APPLICATION

By mentioning such details as the path, the rocky places, and the patch of thorns, Jesus evidently intends to apply the lesson of the seed and soil to the persons hearing the message of the kingdom (Matthew), the Word of God (Luke). Matthew makes use of the present tense of the Greek participles (hearing and understanding); these participles refer to people who are asked to listen to and accept the Word of God. The passage also explains how four distinct types of hearers listen to God's Word.[18]

Matthew, as well as Luke, introduces the word *heart*. That is, "the evil one comes and snatches away what was sown in his heart" (13:19). The Word of God reaches the heart of the listener, but before the Word can have any effect at all, the evil one (Matthew), Satan (Mark), or the devil (Luke) comes and snatches it away. In the parable, the birds swoop down onto the path and devour the kernels of grain. Says Mark, "Some people are like seed along the path, where the word is sown. As soon as they hear it, Satan comes and takes away the word that was sown in them" (4:15). We would say, "In one ear and out the other," or, "Like water off a duck's back." Some people politely listen to the gospel, but they are hearers only. The gospel is not precious to them, for their hearts are as hard as the footpath along the grainfield. They completely ignore the summary of God's Law, "Love the Lord your God with all your *heart*" (Matt. 22:37).

At first it appears that the seed sown on rocky places gets an early start. The summer heat, captured in the rock substratum, is now gradually released in the colder months of November and December. There is sufficient rainfall, so that the necessary warmth and moisture make early germination possible. The green shoots spring up quickly, and while the rest of the field is still barren, they make quite an impressive show. The trained eye of the farmer sees the difference. He knows that the appearance of the green stalks of grain on the rocky places is deceptive; when the rains have ceased, and the sun in the spring of the year rises with increasing heat, the plants wither. They have no roots that go deep down into the soil to supply the plants with water. The plants shrivel up and die.

In the interpretation and application of this segment of the parable, both Matthew and Mark bring out the aspect of immediacy. "Others, like seed sown on rocky places, hear the word and at once receive it with joy. But since they have no root, they last only a short time. When trouble or persecution comes because of the word, they quickly fall away"

(Mark 4:16, 17). The immediacy is reflected in the quick germination of the kernels sown on rocky soil.

Whereas Matthew and Mark attribute the falling away to trouble and persecution, Luke speaks of a "time of testing" (Luke 8:13). The evangelists mention hardship that causes people to have second thoughts about religion. When the time has come to take a stand and to pay the price, they change their interest and involvement in the faith they once embraced with joy. One word describes them: *superficiality*. The sun, usually considered the source of happiness and joy, is portrayed here in terms of trouble and persecution.[19] The reason for this apparent harshness is the lack of moisture. The righteous person, on the other hand, flourishes as a tree planted by a stream of water (Ps. 1:3). Shallow persons lack conviction, courage, stability, and perseverance. They are influenced by every wind of doctrine that blows their way. Because they lack depth, their spiritual life is of passing significance.

The seed sown among the thorns seems to have a better chance for growth and development than that which was sown on shallow soil. At first, after a period of germination, the plants begin to stool out. In fact, by the spring of the year they look quite promising and cannot be distinguished at all from the other plants. But when the sun's heat gains strength and warms the earth, the roots of the thorns and thistles come to life. After a winter's rest they are ready for a new season, and in a matter of weeks the thorns and thistles have overtaken the wheat plants in height. They deprive them of moisture and soil nutrients and literally choke them to death.

The soil in which the seed has been sown is neither hard like a trodden path nor shallow with a rocky substratum. Rather, it is good soil—fertile and moisture-retaining. The only drawback is that the soil has other permanent residents, other roots. The seed that is sown in fertile soil with plenty of moisture must before long compete with growing and developing roots below the surface, and with verdant thistles and thorns above the surface. In short, two types of plants are struggling for a place in the sun, and the type whose roots were put down first is gaining the upper hand.

"Still others, like seed sown among thorns, hear the word; but the worries of this life, the deceitfulness of wealth and the desires of other things come in and choke the word, making it unfruitful" (Mark 4:18, 19). People who lead a double life—religion on Sunday and an irreligious life during the week—will soon discover that the "worries of this life, the deceitfulness of wealth and the desires for other things" take over, so that their faith becomes worthless. The message of the gospel cannot flourish and bear fruit; instead, worldly interests choke it out. These people have led a double life from the beginning. They have found security in riches and possessions; they have purposely relegated their faith to a secondary place. They are the "both/and" people who eventually reap a harvest of thorns and thistles without a single grain of wheat. Even what they have is taken from them.

These three sketches of the field should not discourage the farmer. Likewise, the three portrayals of people whose faith has become fruitless should not dishearten the true believer; they are refusals to heed the Word, denials in times of persecution, and deadly snares of worldliness. By contrast, the seed that is sown in the good soil produces an abundant harvest, a bumper crop. The people who in faith respond to the gospel are without number, a countless multitude. "But the one who receives the seed that fell on good soil is the man who hears the word and understands it. He produces a crop, yielding a hundred, sixty or thirty times what was sown" (Matt. 13:23).[20] Mark gives an ascending order of "thirty, sixty, or even a hundred times." Luke merely lists "a hundred times" in the parable proper, but in the interpretation he writes, "But the seed on the good soil stands for those with a noble and good heart, who hear the word, retain it, and by persevering produce a crop" (8:15). What Luke means by "retain" is given in Mark as "accept" and in Matthew as "understand."

Who, then, is the person with a good and noble heart? Matthew provides the answer. Says he, "the man who hears the word and understands it." Of course, Matthew calls to mind the quotation from Isaiah. The man with a noble and perfect heart does the will of God and in answer to God's call "Whom shall I send?" responds confidently, "Send me, O Lord." He is the hearer and the doer of the Word. He understands because his heart is receptive to God's truth. His whole being—his will, his intellect, and his emotions—is touched by that Word. A spiritual growth takes place, and the believer bears fruit; he does the will of God.[21]

What does the parable teach? Some scholars have called the parable of the sower the parable of parables. This does not mean that this parable is the most outstanding in the Synoptic Gospels but rather that it contains four parables in one. Yet all four are merely aspects of one particular truth: the Word of God is proclaimed and causes a division among those who hear; God's people receive the Word, understand it, and obediently fulfill it. Others fail to listen because of a hardened heart, a basic superficiality, or a vested interest in riches and possessions. These people fail to bear fruit, and even what they have—spiritually speaking—will be taken from them. The parable therefore touches people who are truly in the church and those who are "on the outside." This is the main thrust of the parable. All the details in the parable focus attention on that one point. The faithful proclamation of the gospel will never fail to bring forth fruit, "producing a crop, thirty, sixty, or even a hundred times what was sown."

5 Seed Growing Secretly

> **Mark 4:26–29**
> [26]He also said, "This is what the kingdom of God is like. A man scatters seed on the ground. [27]Night and day, whether he sleeps or gets up, the seed sprouts and grows, though he does not know how. [28]All by itself the soil produces grain—first the stalk, then the head, then the full kernel in the head. [29]As soon as the grain is ripe, he puts the sickle to it, because the harvest has come."

The Gospel of Mark is not known for discourses; instead, it is a narrative in which the author vividly portrays Jesus as a man of action. Yet Mark does incorporate didactic material, such as the discourse on the signs of the end of the age (chapter 13) and three parables of growth (chapter 4). Mark is not interested in expanding the number of parables. He seems to indicate that he has been selective in his choice of available material.[1] Mark has chosen the parables of the sower, the seed growing secretly, and the mustard seed. These parables obviously detail the planting of seed, growing and maturing, and reaping and harvesting.[2] Mark uses the parables to illustrate the nature of God's kingdom taught by Jesus.

SETTING

Because it lacks a number of details, the story of the seed growing secretly is in itself somewhat simplistic. Nothing is said about soil preparation, rainfall, sunshine, weed control, or organic fertilizer. The life of the farmer seems to parallel that of sowing seed, sleeping at night, and

41

becoming active in the morning. At harvesttime he puts the sickle into the grain.

The parable bypasses all the details, significant as they may be, and places the emphasis on sowing, growing, and mowing. We should not assume that the farmer spent his days idly. Of course not; he had work to do. Plowing, fertilizing, and weeding took much of his time. Besides the daily chores, he had to do the buying and selling, planning and preparation for the harvest. All this is understood and taken for granted in the parable. We also note that God will provide the necessary rainfall.[3] He is in control of the natural elements.

That is exactly the point. From the moment he has sown the seed the farmer must leave the sprouting, the growing, the pollinating, and the maturing to God. He can describe the process of growing wheat, but he cannot explain it. After the wheat has been sown, it absorbs the moisture of the soil, swells, and sprouts. After a week or two, the first little blades appear above the surface; gradually the plants begin to stool, increase in height, and develop heads. Then, when the plants die, their color turns from green to gold; the grain ripens and the time to harvest has come. The farmer cannot explain this growth and development.[4] He is only a worker who at the proper time sows and reaps. God holds the secret of life. God is in control.

INTERPRETATION

The parable of the seed growing secretly is found only in the Gospel of Mark. Matthew and Luke do not contain it, and we have no further information other than what is found in these few verses of Mark 4:26–29.[5] The parable is introduced by the sentence, "This is what the kingdom of God is like."

Interpretations of this parable have varied. Some commentators explain the account allegorically: Christ has sown and in time will come to reap; the rest of the parable refers to the invisible working of the Holy Spirit in the church and in the soul.[6] Others have stressed one of the following: the seed; the period of growth; the harvest; or the contrast between sowing and harvesting.[7] Surely, all these interpretations—even the allegorical (with qualifications)—have advantages.

John Calvin looked beyond the Originator of this parable and saw the ministers of the Word sowing the seed. They should not become discouraged, said Calvin, when they do not see immediate results. Jesus teaches them to be patient and reminds them of the process of growth in nature. They should not fret and fuss, but after they have proclaimed the Word, they ought to go about their ordinary task of the day—go to

bed at night and get up in the morning and do the things they are supposed to do. Just as the wheat comes to maturity at the right time, so
the fruit of the preacher's labors will eventually appear. Ministers of
the gospel should take courage and continue their work eagerly and
faithfully.[8]

God is at work in the seed's germination, its growth, development,
and ripening process. "The fruit is the *result* of the seed; the end is *implicit*
in the beginning. The infinitely great is already active in the infinitely
small."[9] It is well to call to mind Paul's jubilant saying, that he is confident of this, "that he who began a good work in you will carry it on to
completion until the day of Christ Jesus" (Phil. 1:6).

In the parable, the farmer is only an assistant in divine employ. He
sows the seed and day by day does the necessary work—he goes about
his business. He is confident that the harvest will eventually come. In
fact, he knows from experience how many days it takes from the time
he sows to the time of harvest.[10] And when the crop is ripe he does not
wait another day. Harvesttime has come. Likewise, the ministers of the
Word are in divine employ, proclaiming the good news of salvation in
Christ Jesus. They too must stand aside while God performs the secret
work of growth and development. In God's time, the minister will see
results when harvesttime has come.

The parable of the seed growing secretly is really a parable of
sequence: harvesting follows sowing in due time. The manifestation of
God's kingdom follows the faithful ministry of God's Word. The one
leads to the other, and nothing happens without the secret working
power of God. "The lesson is: the victory is sure; harvest is approaching
and will certainly arrive at the very moment decided in God's eternal
plan. Then God's kingdom will be revealed in all its splendor."[11]

The last words of the parable are somewhat reminiscent of Joel 3:13,
"Swing the sickle, for the harvest is ripe." Unmistakably, it refers ultimately to the judgment day when the Lord, according to Revelation
14:12–16, sends out his angels to gather the harvest of the earth. In the
meantime, those who are sent forth to proclaim the Word ought to learn
patience from the farmer. "Be patient then, brothers, until the Lord's
coming. See how the farmer waits for the land to yield its valuable crop"
(James 5:7). Lack of patience is a human characteristic. It even appears
in John's description of the souls of those who had been slain because
of the Word of God. They call out in a loud voice, "How long, Sovereign
Lord?" And the answer they receive is that they should wait a little longer
(Rev. 6:9–11). God is in control and determines when the time for harvest has arrived. No one, not even Jesus, knows that day and hour (Matt.
24:26).

6 Wheat and Weeds

> **Matthew 13:24–30**
> [24]Jesus told them another parable: "The kingdom of heaven is like a man who sowed good seed in his field. [25]But while everyone was sleeping, his enemy came and sowed weeds among the wheat, and went away. [26]When the wheat sprouted and formed heads, then the weeds also appeared.
>
> [27]"The owner's servants came to him and said, 'Sir, didn't you sow good seed in your field? Where then did the weeds come from?'
>
> [28]"'An enemy did this,' he replied.
>
> "The servants asked him 'Do you want us to go and pull them up?'
>
> [29]"'No,' he answered, 'because while you are pulling the weeds, you may root up the wheat with them. [30]Let both grow together until the harvest. At that time I will tell the harvesters: First collect the weeds and tie them in bundles to be burned, then gather the wheat and bring it into my barn.'"

The parable of the wheat and weeds is unique to Matthew's Gospel, just like the parable of seed growing secretly is found only in Mark. The word *weeds* is not an adequate translation of the original Greek word *zizania*, which refers to "a troublesome weed in the grain fields, resembling wheat."[1] It cannot be determined whether the word refers to the poisonous or to the nonpoisonous variety of this weed. Whatever the case, the plant has the appearance of wheat and grows exclusively in cultivated fields.[2] In fact, the plant has degenerated from the wheat plant. The weed may be compared to wild oats, which grows freely in North America's wheat fields and which is difficult to eradicate.

The Farmer's Field

After the parable of the sower and its interpretation, Matthew reports that Jesus told the crowd another parable, a story of a rather well-to-do farmer. This farmer has servants and also employs harvesters at the proper time.

Like any efficient farmer, this landowner has obtained good seed. Obviously he is not interested in sowing weed seeds—that would cause him untold grief. Good seed is weed-free. The farmer has sowed good seed in his field (when and how this was done is not important to the story).

As soon as he has finished the task of sowing winter wheat, his enemy comes. He arrives under the cover of darkness, while everyone is sleeping, and sows weed seeds on top of the wheat. Certainly he does not have to cover the entire field. Here and there he scatters the seed. No one will know until the following spring that weeds are growing alongside the wheat plants.[3] The weeds look exactly like the wheat. When the plants form heads, everyone can distinguish the wheat from the weeds—"by their fruit you will recognize them" (Matt. 7:20).

By that time it has become impossible to do anything about the problem. Anyone walking into the grainfield to remove the weeds will trample the wheat. Moreover, the roots of the wheat and the weeds are so intertwined that pulling up the weeds will also uproot the wheat.

The servants of the farmer alert him to the problem and even show their willingness to do something about it. They want to know where these weeds have come from. The farmer merely informs them that an enemy has done this and that they should leave everything until the harvest. At that time the harvesters will receive instructions to collect the weeds, to tie them in bundles, and to gather the wheat for storage in his barn. The farmer will use the weed bundles—seed and straw—for fuel. He therefore turns a disadvantage into an asset: fuel for the winter.

Even though the farmer makes the most of a bad situation, he knows that the weeds have taken up moisture and nutrients that should have gone to the wheat plants. His yield of grain is thus substantially less than he expected. In spite of all his farming skill, he has been unable to tell the difference between the wheat and the weeds until the plants started to form heads and harvesttime was approaching.[4] At last, months after the deed has been committed, the farmer realizes that his enemy has insidiously attacked him. He has to face the consequences of the scheme perpetrated by his enemy.

INTERPRETATION

Matthew 13:36–43

[36]Then he left the crowd and went into the house. His disciples came to him and said, "Explain to us the parable of the weeds in the field."

[37]He answered, "The one who sowed the good seed is the Son of Man. [38]The field is the world, and the good seed stands for the sons of the kingdom. The weeds are the sons of the evil one, [39]and the enemy who sows them is the devil. The harvest is the end of the age, and the harvesters are angels.

[40]"As the weeds are pulled up and burned in the fire, so it will be at the end of the age. [41]The Son of Man will send out his angels, and they will weed out of his kingdom everything that causes sin and all who do evil. [42]They will throw them into the fiery furnace, where there will be weeping and gnashing of teeth. [43]Then the righteous will shine like the sun in the kingdom of their Father. He who has ears, let him hear."

According to Matthew, Jesus' disciples asked for an explanation of the parable of the weeds.[5] In relatively few words the explanation is given. In paradigm form it reads as follows:

1. "The one who sowed the good seed   is the Son of Man.
2. The field   is the world, and
3. the good seed   stands for the sons of the kingdom.
4. The weeds   are the sons of the evil one, and
5. the enemy who sows them   is the devil.
6. The harvest   is the end of the age, and
7. the harvesters   are angels."

Although Jesus provides the interpretation of the parable, the composition of the explanation is from the hand of Matthew. Matthew takes the teaching of Jesus and arranges his words in a list of seven concepts.[6] (Arranging names and data is a characteristic of Matthew's writing style, as is evident from the first chapter of his Gospel.)

In the interpretation, no mention is made of the fact that the enemy came while people were sleeping. Also, the reference to the growing and maturing of wheat and weeds is omitted, and nothing is said about the gathering of wheat into the barn and the bundling of weeds for the fire. Jesus omits the reference to the servants in his interpretation. Perhaps he did this to focus attention on the deeper significance of the parable: the conflict between good and evil, between God and Satan. And in this conflict Satan loses the battle. Likewise, the conversation between the servants and the farmer seems to have no significance for the interpretation of the parable. The conversation is left out; the reference to it is given by way of a summary in which the pulling out of the weeds and their burning in the fire becomes an important point (Matt. 13:40). In fact, the conclusion of the interpretation is a view of things to come at the end of the age. Jesus in effect says, "By way of the Old Testament Scriptures, let me tell you what is going to happen."

> [41]The Son of Man will send out his angels, and they will weed out of his kingdom everything that causes sin and all who do evil. [42]They will throw them into the fiery furnace, where there will be weeping and gnashing of teeth. [43]Then the righteous will shine like the sun in the kingdom of their Father. He who has ears, let him hear.
>
> Matthew 13:41–43

As usual, Jesus' teaching directly and indirectly reflects the Old Testament Scriptures.[7] Jesus seems to refer to the prophecy of Zephaniah ("I will sweep away everything from the face of the earth, . . . both men and animals" [1:2, 3]) when he speaks of weeding out of his kingdom everything that causes sin and all who do evil. The phrase "They will throw them into the fiery furnace" resembles Daniel 3:6 ("be thrown into a blazing furnace"). The concept itself is akin to Malachi 4:1, "Surely the day is coming; it will burn like a furnace. All the arrogant and every evildoer will be stubble." The sentence, "Then the righteous will shine like the sun," resembles Daniel 12:3, "Those who are wise will shine like the brightness of the heavens and those who lead many to righteousness, like the stars for ever and ever." And to be complete, we should also look at Malachi 4:2: "But for you who revere my name, the sun of righteousness will rise."

Unmistakably, Jesus' interpretation conveys a resounding echo of the words and sentiments of the prophets. The parable of the weeds is actually a parable in which Jesus teaches the coming judgment; it may well be called the parable of the harvest.

The servants wish to pull up the weeds, although they would in the process uproot the wheat—the root system of the weeds is much more developed than that of the wheat. But the farmer says: wait until the harvest, then the harvesters will separate the weeds from the wheat.

The farmer knows his business. If he permits the servants to pull up the weeds, he will lose his wheat crop, since the wheat plants cannot be separated from the weeds. If he lost his crop, the farmer would give his enemy all the satisfaction he wanted.

Instead, the farmer decides to leave the whole field to mature. At the time of the harvest the separation will take place. Both the weeds and the wheat will mature until the harvest.

The weeds are the sons of the evil one and the good seeds stand for the sons of the kingdom. How these two—the evil and the good—mature is not explained, and we do well not to go beyond the parable in finding an answer.[8]

While these two are growing and maturing, the farmer is unable to take steps to remedy the situation. This inability does not stem from ignorance. On the contrary, the farmer, fully in control of the situation, waits it out. He knows what to do. He knows where the weeds came from and how they were sown into his field—by night, while everyone was sleeping.

Jesus, in interpreting the parable, says that the farmer who sows the good seed is the Son of Man. This Son of Man is Jesus himself, who being made in human likeness has taken on the appearance of a man (Phil. 2:7, 8). He has come to sow the good seed, the sons of the kingdom, the new humanity in Christ. The field where the seed is sown is the world. That is where the drama of good and evil takes place. The enemy who sows the seed is the devil, and the weeds are the sons of the evil one.

It is interesting to note that the field, the world, belongs to the farmer—to Jesus. In that field grow wheat and weeds. It does not matter where man lives on this earth. Wherever he lives he finds himself on property that belongs to Jesus.[9] He is either wheat or weed, one or the other. He is either a son of the kingdom or a son of the evil one. Both the wheat and the weeds mature until the farmer sends the harvesters into the field.

When the end of the age has come, the harvesters, who are God's angels, separate the good from the bad, the wheat from the weeds, the sons of the kingdom from the sons of the evil one. In the conflict between God and Satan, Satan loses out. Satan's seed—everything that causes sin and all who do evil—is weeded out and thrown into the fiery furnace. The sons of the kingdom, on the other hand, will shine like the sun in the kingdom of their Father. They are the righteous. They are the blessed. They endure.

APPLICATION

Jesus' parable contrasts the good and the bad, and teaches that in the end the good will triumph. In the parable the servants question the farmer about the source of the weeds: "Where then did the weeds come from?" The farmer's somewhat terse reply is: "An enemy did this." The servants, of course, could have vented their anger against the enemy,[10] but instead they turn their attention to the weeds and make known their wish to pull them out. The farmer says, "No, wait!"

The servants reflect the impatient mood of many Christians in God's kingdom. Under the banner of maintaining the purity of the church, zealous believers have caused untold damage by passing judgment on fellow Christians, and by cutting them off from the church.

Any gardener knows that at times it is impossible to tell the difference between a plant that produces a beautiful flower and a plant that turns out to be a troublesome weed. In the words of the old rhyme,

> There is so much good in the worst of us,
> And so much bad in the best of us,
> That it hardly becomes any of us
> To talk about the rest of us.[11]

No one should understand the parable to teach elimination of discipline or a disapproval of enforcing and applying the Law. On the contrary, Scripture teaches most clearly that discipline must be maintained and that the Law must be upheld. Jesus explicitly teaches the doctrine of discipline in Matthew 18:15–17. He outlines the process by indicating that discipline must, however, be conducted in a loving and gentle spirit. And the process must proceed cautiously and patiently. Discipline must always aim at saving and restoring the person involved.

Paul in Romans 13 teaches that "the authorities that exist have been established by God. Consequently, he who rebels against the authority is rebelling against what God has instituted, and those who do so will bring judgment on themselves. For rulers hold no terror for those who do right, but for those who do wrong" (13:1–3). God has entrusted authority to rulers to uphold the law, punish the evildoer, and deter crime.

The parable, however, instructs us to be patient and not to act as self-appointed judges. "Be patient and stand firm, because the Lord's coming is near. Don't grumble against each other, brothers, or you will be judged. The Judge is standing at the door!" (James 5:8, 9).

At first sight, the parable may leave the impression that there are two kinds of people in this world, the good and the bad, and that the good always remain good and the bad always remain bad. This, however, is not quite correct. Scripture does not teach that God creates good men and Satan creates bad men. God creates people—they are his handiwork—and he regenerates those whom he has chosen through the gracious work of his Spirit. Wicked people, although created by God, have been corrupted by Satan and are being used by him to influence God's regenerated people.[12] They are the weeds among the wheat. Weeds and wheat mature side by side until the harvest. Then they will be separated.

The parable of the weeds contains a compact list of terms similar in form to a glossary. The apparent simplicity in explaining the terms almost seems to be a challenge to do the same thing to the other parables Jesus taught. Many commentators have seen this as an open invitation to explain the parables as Jesus did. For example, in explaining the parable of the five wise and five foolish virgins (Matt. 25:1–13), commentators in the early church gave various explanations for the word *oil*. For Clement of Alexandria, oil was the Father's compassion; for Hilary, oil signified the fruit of good works; for Augustine, oil denoted joy. But Chrysostom suggested that oil meant giving help to the needy; and Origen considered oil to be the word of teaching.[13] During the Middle Ages and the Reformation, Bede said that oil represented repentance, but for Luther it was grace.[14]

Obviously, commentators do not have the wisdom Jesus displayed in interpreting the parables. They should be careful, therefore, not to read into a parable thoughts and concepts that the parable does not intend to teach. Indeed, they do well to find the basic teaching of the parable in the parable itself or in its context, and to limit their interpretation to the point the parable conveys.

7 Mustard Seed

> ### Matthew 13:31, 32
> [31]He told them another parable: "The kingdom of heaven is like a mustard seed, which a man took and planted in his field. [32]Though it is the smallest of all your seeds, yet when it grows, it is the largest of garden plants and becomes a tree, so that the birds of the air come and perch in its branches."
>
> ### Mark 4:30–32
> [30]Again he said, "What shall we say the kingdom of God is like, or what parable shall we use to describe it? [31]It is like a mustard seed, which is the smallest seed you plant in the ground. [32]Yet when planted, it grows and becomes the largest of all garden plants, with such big branches that the birds of the air can perch in its shade."
>
> ### Luke 13:18, 19
> [18]Then Jesus asked, "What is the kingdom of God like? What shall I compare it to? [19]It is like a mustard seed, which a man took and planted in his garden. It grew, became a tree, and the birds of the air perched in its branches."

Jesus told two parables to indicate the phenomenal growth of the kingdom of heaven: the parable of the mustard seed and the parable of the yeast. These two form a pair, and are really two sides of the same coin. The parable of the mustard seed portrays the extensive growth of the kingdom, and that of the yeast describes the intensive growth of the kingdom.[1]

Matthew placed the two parables in his parable chapter (chapter 13); he did this most likely for topical reasons. Luke, on the other hand, by incorporating the parables in the so-called travel narrative (Luke 9:51–19:27), may reflect a more historical sequence, although we cannot ascertain this in any way. We may assume that Jesus taught these two parables together on the same occasion.[2]

Sowing and Growing

Twenty-five schoolchildren accompany their teacher to Washington, D.C., to see the White House. When they return to their classroom, the teacher asks every child to write a short essay on the trip to the White House. Twenty-five essays reflect twenty-five aspects of the presidential dwelling. One child may write, "The White House is like this," followed by a description of a most relevant feature in his eyes. Another child, however, may use the same introduction but in the essay portray an entirely different perspective on the White House.

Jesus acquainted his followers with the many characteristics of the kingdom of God. By means of parables, he sought to describe the individual facets of God's royal rule. Thus he introduces his parables with the phrase "The kingdom of heaven is like . . . ."

The parable of the mustard seed, in contrast to that of the wheat and weeds, is very brief. In relatively few words Jesus portrays the amazing size of the mustard tree ("tree" in Matthew and Luke; "plant" in Mark), which developed from the smallest seed planted in gardens. Obviously, Jesus stresses the difference between the smallness of the seed and the greatness of the plant. He does not say a word about the qualities of the mustard plant. He could have mentioned its use in food and medicine, its color, and its taste, but this is not the point of the parable.

Jesus uses an example out of everyday life. In our modern society of canned, bottled, and packaged food, gardens are unknown to many people. But in Jesus' day most everyone had his own garden plot. Even the clergy of that day tithed spices—mint, dill, and cummin—from their gardens (Matt. 23:23). In every garden, the mustard plant had a place. The plant may most often have been grown in a field bordering a garden plot because of its demand for space. In Matthew the gardener plants the seed in a field, in Luke in a garden, and in Mark in the ground.

The gardener took only one of the mustard seeds. His fingers seemed far too big to hold such an insignificantly small seed. He sowed the seed in his field because he knew that tiny speck had the capabilities of growing into a plant the size of a tree.[3] He needed only one plant. And he knew the contrast between seed and plant.[4] In fact, the insignificant size of the mustard seed had become proverbial in the first century. Jesus at one time said: "If you have faith as small as a mustard seed, you can say to this mountain, 'Move from here to there'" (Matt. 17:20).[5] Both Matthew and Mark explicitly say that the mustard seed "is the smallest of all your seed."[6] The contrast, therefore, is brought out all the more, because the statement is balanced by the description of the mature plant: "the largest of garden plants and becomes a tree." That utterly small, insignificant speck of seed, entrusted to the field, becomes a tree. A miracle!

Concluding the parable, Jesus alludes to the Old Testament passages of Daniel 4:12 and Ezekiel 17:23 and 31:6. The passage from Daniel was well known to Jesus' audience because it referred to Nebuchadnezzar's dream of a tree that became so strong that its top reached to heaven. Under that tree beasts of the field found shade, and on its branches the birds of the air came to perch. Jesus, who speaks the words of God (John 3:34), teaches Scripture indirectly by way of a verbal allusion, and calls attention to a messianic parable in Ezekiel 17:23, "On the mountain heights of Israel I will plant it; it will produce branches and bear fruit and become a splendid cedar. Birds of every kind will nest in it; they will find shelter in the shade of its branches."[7]

Effect

By means of the parable, Jesus teaches that God's kingdom may seem unimportant and insignificant, especially in Galilee in A.D. 28. But the gospel of the kingdom proclaimed by a carpenter-turned-preacher will have a tremendous impact upon the world at large. Jesus' followers consisted of a few "uneducated" fishermen who were told to make disciples of all nations. These followers set the world on fire with the message of salvation, which today is proclaimed in nearly all the known languages of the world. The tiny seed sown in Galilee at the dawn of the new age of Christianity has become a tree that today provides shelter and rest to people everywhere. And yet the day is not spent.

The tree has not yet reached maturity; it is still growing.[8] We look at the phenomenon of the growing tree and know that God is at work developing his kingdom. We know that countless people on this globe have not heard the good news of God's forgiving love. Entire nations are virtually devoid of the shade and shelter extended by God's kingdom. The tree's branches must continue to grow and extend to those regions that still need the gospel so that multitudes may find refuge and rest.[9] And when the gospel of God's kingdom has been preached to all the nations of the world, then the end will come (Matt. 24:14) and the tree will be fully grown.

8 Yeast

Matthew 13:33
³³He told them still another parable: "The kingdom of heaven is like yeast that a woman took and mixed into a large amount of flour until it worked all through the dough."

Luke 13:20, 21
²⁰Again he asked, "What shall I compare the kingdom of God to? ²¹It is like yeast that a woman took and mixed into a large amount of flour until it worked all through the dough."

Visual education was one of Jesus' pedagogical rules. Whenever he taught people about God's kingdom, he used examples taken directly from everyday life. As he grew up in Nazareth, he saw his mother bake bread. First she got the pots and pans ready; then she took flour, water, and yeast and added a pinch of salt. She mixed the ingredients together and then left the batch of dough alone. Her work for the moment was done; the yeast would take over and cause the dough to rise. When the process of fermentation was over, she would bake the bread.

Jesus told the story of a woman baking bread—a scene borrowed from daily life. The woman took a rather small quantity of yeast, mixed it with a large quantity of flour, and baked enough bread to feed one hundred persons at a single meal. Both Matthew and Luke indicate that the woman took three *satas* of flour. A *sata* is the equivalent of about 13.13 liters. Thus the woman, taking some 39 liters of flour—more than 50 pounds in weight—intended to bake bread in large quantities. It is too much, of course, for the daily use of a small family.[1] But Sarah, Abraham's wife, baked that much when three men visited them at Mamre (Gen. 18:6). And in at least two other references the amount of three

54

measures *(seahs,* or one *ephah)* is mentioned for baking bread (Judg. 6:19; 1 Sam. 1:24).

One could argue that modern translations obscure the basic meaning of the verse by rendering the Greek word *zumē* as yeast and not as leaven. Apart from Jewish people, hardly anyone is familiar with the word *leaven,* and for that reason the yeast concept is introduced: "The kingdom of heaven is like yeast that a woman took and mixed into a large amount of flour until it worked all through the dough" (Matt. 13:33). Yeast as we know it today is clean, fresh, and wholesome. It is made from a cultivation of a mineral salt-sugar solution to which starch is added. Leaven, however, was produced by storing a piece of dough from the previous week and by adding juices to promote the process of fermentation. Should the leaven become infected with a harmful bacterial culture, it would be passed on in the bread until the process was broken when people ate unleavened bread for a week, as they did during Passover.[2]

Jesus' intention is not to call leaven something evil. He uses the concept of leaven because of its hidden power. Yeast and leaven cause the dough to rise by permeating the entire batch. The yeast or leaven, after it was mixed in with the flour, could not be found anymore. It was hidden and invisible.

This rather short parable has been interpreted in numerous ways. Jerome, for example, identified the woman with the church.[3] The three measures of flour have been explained as the three branches of the human race (descendants of Shem, Ham, and Japheth); the Greeks, Jews, and Samaritans; or heart, soul, and mind.[4] These interpretations are speculative, imaginary, and of little more than passing value.

The point of the parable is that the yeast, once added to the flour, permeates the entire batch of dough until every particle is affected. The yeast is hidden from sight, and yet its effect is visible to all. That is how the kingdom of God demonstrates its power and presence in today's world.

In the parable of the mustard seed, Jesus makes known the extent and outward spread of the kingdom. In the parable of the yeast, Jesus focuses attention on the internal power of the kingdom that leaves nothing unaffected.

The mustard seed parable illustrates the church's global evangelistic program in obedience to Christ's commission. He told his followers to make disciples of every nation. The yeast parable further illustrates that this obedience to Christ entails Christianizing every sector and segment of life. The follower of Christ lets his light shine before men, that they may see his good deeds and praise his Father in heaven (Matt. 5:16). He alleviates the suffering of the poor and afflicted; he champions the cause of justice in behalf of the oppressed; he demands honesty from those elected or appointed to rule the nation; he elevates the standards of morality and decency; he defends the sanctity of life; he upholds the laws of the land; he requires integrity in business, commerce, industry, labor, and the professions (medical, legal, religious); and in the area of education he meaningfully explains that in Christ "are hidden all the treasures of wisdom and knowledge" (Col. 2:3). Christ's follower makes the teachings of Scripture relevant everywhere. "That this 'yeast' of the rule of Christ in human hearts, lives, *and spheres* has already exerted a wholesome influence in thousands of ways, and that this influence is still continuing, is clear to all who have eyes to see."[5] He who has ears, let him hear.

What precisely did Jesus mean by the expression "kingdom of heaven"? Is it a synonym for *church?* God's people individually and corporately confess the name of Jesus Christ as their Savior. Together they constitute the church. In that church they receive gifts and powers enabling them to keep God's Law cheerfully, to proclaim the gospel of salvation universally, and to further the rule of God effectively.[6] The church then consists of Christians who apply the teachings of Christ in every sphere of life. By doing this they promote the kingdom of God in which the rule of Christ is recognized. In short, every area of life affected by the teaching of Christ (the yeast) belongs to the kingdom.

9 Hidden Treasure and Pearl

> **Matthew 13:44**
> [44]"The kingdom of heaven is like treasure hidden in a field. When a man found it, he hid it again, and then in his joy went and sold all he had and bought that field."
>
> **Matthew 13:45, 46**
> [45]"Again, the kingdom of heaven is like a merchant looking for fine pearls. [46]When he found one of great value, he went away and sold everything he had and bought it."

In his series of seven parables, Matthew is quite elaborate on the first two (the sower, and the wheat and weeds), providing an interpretation for each. The other five are shorter and more pointed in content. The parables of the hidden treasure and of the pearl consist of two sentences each; and part of the first sentence of each parable is the familiar introductory phrase, "The kingdom of heaven is like . . ." The main point of the parable, of course, is found in the second sentence.

These parables occur only in Matthew's Gospel and form a pair. Whether Jesus taught the two parables in sequence or whether Matthew in arranging his material topically placed them together is unknown; the fact remains that the two belong together.[1]

Strictly speaking, the introductory sentences of the two parables are not quite balanced. In the one the kingdom of heaven is like a treasure, and in the other it is like a merchant. We should not, however, approach the two parables with an analytic Western mind. Instead, we should try to grasp the basic meaning of the parables as understood by the disciples who first heard them.

SETTING

Jesus told the parable of a man who found a treasure hidden in a field. He quickly buried it again and joyfully went home to sell all that he owned in order to buy the field.

Children often fantasize that in some field or old building or barn they will discover a treasure that has escaped everybody else's attention. In our sophisticated society, we call this unrealistic; we think such things do not happen anymore. Yet from time to time discoveries are made: a shepherd boy near the Dead Sea found scrolls that were two thousand years old; a diver off the Florida coast located a sunken seventeenth-century Spanish vessel filled with silver and gold; and a farmer plowing his field in Suffolk, England, struck a container that held beautiful silver dishes dating from Roman times.[2]

A treasure has been hidden in a field. Who put it there and how long ago are questions that cannot be answered. We do know that in ancient Palestine, a country frequently ravished by war, people often hid their treasure or part of it in a field rather than in a house. In a house, thieves would be able to find it; in a field, the treasure would be safer. But if the owner was killed during a war, he would carry his secret with him to the grave, and no one would ever know where he had hidden the treasure.

The man who found such a treasure may have been a hired hand or a renter. He may have been plowing the field, digging a ditch, or planting a tree. Whatever the case, he hit something underground that was hard and did not sound like a rock. He dug it out and found a treasure. We are not told what the treasure was, but the man was dumbfounded. He had never seen such a valuable treasure before. It could be his if he owned the field.

Within seconds he made a plan. He quickly put the treasure back in its place, covered it up, and went home. He knew that the present owner of the field had not put the treasure there. Therefore, if the owner sold him the field, he would have the treasure in his own possession. Then it would be rightfully his.[3] He needed finances and was willing to sell all that he possessed. People may have shaken their heads about such rashness, but the man knew what he was doing. With the money he would buy the field to get the treasure.

With a few strokes of his verbal brush Matthew paints Jesus' parable of the pearl. A merchant is looking for pearls and finds one of exceptional value. He goes away, sells all that he owns, and buys the one pearl.

By itself, the story is a close parallel to that of the man who found a treasure. The same dedication is found in both parables. Each man must have the object of his desire even if it costs him his livelihood. Both men literally sell all that they have in order to obtain the treasure or the pearl.

In Old Testament times pearls apparently were not known, but by the first century of the Christian era pearls had become a status symbol of wealthy people.[4] Jesus told his audience, "Do not throw your pearls to pigs" (Matt. 7:6), and Paul wanted the women of his day to dress modestly, "not with braided hair or gold or pearls or expensive clothes" (1 Tim. 2:9). In the Book of Revelation a voice from heaven says, "The merchants of the earth will weep and mourn over her because no one buys their cargoes any more—cargoes of gold, silver, precious stones and pearls" (Rev. 18:11, 12).

In the times of Jesus and the apostles, pearls were in great demand. Merchants had to go to the Red Sea, the Persian Gulf, and even India in order to find them. Inferior pearls came from the Red Sea; the better ones came from the Persian Gulf and the coasts of Ceylon and India.[5] A merchant had to travel in his search for bigger and better pearls.

The man portrayed by Jesus is looking for fine pearls. We do not know how far he has traveled, but on a given day he finds one particular pearl of great value. For him, this is the chance of a lifetime. He will not be happy until that pearl is his. He mulls it over, makes all kinds of calculations, evaluates his assets, and decides to sell all his belongings in order to buy that one perfect pearl.

We should note that the merchant does not go from one pearl fisher to the next in deliberate search of one outstanding pearl. As he is looking for pearls in the course of normal business, he spots the finest pearl he has ever seen. Like the man discovering the treasure, the merchant suddenly sees the pearl. It is a now-or-never proposition: sell everything and buy! A typical oriental trader, the merchant keeps a straight face while making the transaction. When he has the pearl in his possession, it is time to celebrate.

> "It's no good, it's no good!" says the buyer; then off he goes and boasts about his purchase.
>
> Proverbs 20:14

APPLICATION

The friends and acquaintances of the two men in the parables must have shaken their heads when they saw that everything the men owned was for sale. They must have been surprised when soon afterward they learned of the possessions the men had gained. And they would have to respect them; these two individuals knew what they were doing.

The two men, however, did not speculate. There was no risk involved in buying the field and purchasing the pearl; the items bought would keep their value. What they did was most sensible. They had stumbled upon these items unintentionally, and to bypass them would be foolish. The opportunities were presented to them, and all they had to do was acquire the treasure and the pearl.

In buying the field and the pearl, the two men did not make a sacrifice, even though they sold everything they owned. "There is a basic difference between a purchase price and a sacrifice. Purchase is directed towards acquiring an object of equivalent value. Sacrifice on the other hand is a giving that expects no reward."[6] Both the man who found the treasure and the pearl merchant paid the full justifiable price of the purchased items. They heard opportunity knock and were ready to pay the price. They gave all they had in order to gain the one thing they desired.

What, then, do the parables teach? Church fathers such as Irenaeus and Augustine identified the treasure and the pearl with Christ. They saw correctly. The recent convert to Christianity says exactly the same thing: "I found Christ." Filled with joy, he returns to his own environment, gives up his lifestyle, and devotes himself completely to his Lord. Some people sell their business in order to pursue a theological education, seek ordination, and be commissioned as minister or missionary of the gospel of Christ.

It is Christ who offers the treasure and the pearl to people traveling along life's highway.[7] Some of these travelers are searching. Some are wandering. Suddenly they meet Jesus and find in him a priceless treasure. Their response to Jesus is one of total self-surrender. Joyfully they sell all that they have in order to have Jesus. Of course, salvation is full and free and cannot be purchased. It is a gift. What is meant is that Jesus demands the believer's heart. In the words of the hymn writer:

> All to Jesus I surrender,
> All to Him I freely give;
> I will ever love and trust Him,
> In His presence daily live.
>
> I surrender all, I surrender all.
> All to Thee, my blessed Savior,
> I surrender all.

10 Fishnet

> **Matthew 13:47–50**
> [47]"Once again, the kingdom of heaven is like a net that was let down into the lake and caught all kinds of fish. [48]When it was full, the fishermen pulled it up on the shore. Then they sat down and collected the good fish in baskets, but threw the bad away. [49]This is how it will be at the end of the age. The angels will come and separate the wicked from the righteous [50]and throw them into the fiery furnace, where there will be weeping and gnashing of teeth."

Only Matthew's Gospel contains the parable of the fishnet.[1] It is clearly a companion parable to that of the wheat and weeds; the interpretations of both are focused on the judgment day. Yet important differences are most evident. In the parable of the weeds Jesus stresses the idea of patience. This idea is not present in the parable of the fishnet.[2]

The weed parable is far more descriptive than that of the fishnet. It mentions the farmer, his servants, and the harvesters, but in the parable of the fishnet only fishermen and their labors are described. Weeds are *sown* into the field after the farmer has planted his crop, while edible and inedible fish are *always together* in the Galilean Lake. The parable of the weeds describes the field conditions of the present and the harvest as a future event. The fishnet parable, on the other hand, portrays the separating of the fish in terms of the present.[3]

FISHING

Most of Jesus' disciples were fishermen by trade; they had left their nets and boats to follow Jesus and to become fishers of men. When Jesus told them the parable of the fishnet, they understood every nuance of the story. Jesus touched upon their very livelihood of earlier days.

The northern edge of the Lake of Galilee is one of the best fishing areas in Israel. Plants swept along by the rapidly descending waters of the Jordan River are deposited at its northern inlet. These plants attract and feed a large and varied fish population. At least twenty-five native species have been identified in the lake.[4] The village of Bethsaida, meaning "house of fishing," was the home of Peter, Andrew, and Philip (John 1:44). It was situated along the north shore of the Lake of Galilee to the east of the Jordan.

Although there were various fishing methods in Jesus' day, a rather effective method was the use of the dragnet. This net was about 2 meters in height and up to 100 meters in length. Corks held up the top of the net, while the bottom was weighted down. At times fishermen fastened one end of the net on shore while a boat pulled the other end into the lake, traveling in a half circle and bringing the net back to shore. At other times two boats went out from shore, forming a semicircle with the net, drawing it together to catch the fish and gather them into the boats. The use of the dragnet required the united effort of a half-dozen men or more. While some rowed, others cast out or pulled in the net; still others would beat the water to drive the fish into the net.[5] Experienced fishermen would try to locate a school of fish before setting out the net. But once the net was set, the men pulled in all the fish that were in the net. Their catch was always a mixed one; obviously they could not be selective while catching the fish.[6]

The net drew in the edible fish as well as the inedible, the good as well as the bad. All kinds and sizes of fish were flapping their tails as they were pulled to shore. Many kinds of fish were declared unclean according to Jewish dietary laws. Fish without fins and scales could not be eaten (Lev. 11:10) and had to be thrown back into the water. The small fish were also released. Only fish that were marketable were kept and put in suitable containers. Sorting the fish ultimately determined the weight of the catch; until sorting time, no one knew the exact yield.

EXPLANATION

Jesus uses the parable of the fishnet to depict the day of judgment. He addresses his disciples who knew how to catch and sort fish. He speaks their language and thus effectively communicates a spiritual truth. And yet Jesus gives a brief interpretation of this parable. "This is how it will be at the end of the age. The angels will come and separate the wicked from the righteous and throw them into the fiery furnace, where there will be weeping and gnashing of teeth" (Matt. 13:49, 50). The words are almost identical to those given by Jesus in his interpretation of the parable of the wheat and weeds. "As the weeds are pulled up and burned in the fire, so it will be at the end of the age. The Son of Man will send out his angels, and they will weed out of his kingdom everything that causes sin and all who do evil. They will throw them into the fiery furnace where there will be weeping and gnashing of teeth" (Matt. 13:40–42).

To say that the interpretation of the dragnet does not fit the terms of the parable because inedible fish are thrown back into the water, and not into a fiery furnace, is illogical. One might just as well say that the interpretation of the parable of the wheat and weeds is ill-suited because weeds do not gnash their teeth. Jesus uses symbolic language and transfers the message of the parable to man's spiritual destiny: heaven or hell. In the parable of wheat and weeds man's destiny is either heaven, where the righteous shine like the sun, or hell, where there is weeping and grinding of teeth.

The interpretation given omits all the descriptive details of the fishermen casting their net and bringing their catch to shore; only the separating of the good fish from the worthless is explained. It is therefore wise not to impose one's own interpretation upon the details of the parable.[7] The particulars belong to the overall picture of bringing in the harvest. The net brings in all the fish that are caught, and the fishermen simply cannot be selective while drawing in the net. Thus Jesus' followers, appointed as fishers of men, are unable to be selective concerning when and to whom they proclaim the gospel. To borrow the wording from another parable, Christ's servants go out into the streets and gather all the people they can find, both good and bad (Matt. 22:10). The appeal of the gospel is directed to all people without discrimination.

The parable of the fishnet depicts the fishermen who cast the net, gather the catch, and separate the fish.[8] In the interpretation the angels come and separate the wicked from the righteous. The implication is that the fishermen, too, belong to the multitude from which the angels glean the wicked. The wicked are taken out of the multitude of the righteous.

The term *wicked* is comprehensive; it refers to those people who outwardly adhere to the church but inwardly have no connection with the true church. They may confess with their mouths the Apostles' Creed, but in their hearts they lack true faith in Jesus Christ.

These people are like those depicted in the parable of the sower: those with hardened hearts (the trodden path); shallow Christians (the rocky soil); and the lovers of worldly goods and pleasures (the weed patch). They are in the church but not of it. In the judgment day, God's angels will come and separate them from God's people, and throw them into the burning fire reserved for them.

What does the parable teach? Followers of Jesus, go about your daily task: witness to your fellowmen, whoever they may be; bring them together to the church; constantly remind them of the need for faith and repentance; and direct their attention to the judgment day, at which time the final separation of the wicked and the righteous will take place.

Matthew appropriately closes the series of seven parables (the number 7 symbolizes completeness) with the one of the fishnet. This last parable once again voices the theme of the day of days, in which the final judgment will take place.[9] The writer of the Epistle to the Hebrews summarizes it succinctly: "Just as man is destined to die once, and after that to face judgment, so Christ was sacrificed once to take away the sins of many people" (Heb. 9:27, 28).

11 Unforgiving Servant

> **Matthew 18:21–35**
>
> [21]Then Peter came to Jesus and asked, "Lord, how many times shall I forgive my brother when he sins against me? Up to seven times?"
>
> [22]Jesus answered, "I tell you, not seven times, but seventy-seven times.
>
> [23]"Therefore, the kingdom of heaven is like a king who wanted to settle accounts with his servants. [24]As he began the settlement, a man who owed him ten thousand talents was brought to him. [25]Since he was not able to pay, the master ordered that he and his wife and his children and all that he had be sold to repay the debt.
>
> [26]"The servant fell on his knees before him. 'Be patient with me,' he begged, 'and I will pay back everything.' [27]The servant's master took pity on him, canceled the debt and let him go.
>
> [28]"But when that servant went out, he found one of his fellow servants who owed him a hundred denarii. He grabbed him and began to choke him. 'Pay back what you owe me!' he demanded.
>
> [29]"His fellow servant fell to his knees and begged him, 'Be patient with me, and I will pay you back.'
>
> [30]"But he refused. Instead, he went off and had the man thrown into prison until he could pay the debt. [31]When the other servants saw what had happened, they were greatly distressed and went and told their master everything that had happened.
>
> [32]"Then the master called the servant in. 'You wicked servant,' he said, 'I canceled all that debt of yours because you begged me to. [33]Shouldn't you have had mercy on your fellow servant just as I had on you?' [34]In anger his master turned him over to the jailers to be tortured, until he should pay back all he owed.
>
> [35]"This is how my heavenly Father will treat each of you unless you forgive your brother from your heart."

THE STORY

Does Jesus ever turn anyone away who comes to him in repentance and faith? Of course not, never—no matter how great a sin he has committed. That's our answer. And we know this because "the Bible tells us so." But how many times must we forgive our neighbor? It is one thing for Jesus to forgive a person who has committed a heinous crime. It is quite another thing for us to forgive our neighbor who constantly falls into the same sin.

Peter, trained in the Law and the Prophets as well as Jewish tradition, knew that he had to forgive his fellowman. He knew his duty. But what is the limit? Are there limits at all? Peter thought that he should go as far as seven times. That should be sufficient, he thought, and Jesus would most likely say, "Yes, Peter, that is enough." Does not unlimited mercy encourage a life of sin? Would Jesus not agree with Peter, "Enough is enough"?

But Jesus' answer is, "I tell you, not seven times but seventy-seven times." Jesus multiplies the two numbers 7 and 10—numbers that symbolize completeness—and adds another 7. He means to say, not seven times but seventy-seven times—that is, completeness times completeness and completeness.[1] He conveys the idea of infinity. God's mercy is so great that it cannot be measured; so you, Peter, should likewise show mercy to your neighbor.

To explain the magnitude of God's forgiving love that must be reflected in his people, Jesus teaches the parable of the unforgiving servant. He tells a story, and he tells it well.

A king called his officials (servants) together for an appointed day of accounting.[2] One of them owed him the astonishing sum of ten thousand talents, an amount that connotes millions in our currency. In fact, the word for ten thousand has an underlying basic meaning of that which is numberless, countless, infinite.[3] Moreover, the talent in those days was the largest denomination in the monetary system. By comparison, Herod the Great's annual revenue from his entire kingdom was about nine hundred talents. The areas of Judea, Idumea, and Samaria paid six hundred talents in taxes annually; Galilee and Perea paid two hundred talents; and Batanea with Trachonitis as well as Auranitis paid one hundred talents.[4] A minister of finance responsible for an area much larger than that of Herod would have to pay the revenue of ten thousand talents.

Clearly, the financial minister owed his master a tremendous sum. We are not told what he had done with the money; that is not important here. He owed the sum of ten thousand talents, and he had to pay. He knew that he would never get the money together on accounting day.

When he stood before his master, he heard the verdict: he, his wife, his children, and all his possessions would be sold to repay the debt. That was too much for him. He flung himself at the feet of the sovereign, begged for mercy, and cried out, "Be patient with me and I will pay back everything." He pled for mercy, not for remission. He promised restitution, knowing that he could only make a beginning and no more. In response, he received what he had least expected—acquittal. His master took pity on him, canceled the debt, and let him go.[5] Incredible! What joy! What kindness!

This is only the first act of the play.[6] The second act is parallel to the first: the minister of finance became master and met another official of the king.

Descending the steps of the royal palace, the acquitted public servant encountered a fellow servant who owed him the sum of one hundred denarii. Really, that was nothing—a few days of work and he would have it. But the public servant grabbed the man by the throat and demanded immediate payment. "Pay back what you owe me!"[7] The indebted man flung himself at the feet of the minister of finance and begged, "Be patient with me and I will repay." He did not have to say, "I will pay it *all*," because the amount was so small. It was self-evident that he would pay back everything. But the minister of finance refused the man's plea, threw him in prison, and expected someone to bail him out to pay the debt.

The third act introduces witnesses of the second act; also, it is the second and last confrontation of king and public servant.

Nothing was done covertly; palace secrets were hard to keep. Others saw what had happened and could not keep it to themselves. They had to tell the king. The king, when he heard the story, was angry. He summoned the public servant and rebuked him. "You wicked servant, I canceled all that debt of yours because you begged me to. Shouldn't you have had mercy on your fellow servant just as I had on you?" With that he turned him over to the jailers to have him tortured until all his debts were paid.[8]

The conclusion is that everyone who has experienced forgiveness must be ready to forgive anyone who is indebted to him and to do so wholeheartedly.

THE LESSON

This vivid story, told in colorful detail, accentuates the contrast between God's infinite love and mercy and man's stingy behavior that he attempts to justify on the basis of law. Jesus uses this parable to tell

Peter something about the magnitude of God's forgiving love toward sinful man. Man's sin is so great that God has to forgive him infinitely more than the numerical count of seventy-seven times. The depth of God's mercy simply cannot be measured. It can only be approximated, and vaguely at that, by telling the story of the public servant who owed his master a sum that ran into the millions.

Although the word *justice* is not found in the parable, the concepts expressed are those of mercy and justice. They are biblical concepts because they repeatedly occur in the Old Testament, developed especially by the psalmists and prophets.[9]

> I will sing of your love and justice;
>   to you, O Lord, I will sing praise.
>
> Psalm 101:1

Jewish people knew very well that they had to exercise mercy and compassion. God told them expressly, "If you lend money to one of my people among you who is needy, do not be like a moneylender; charge him no interest. If you take your neighbor's cloak as a pledge, return it to him by sunset, because his cloak is the only covering he has for his body. What else will he sleep in? When he cries out to me, I will hear, for I am compassionate" (Exod. 22:25–27).[10] And justice was expressed in a variety of ways. For example, the demands of the Year of Jubilee were pressed, during which year land belonging to the dispersed was returned to the original owner. And even people sold into slavery were set free.[11] In brief, the Jew of Jesus' day knew that mercy and justice could not be treated separately. They were interrelated.

It is for this very reason that Jesus tells the parable of the unforgiving servant. He teaches that the exercise of mercy is not an occasional setting aside of justice. Jesus teaches the application of both mercy and justice. Too often we perceive justice as the norm that must be applied rigorously, and mercy as an occasional abandonment of that norm. We exercise this option as a "right," and frequently are commended for showing leniency.[12] We recognize that justice has a built-in provision for mercy, but on the whole we feel it is not to be shown too often.

In Old Testament times, however, God instructed his people to regard mercy and justice as equal norms. Both norms must be operative and functional, for they reflect how God deals with his people. In time, however, the emphasis shifted. The writings of the intertestamental period proclaim that on the judgment day justice shall prevail and mercy shall end. "Then the Most High shall be seen on the judgment-seat, and there shall be an end of all pity and patience. Judgment alone shall remain" (2 Esdras 7:33, 34 NEB).

APPLICATION

In our society, we have at times stressed mercy at the expense of justice. Coddling the criminal has been practiced to such an extent that the "rights" of the offender are scrupulously observed while the rights of the offended are completely ignored. Scripture does not teach that mercy eliminates justice; nor does it teach that justice nullifies mercy. The two are equally valid norms.

How did Jesus show Peter that he must forgive his neighbor times without number? He told the story of the man whose debt was overwhelmingly great and who pled for mercy when justice was administered. His master canceled the debt and showed infinite mercy. The man was free and could keep his wife, children, and possessions.[13] He was debt-free!

Jesus does not tell a story of a man who repeatedly, day after day, stands before his master to ask forgiveness for sins he repeatedly commits. Instead, to give expression to our debt with God, he teaches the story of the man who owed his master a tremendous debt. "If you, O LORD, kept a record of sins, O Lord, who could stand? But with you there is forgiveness; therefore you are feared" (Ps. 130:3, 4). Man's hopelessness is revealed when he stands before God.[14] His sin is overwhelming because he has transgressed God's Law. He deserves death. But he knows that God is a God of mercy. When David had disobeyed God by numbering the people of Israel and Judah, in meting out justice God gave him three choices: three years of famine, three months of persecution, or three days of pestilence. David replied, "Let us fall into the hands of the LORD, for his mercy is great" (2 Sam. 24:14; 1 Chron. 21:13). God revealed David's sin to him, handed him the verdict, waited for his response, and showed mercy.

In the second act of the story, Jesus shows that forgiven man must reflect God's mercy and compassion. If Jesus had not depicted the public servant on his knees pleading for mercy and had only told the second half of the story, with the man forcing his fellowman to pay his debt, we would have said that justice prevailed even though the measure may have been harsh.[15] But the man had been forgiven an enormous debt, and now faced a fellow servant who, owing him a trifle, asked for mercy. Would he forgive?

The late Corrie ten Boom, well-known speaker and author, was imprisoned in a German concentration camp during World War II, suffering much from one of the German guards. Years later she testified of her joy in the Lord one day at a meeting in postwar Germany. After the meeting, while people were talking to her, that same German guard approached Corrie and asked her to forgive him. In a flash of recognition, she recalled the pain and anguish of her imprisonment that she had suffered at the hands of that prison guard. Now he stood in front of her seeking mercy. And he who did not deserve it received forgiveness. Mercy triumphed!

The public servant portrayed in the parable would not forgive. He applied the principle of justice without mercy. Instead of letting mercy triumph, he chose to have justice triumph. That was his mistake. James writes, "judgment without mercy will be shown to anyone who has not been merciful" (2:13). The servant refused to reflect the compassion his master had shown him. Because he did not show mercy to his fellowman, but demanded justice, he had to face his master the king once more. By demanding justice, the servant cut himself off from his master and his fellowman.[16]

In the last act of this drama, the unforgiving servant faces an angry master. What the servant had done to his debtor, the master now does to him: justice is administered without mercy. The servant has cast himself into everlasting misery.

God cannot overlook a refusal to show mercy, for this is contrary to his nature, his Word, and his testimony. God pardons by accepting the sinner as if he had never sinned at all. God forgives the sinner's debt and he remembers his sin no more (Ps. 103:12; Jer. 31:34). And God expects the forgiven sinner to do the same. He is therefore God's representative in showing the divine characteristic of pardoning grace.

The conclusion of the parable is not couched in unfamiliar words. When Jesus taught the Lord's Prayer, he followed it by saying, "For if you forgive men when they sin against you, your heavenly Father will also forgive you. But if you do not forgive men their sins, your Father will not forgive your sins" (Matt. 6:14, 15).[17]

12 Workers in the Vineyard

> **Matthew 20:1–16**
>
> [1]"The kingdom of heaven is like a landowner who went out early in the morning to hire men to work in his vineyard. [2]He agreed to pay them a denarius for the day and sent them into his vineyard.
>
> [3]"About the third hour he went out and saw others standing in the marketplace doing nothing. [4]He told them, 'You also go and work in my vineyard, and I will pay you whatever is right.' [5]So they went.
>
> "He went out again about the sixth hour and the ninth hour and did the same thing. [6]About the eleventh hour he went out and found still others standing around. He asked them, 'Why have you been standing here all day long doing nothing?'
>
> [7]"'Because no one has hired us,' they answered.
>
> "He said to them, 'You also go and work in my vineyard.'
>
> [8]"When evening came, the owner of the vineyard said to his foreman, 'Call the workers and pay them their wages, beginning with the last ones hired and going on to the first.'
>
> [9]"The workers who were hired about the eleventh hour came and each received a denarius. [10]So when those came who were hired first, they expected to receive more. But each one of them also received a denarius. [11]When they received it, they began to grumble against the landowner. [12]'These men who were hired last worked only one hour,' they said, 'and you have made them equal to us who have borne the burden of the work and the heat of the day.'
>
> [13]"But he answered one of them, 'Friend, I am not being unfair to you. Didn't you agree to work for a denarius? [14]Take your pay and go. I want to give the man who was hired last the same as I gave you. [15]Don't I have the right to do what I want with my own money? Or are you envious because I am generous?'
>
> [16]"So the last will be first, and the first will be last."

Known by the title, "Workers in the Vineyard,"[1] this story is one of Matthew's kingdom parables. However, this parable does not end with the message, "Go and do likewise" in God's kingdom. Its focus is not on labor relations and the economics of establishing a fair wage. Rather, the words and deeds of the employer, theologically speaking, point to God who freely gives good gifts to man. The story indeed echoes a line from one of David's psalms, "Taste and see that the LORD is good" (Ps. 34:8).

WORK AND WORKERS

Although the parable gives no specific time of year when the workmen are needed in the vineyard, the assumption that it is the month of September,[2] during which grapes are harvested, may not be too far-fetched. The period from sunrise to sunset in Israel during the month of September is approximately 6:00 A.M. to 6:00 P.M. Discounting periods of rest for meals and prayers, Jewish workers in Jesus' day considered ten hours the normal length of a working day.[3] In Israel the temperatures during the middle of the day are still rather high in September, so that workers out in the field or vineyard literally experience "the heat of the day."

The owner of a sizable vineyard has determined to harvest his grapes on a particular day. All his servants who work for him throughout the year go out to the vineyard at six in the morning, while the owner visits the marketplace in the nearby town or village at the crack of dawn. He needs a number of unemployed workers who are willing to do a day's work for the reasonable sum of one denarius.[4] Already at that early hour, between 5:00 A.M. and 6:00 A.M., some able-bodied men are standing around waiting for an employer to come by who will provide work for them. The owner of the vineyard talks to them, mentions the daily wage of one denarius—to which all agree—and takes them to the vineyard for a ten-hour workday. The workmen, because they have no steady employment, are utterly dependent on the employer who happens to need them for a short period of time. Clearly they are much more dependent on the good graces of the employer than the employer is on them.

In Jesus' day it was a privilege for the workman to be placed in a position to earn wages. By providing work for him the employer showed him a measure of kindness. It was an act of grace on the part of the employer.[5] Spending idle hours in the marketplace meant that the laborer and his family had to rely on charity. The workman had no resources of his own, and gifts from the rich did not always come. Consequently, a full day's work was a boon to the workman and his family.

While the servants and the workmen are busy at work in the vineyard, the owner returns to the marketplace to see if he can find still more workers. It is now between eight o'clock and nine o'clock, and many workmen are passing the time in the marketplace. The employer asks them to spend the rest of the day in his vineyard. He is promising them a fair wage, although he does not specify the amount. The workmen, knowing the reputation of the vineyard-owner, put their trust in him. They will not be disappointed at the end of the day.

As the work progresses and the owner with the foreman calculates the number of man-hours required to finish the task before nightfall, the need for additional workers becomes evident. The owner of the vineyard knows exactly when certain grapes must be picked. If they are left one or two extra days on the vine, the sugar content will be too high. The market value of grapes of superior vintage depends on the correct amount of sugar in the grapes. If the harvest day happens to be a Friday, the landowner does everything in his power to hire additional workers to complete the task before the Sabbath.[6]

Trips to the nearby marketplace are made at regular intervals, at noon and three in the afternoon, with varying degrees of success. By late afternoon it becomes apparent that the project cannot be completed before dark unless extra workmen come in. The owner returns to the marketplace at five o'clock and finds a number of men standing around. He inquires why they are in the marketplace at this hour of the day. The reply is that no one has come to offer them work. The employer says: "You also go and work in my vineyard." No mention is made of remuneration.

The owner of the vineyard knows that workers are permitted to eat as many of the grapes as they desire. He expects to lose nearly 3 percent of the yield this way. By hiring workers late in the afternoon, however, he does not run the risk of losing too many grapes. He expects them to apply their energy to the harvesting of the crop. "You also go and work in my vineyard."

Hours and Wages

Throughout the parable, the employer is the dominant figure. He visits the marketplace at the break of dawn, hires the laborers, notices the need for additional workers, and returns repeatedly to the marketplace for still more employees. It is he who instructs his manager to pay the workers, and he himself addresses those laborers who think they have been wronged. The owner is in control of the situation from beginning to end. In fact, he is the one to whom the kingdom of heaven is compared in the introductory sentence.[7]

Various questions may be raised concerning the management of the vineyard. For example, why did the owner return to the marketplace at least four times to hire additional workmen? We would have expected the owner to make careful estimates at the beginning of the day and to hire the exact number of laborers needed to complete the work before nightfall. But we may not apply Western analysis to a story set in an oriental culture. The law of supply and demand was undoubtedly observed. No employer would engage more workers than he needed. Moreover, laborers hired at later periods in the day come to the vineyard unhampered by fatigue and with energy to spare. The employer receives high returns from workers who give him all their energy in half a day or less.

Laborers could be hired by the hour and could expect to be paid immediately upon termination of their work.[8] The workers standing in the marketplace throughout the day could have returned home at dawn when no one came to hire them. Instead, they waited for employers to come and call them in for only part of the day. These workers were no loafing busybodies who spent their time in gossip. They had families to support and therefore eagerly waited for an employer who would engage their services. Even at five in the afternoon they were still waiting, hoping either to be employed for just one hour or to make arrangements for the following day. In their own way, the laborers demonstrate faithfulness, dedication, and dependability.

Workers were paid at the end of the day. Employers were to heed the biblical injunctions not to hold back the wages of a hired man overnight (Lev. 19:13) and not to take advantage of a hired man who was poor and needy. "Pay him his wages each day before sunset, because he is poor and counting on it. Otherwise he may cry to the Lord against you, and you will be guilty of sin" (Deut. 24:15). The owner of the vineyard, mindful of these injunctions, instructs his manager to pay the laborers their wage. He is portrayed as a just and trustworthy man. He has guaranteed only the laborers hired at six in the morning one denarius each for the day. Those employed at nine are told that he will pay them whatever is right. And those engaged later in the day are not even told about wages. They come to the vineyard, fully trusting that the owner will pay them something in the evening.

The landowner is a man of his word. When he instructs his foreman to pay the workers their wages, he makes one stipulation: begin with those hired last and successively go on to those hired first. What a surprise when those hired at five in the afternoon receive a denarius![9] They are happy, joyful, and filled with gratitude. They know the landowner not only as trustworthy and honest but also as a generous man. All the workers who were hired throughout the course of the day receive the same wage and testify of the goodness and generosity of the employer.

The workers hired at the break of dawn, however, who have endured the heat of the day, expect to receive more than one denarius each. They also wish to experience the landowner's generosity. But their wish is not fulfilled. They receive one denarius each as agreed before they began their work. They see the whole matter as unfair; and they make their displeasure and disappointment known by grumbling against the landowner. They do not address him courteously at all. Angrily, they list their grievances: we worked hard all day long, perspiring in the heat, and receive one denarius; others come at five in the afternoon, work for one hour, and also receive one denarius.

The employer does not take offense. He addresses one of the laborers, obviously the spokesman, and calls him "friend." The connotation is one of reproach, yet the tone is friendly.[10] In answering the grumbling worker, the landowner is master of the situation. "Friend, I am not being unfair to you. Didn't you agree to work for a denarius?" The dissatisfied laborer may go to court, but he does not have a case, for the evidence is against him. He agreed to work a full day for one denarius, which he received. His accusation of injustice is nothing more than a cover for envy and greed. The employer does not argue, does not explain, and does not justify himself. He merely asks questions that the hearer is forced to answer in the affirmative. "Didn't you agree to work for a denarius?" To ask the question is to answer it. "Don't I have the right to do what I want with my own money?"

The point at issue is not fraud or deception. On the contrary, no one is unfairly treated. Most of the workers experience the landowner's generosity. If there is one person who sacrifices economy in the interest of benevolence, it is the landowner. He would have been much better off if he had paid the workers the exact amount earned.[11] He is faulted for his genuine generosity. "Or are you envious because I am generous?" he asks. With that last question the employer removes the facade of the disgruntled employees. He has demonstrated goodness and kindness, while they show envy and greed. They remain totally blind to the owner's benevolence until the mask that veiled their discontent is removed by the question, "Or are you envious because I am generous?"

This is how it is in the kingdom of heaven, Jesus says. Because God is so good, the principle of grace triumphs. The principle in the world is that he who works the longest receives the most pay.[12] That is just. But in the kingdom of God the principles of merit and ability may be set aside so that grace can prevail.

GRACE

The parable does not intend to teach a lesson in business or eco-nomics. It is not to be used as an example of human relations in the area of labor and management. The lesson the parable conveys is this: grace supersedes impartial justice and profitable business practices. The employer in the parable went to the marketplace at various times during the day and saw behind each worker a family in need of support. He knew that a fraction of a denarius would not be sufficient for the daily needs of a family. At the end of the day, the employer paid the laborers who were hired during the course of that day not in relation to the hours they had worked but in accordance with the current need of their dependents. He was a most benevolent person.

When Jesus taught the parable, he faced an audience generally trained in the Jewish doctrine of merit. His contemporaries believed that man must accumulate to his credit numerous good deeds so that he might convert them into rewards before God. He could come to God, therefore, and claim rewards. That was the doctrine of works in the time of Jesus.[13] These people should have known the grace of God that they extolled in psalm and prayer. Nevertheless, they stressed the meritorious value of works.

In teaching the parable, Jesus showed that God does not deal with all men in accordance with the principles of merit, justice, and economics. In a sense, God is not interested in making profit. God does not deal with man on the basis of "tit for tat" or "one good deed merits another." God's grace simply cannot be divided into neatly proportioned quantities adjusted to merits that man has accumulated. There used to be a coin in circulation called the *pondion,* which was worth one-twelfth of a denarius.[14] The grace of God, however, does not circulate in percentages, because "from the fullness of his grace we have all received one blessing after another" (John 1:16).

APPLICATION

> God is so good;
> God is so good;
> God is so good;
> Is so good to me.

This simple song sung in many languages around the world vividly expresses the basic meaning of the parable. In the kingdom of heaven God's goodness prevails and is shown to those people who have entered the kingdom by grace alone. The fact that the landowner paid a denarius to those who were told they would receive "whatever is right" and also to those who were not told anything at all was nothing but pure goodness. All the workers received the same wage that was sufficient for the support of their families. And those workers who had agreed to work for the sum of one denarius a day had to concede that the landowner was a just man who honored his commitments. Justice and goodness, exemplified in the parable, are fundamental characteristics in the kingdom of God.

The immediate context of the parable concerns Peter's question and Jesus' response. Peter asked what he and his fellow disciples would receive for following Jesus: "We have left everything to follow you! What then will there be for us?" Jesus replied that his followers would receive untold spiritual blessings:

> I tell you the truth, at the renewal of all things, when the Son of Man sits on his glorious throne, you who have followed me will also sit on twelve thrones, judging the twelve tribes of Israel. And everyone who has left houses or brothers or sisters or father or mother or children or fields for my sake will receive a hundred times as much and will inherit eternal life. But many who are first will be last, and many who are last will be first.
>
> Matthew 19:28–30[15]

Jesus illustrates the meaning of this last sentence—"but many who are first will be last and many who are last will be first"—by means of the parable of the vineyard workers. Thus, he concludes the parable with the same words, although in reversed order, "So the last will be first, and the first will be last."

By means of this saying Jesus does not intend to indicate to Peter and the other disciples that the position of the first and last in the kingdom will be reversed. Rather, the parable shows the saying to mean that in the kingdom of heaven equality is the rule. Even though the work itself may vary, the work performed by the disciples—and, for that matter, by any one of Jesus' followers—is transcended by a reward equal for all. God's gift is sheer grace.[16] His grace is sufficient for all.[17]

The original audience consisted of the disciples of Jesus. Whether others were present at that time cannot be ascertained. The disciples, as children of their time, were steeped in the doctrine of merit. They needed to discard this teaching for two reasons: to fully appreciate the goodness of God and to see that their own place in the kingdom was a gift of grace. Moreover, in the course of time they would be welcoming Gentiles into the church. For example, Peter would be sent to the house of Cornelius, the Roman centurion, to preach the gospel, to baptize the believers, and to praise God for granting "repentance unto life" to the Gentiles (Acts 11:18). Gentiles would receive the same gift God had given to the Jews who believed in Jesus. Paul calls this a mystery and concludes that "through the gospel the Gentiles are heirs together with Israel, members together of one body, and sharers together in the promise in Christ Jesus" (Eph. 3:6).

Who, then, are the grumblers? Although the parable should not be interpreted allegorically,[18] the question concerning the significance of the grumblers is valid. The grumblers may be compared to the elder brother in the parable of the prodigal son. Together they reflect the attitude of some Pharisees who, because of their zeal in observing the Law of God, counted on a first-rank position in God's kingdom. Pharisees expected God to reward them for their labors and to withhold blessing from undeserving sinners. Jesus showed them (assuming that they were in the audience) by means of this parable that God is a God of justice who honors his Word, but he also offers "uncovenanted mercies" to people who do not deserve them but who nevertheless are recipients of his grace.[19]

The parable teaches that when man comes to God, he does not receive a carefully calculated portion of divine grace. Rather, God liberally grants him the gifts of forgiveness, reconciliation, peace, joy, happiness, and assurance. All his needs are met "according to his glorious riches in Christ Jesus" (Phil. 4:19). For Christians, the inclusion of converts in the church of Jesus Christ must be cause for joy. It must not be a matter of skepticism. History teaches, however, that such skepticism has occurred repeatedly. When George Whitefield and John and Charles Wesley brought the gospel to the lower-class society of the eighteenth century, they were criticized and resented by the conventional Christians.[20] William Booth, who had compassion on the poverty-stricken slum dwellers of London and who gave them "soup, soap, and salvation," was condemned by the self-righteous church people of his day.

This parable will always be unacceptable to people who wish to regulate salvation according to man-made rules and stipulations. But the kingdom of heaven, as Scripture teaches, is free from human bureaucracy. God's grace is full and free to all who come to him in faith. And all who are recipients of this grace proclaim with the psalmist: "Give thanks to the LORD, for he is good; his love endures forever" (Ps. 107:1).

13 Two Sons

Matthew 21:28–32

²⁸"What do you think? There was a man who had two sons. He went to the first and said, 'Son, go and work today in the vineyard.'

²⁹"'I will not,' he answered, but later he changed his mind and went.

³⁰"Then the father went to the other son and said the same thing. He answered, 'I will, sir,' but he did not go.

³¹"Which of the two did what his father wanted?"

"The first," they answered.

Jesus said to them, "I tell you the truth, the tax collectors and the prostitutes are entering the kingdom of God ahead of you. ³² For John came to you to show you the way of righteousness, and you did not believe him, but the tax collectors and the prostitutes did. And even after you saw this, you did not repent and believe him."

The parable of the two sons is found only in the Gospel of Matthew. It is marked by simplicity and can be summarized in the familiar words of James, "Do not merely listen to the word, and so deceive yourselves. Do what it says" (1:22). It teaches that the person who refuses to do what is asked of him but who subsequently changes his mind and does the task is better than the one who promises to take care of his obligations but never fulfills them.

Matthew's Gospel places the parable immediately following the incident of chief priests and elders questioning Jesus' authority. Jesus in turn asked them a counterquestion on the baptism of John, whether it was from heaven or from man. And their answer was, "We don't know." Jesus' reply to their query on his authority was, "Neither will I tell you by what authority I am doing these things."

While teaching in the temple courts with the chief priests and elders still in the audience, Jesus continued the trend of thought with a story about a father and his two sons. The father owned a vineyard, which was one of the sources of income for the family. Hence, all members of the family did the work in the vineyard on a communal basis. The father went to the first son and told him to go and work in the vineyard that particular day.[1] It is immaterial whether it was early spring when the vines were pruned, or summer when the weeds were cut down, or autumn when the grapes were harvested. The request and the response to the request are essential. "Son, go and work today in the vineyard." The son showed no courtesy at all toward his father. He answered, "I will not."[2] He failed to address him as "sir," and did not even bother to give an excuse for his unwillingness to go.

The father had to go to the second son with the same request in order to get the work done in the vineyard.[3] This son, in polite oriental fashion, addressed his father correctly and said, "I will, sir." However, he did not go. He promised his father a full day's work. It was a promise he did not intend to honor.

INTERPRETATION

The inevitable question, "Who was the obedient son?" Jesus puts directly to his audience. The chief priests and elders of the people can no longer hide behind feigned ignorance. They are forced to answer, even though they realize that the parable talks about the ecclesiastical hierarchy of Israel. They say that the son who at first refused but later changed his mind did the will of his father.

Jesus illustrates what the story of the father and his two sons really means in the spiritual context of his day. The first son, says Jesus, is the personification of the tax collectors and the prostitutes who are living a sinful life and who have refused to do the will of God. But when John the Baptist came "preaching a baptism of repentance for the forgiveness of sins" (Mark 1:4), the social and moral outcasts of society repented, believed, and entered the kingdom of God. Thus they did the will of the Father.

The second son portrays the attitude of the religious leaders of Jesus' day. They are the ones who do everything for men to see. "They make their phylacteries wide and the tassels on their garments long; they love the place of honor at banquets and the most important seats in the synagogues; they love to be greeted in the marketplaces and to have men call them 'Rabbi'" (Matt. 23:5–7). They are the people who do not practice what they preach. John the Baptist came to them and showed them the way of righteousness. They listened to his words but did not believe. They simply ignored him. They saw, however, that the tax collectors accepted John's message and were baptized. Nevertheless, they rejected God's purpose for themselves, refusing to be baptized by John (Luke 7:30).

The application of the parable is dynamic. Tax collectors and prostitutes had refused to obey the will of God. Yet when they heard the message of repentance, they turned to God in obedience. They were like the son who said, "I will not," but later changed his mind and went to work in the vineyard. They were like Zacchaeus, who said to Jesus, "Look, Lord! Here and now I give half of my possessions to the poor, and if I have cheated anybody out of anything, I will pay back four times the amount" (Luke 19:8).

The religious leaders who presumably were experts in the Law of God put on an outward show of compliance. Inwardly, however, they refused to accept the Word of God, whether it came via the written word of the prophets or the spoken word of John the Baptist and Jesus. They were like the son who said to his father, "I will, sir," but did not go.

Although this parable is relatively short and its message is simple, the lesson it teaches is by no means trivial. It comprises the teaching of the Old and New Testaments: obey the Word of God, heed his voice, and do his will. As Samuel told Saul, "To obey is better than sacrifice, and to heed is better than the fat of rams" (1 Sam. 15:22), so Jesus instructs his disciples, "You are my friends if you do what I command" (John 15:14). Jesus himself openly speaks of his obedience to God the Father: "For I have come down from heaven not to do my will but to do the will of him who sent me. And this is the will of him who sent me, that I shall lose none of all that he has given me, but raise them up at the last day" (John 6:38, 39).

14 Tenants

Matthew 21:33–46

[33] "Listen to another parable: There was a landowner who planted a vineyard. He put a wall around it, dug a winepress in it and built a watchtower. Then he rented the vineyard to some farmers and went away on a journey. [34]When the harvest time approached, he sent his servants to the tenants to collect his fruit.

[35] "The tenants seized his servants; they beat one, killed another, and stoned a third. [36]Then he sent other servants to them, more than the first time, and the tenants treated them the same way. [37]Last of all, he sent his son to them. 'They will respect my son,' he said.

[38] "But when the tenants saw the son, they said to one another, 'This is the heir. Come, let's kill him and take his inheritance.' [39]So they took him and threw him out of the vineyard and killed him.

[40] "Therefore, when the owner of the vineyard comes, what will he do to those tenants?"

[41] "He will bring those wretches to a wretched end," they replied, "and he will rent the vineyard to other tenants, who will give him his share of the crop at harvest time."

[42]Jesus said to them, "Have you never read in the Scriptures: 'The stone the builders rejected has become the capstone; the Lord has done this, and it is marvelous in our eyes'?

[43] "Therefore I tell you that the kingdom of God will be taken away from you and given to a people who will produce its fruit. [44]He who falls on this stone will be broken to pieces, but he on whom it falls will be crushed."

[45]When the chief priests and the Pharisees heard Jesus' parables, they knew he was talking about them. [46]They looked for a way to arrest him, but they were afraid of the crowd because the people held that he was a prophet.

Mark 12:1–12

[1]He then began to speak to them in parables: "A man planted a vineyard. He put a wall around it, dug a pit for the winepress and built a watchtower. Then he rented the vineyard to some farmers and went away on a journey. [2]At harvest time he sent

a servant to the tenants to collect from them some of the fruit of the vineyard. [3]But they seized him, beat him and sent him away empty-handed. [4]Then he sent another servant to them; they struck this man on the head and treated him shamefully. [5]He sent still another, and that one they killed. He sent many others; some of them they beat, others they killed.

[6]"He had one left to send, a son, whom he loved. He sent him last of all, saying, 'They will respect my son.'

[7]"But the tenants said to one another, 'This is the heir. Come, let's kill him, and the inheritance will be ours.' [8]So they took him and killed him, and threw him out of the vineyard.

[9]"What will the owner of the vineyard do? He will come and kill those tenants and give the vineyard to others."

[10]"Haven't you read this scripture: 'The stone the builders rejected has become the capstone; [11]the Lord has done this, and it is marvelous in our eyes'?

[12]Then they looked for a way to arrest him because they knew he had spoken the parable against them. But they were afraid of the crowd; so they left him and went away.

Luke 20:9–19

[9]He went on to tell the people this parable: "A man planted a vineyard, rented it to some farmers and went away for a long time. [10]At harvest time he sent a servant to the tenants so they would give him some of the fruit of the vineyard. But the tenants beat him and sent him away empty-handed. [11]He sent another servant, but that one also they beat and treated shamefully and sent away empty-handed. [12]He sent still a third, and they wounded him and threw him out.

[13]"Then the owner of the vineyard said, 'What shall I do? I will send my son, whom I love; perhaps they will respect him.'

[14]"But when the tenants saw him, they talked the matter over. 'This is the heir,' they said. 'Let's kill him, and the inheritance will be ours.' [15]So they threw him out of the vineyard and killed him.

[16]"What then will the owner of the vineyard do to them? He will come and kill those tenants and give the vineyard to others."

When the people heard this, they said, "May this never be!"

[17]Jesus looked directly at them and asked, "Then what is the meaning of that which is written: 'The stone the builders rejected has become the capstone'?

[18]"Everyone who falls on that stone will be broken to pieces, but he on whom it falls will be crushed."

[19]The teachers of the law and the chief priests looked for a way to arrest him immediately, because they knew he had spoken this parable against them. But they were afraid of the people.

According to Matthew, Mark, and Luke, Jesus told the parable of the tenants during the last week of his earthly life. One evangelist may vary from the other in minor details, but all faithfully transmit the teaching of Jesus. The apocryphal Gospel of Thomas also presents the parable.[1]

The story may be true to fact and lend itself to a portrayal of Israel's ecclesiastical history. The people surrounding Jesus understood the story, for they responded to the parable by saying, "May this never be" (Luke 20:16). Moreover, the Pharisees, chief priests, and the teachers of the Law knew that this parable was directed against them.

STORY

A landowner had a plot of land and decided to plant grapevines on it. After he had planted the tender shoots of the grapevine, he protected them from wild animals such as foxes and boars (Song of Sol. 2:15; Ps. 80:13) by putting a wall around the vineyard. He also equipped the vineyard with a winepress and a watchtower. The watchtower was used during the harvest as a lookout against thieves, and might also serve as a dwelling place for the tenant.

The whole project was a financial venture for the landowner. He planted new vines on untried soil. He rented the vineyard to farmers, but would have to wait four years before the vines began to bear grapes. During this time he would support the farmers, buy manure and supplies for the vineyard, and hope that in the fifth year he might have a profit.[2] A new vineyard was, therefore, a venture not for immediate financial returns but rather for lasting results benefiting successive generations.

The landowner went away on a journey for an extended period. In his absence, the tenants would cultivate the vineyard, prune the branches, and raise vegetable crops between the vines during the first few years. The tenants worked as sharecroppers and were thereby entitled to a portion of the produce. The rest of the income would go to the owner. The tenants had made a contract with the landowner to cultivate the vineyard. For the first four years the owner would have to support them. After those years of toil were past, the vineyard would be a lucrative source of income for the owner.

When the harvesttime approached in the fifth year, the landowner sent his servant[3] to collect the income of the vineyard.[4] Contacts between the owner and the tenants may have been minimal during the first four years. This lack of contact may have resulted in alienation and even in hostile attitudes on the part of the tenants, as depicted in the parable. The exact reason for the bitter animosity is not stated—only the fact of its evidence.[5] The servant was seized, beaten, and sent back to his master. He returned with the physical evidence of a bruised body. The message the owner received was that the tenants had no intention of paying the requested income of the grape harvest. They wanted to keep the total amount for themselves, perhaps in compensation for the years of toil and care given to the vineyard before it yielded a harvest. By sending the servant away beaten and empty-handed, the tenants claimed possession of the total crop.

Because the fruit of the vineyard would be sold, the income requested by the landowner could be paid out at various times during the year. The landowner, therefore, sent another servant to the tenants with the same request. Undoubtedly, he referred to the contract signed by the owner and the tenants, which clearly spelled out the terms. But they received him in the same manner as his predecessor. They struck him on the head, they treated him shamefully, and they also sent him away empty-handed (Luke 20:11). Once more the tenants showed open defiance: they did not want to part with any of the income received from the grape harvest. The owner demonstrated commendable forbearance. He did not meet force with force, nor did he declare the contract null and void, as the tenants had done. After some time, perhaps at the next harvesttime, the owner sent a third servant.[6] Again the tenants refused to yield to the owner's request; they resorted to violence by wounding (Luke 20:12) or killing (Mark 12:5) the servant. But while the landowner kept on sending servants,[7] the tenants, by beating and killing them, made it known that the vineyard remained in their hands. They were the ones who had made it productive; therefore, so they reasoned, they were the ones who were entitled to the produce of the vineyard and even to the vineyard itself.

The owner realized that the tenants were posing as the rightful possessors of his property. As a last resort he sent his son, telling himself that the tenants would recognize authority when his son confronted them. "They will respect my son," he said. Servants simply did not engender the respect that a son commanded.[8] He would send his only son who was the heir to the vineyard.

The tenants, however, were in no mood to give up the vineyard. When they saw the son approaching, they may have thought that the owner had died and that the son had taken his place. That being the case, little would stand in the way of full possession of the vineyard if the son were removed. The tenants then could claim that they had faithfully tended the vineyard, that they had not paid any rent for a number of years, and that the legitimate owner of the property had died.[9] In the legal setting of that time, the tenants would be able to get exclusive ownership of the land. Local judges most likely would favor the tenants and pronounce the transaction legal.

The tenants decided to kill the son and take the inheritance. They initially admitted him to the vineyard, but then in order not to defile the vines with blood, they killed him outside the vineyard.[10] They left him there, assuming that accompanying servants would take care of the burial.

The landowner's patience ran out. The tenants had made a disastrous mistake in killing his son. Forces to eject the tenants and to bring them to justice were initiated, and the owner, claiming full possession of his property, appointed other tenants to care for the vineyard. These were servants who would give him the stipulated share of the crop in due season.

MEANING

The audience readily accepted the story Jesus told. The parable portrayed a realistic situation where an absentee landowner from time to time dispatched a servant to collect the proper share of the vineyard's annual income. The audience knew the circumstances Jesus described in the parable; they could picture the conclusion of the story and concurred in the execution of justice.

Jesus addressed the chief priests, Pharisees, and teachers of the Law as well. As the clergy of that time, they must have been quick to notice the quotation from Isaiah's prophecy:

> I will sing for the one I love
>   a song about his vineyard:
> My loved one had a vineyard
>   on a fertile hillside.
> He dug it up and cleared it of stones
>   and planted it with choicest vines.
> He built a watchtower in it
>   and cut out a winepress as well.
> Then he looked for a crop of good grapes,
>   but it yielded only bad fruit.

> Isaiah 5:1, 2

The Jewish people knew this song by heart; they had learned it in the synagogue worship service, where they sang it from time to time.[11] They also knew the conclusion of the song:

> The vineyard of the LORD Almighty
>   is the house of Israel,
> and the men of Judah
>   are the garden of his delight.

And he looked for justice, but saw bloodshed;
  for righteousness, but heard cries of distress.

Isaiah 5:7

The religious leaders knew that this parable applied to them. They realized that Jesus referred to the prophets God had sent to Israel. They knew that some of these prophets were killed because of the message they brought; one of them, Zechariah, was murdered between the temple and the altar (2 Chron. 24:20, 21; Matt. 23:35). Jesus skillfully taught the audience the meaning of these well-known Old Testament passages. When he spoke of the landowner's son, who, having been sent to the vineyard, was killed by the tenants, he prophetically spoke of his own impending death.[12]

Jesus asked the question of his audience, "Therefore, when the owner of the vineyard comes, what will he do to those tenants?" He used words that resemble those in the Song of the Vineyard (Isa. 5:4, 5). His words were directed against the leaders of the people. They had rejected the message of John the Baptist, and they questioned the authority of Jesus to the point of openly defying him. In effect, they rejected God's final messenger.[13]

The answer to Jesus' question was that swift retribution would be meted out to the murderous tenants. They would be killed and the vineyard rented to other tenants.[14]

Directly addressing the crowd, Jesus appealed to Psalm 118, a passage in Scripture known to all the worshipers who had come to Jerusalem for the Passover feast. This psalm was sung on an appointed day during the feast. Participants in the singing of the choral songs were priests, pilgrims, and proselytes, who sang the words of the psalm before the gates of the temple. A choir of pilgrims would sing the section of the psalm that speaks of the stone rejected by the builders, but that became the capstone (Ps. 118:22–25).[15] Referring to this familiar psalm and especially to the verses relating to the rejected stone, Jesus asked the audience if they had never read in the Scriptures:

The stone the builders rejected
  has become the capstone;
the LORD has done this,
  and it is marvelous in our eyes.

Psalm 118:22, 23[16]

This rhetorical question posed by Jesus had to be answered in the affirmative. Jesus shifted the imagery from the tenants who rejected the servants to the builders who rejected the stone. The tenants by killing the son destroyed themselves, and the builders by laying aside the stone that became the capstone made themselves look foolish. Because of the Lord's doing, the stone became the fitting capstone in an archway of a building. Originally, the stone may have referred to one of the building blocks in Solomon's temple and that became the keystone in the building.[17]

Jesus implied that he was the personification of the landowner's son, as well as of the stone rejected by the builders. Moreover, the teachers of the Law and the other religious leaders were tenants of the vineyard and the builders who put the capstone aside. Thus Jesus spoke of his imminent death and impending exaltation.

THEOLOGY

As reported by the evangelists, the parable has a definite christological focus. The murder of the son brings about the inevitable demise of the tenants, and the rejection of the stone results in its marvelous exaltation. The parable, therefore, teaches the parallel images of the rejection of the son and the rejection of the stone.[18] Both images represent the Son of God.

By mentioning two separate groups of servants sent out by the landowner to collect his share of the vineyard's produce, Matthew apparently hints at the two divisions of the prophets—that is, the former and the latter prophets. He does not provide any further details about the son of the landowner. Mark and Luke, however, call him the "beloved son," which bears the connotation of an only son.[19] The Greek word *agapētos* (beloved son) was used at the time of Jesus' baptism and at his transfiguration. Also, Mark writes that the landowner sent his son last of all. The word *last* is clearly echoed in the opening verses of the Epistle to the Hebrews, "In the past God spoke to our forefathers through the prophets at many times and in various ways, but in these last days he has spoken to us by his Son, whom he appointed heir of all things" (Heb. 1:1, 2).

Furthermore, whereas Mark says that the son was killed inside the vineyard, Matthew and Luke write that the tenants took the son, threw him out of the vineyard, and then killed him. The implication is that the tenants left the body there for bystanders to come and bury the slain. Again the reader detects an echo in the Epistle to the Hebrews: "And so Jesus also suffered outside the city gate to make the people holy through his own blood" (Heb. 13:12).

If the parable had ended with the death of the son and the coming of the landowner to the vineyard, the sacrifice of the son's life would have been inconclusive. The owner could have come to the vineyard immediately after his servants were maltreated. The exaltation of the son could not be portrayed by the vineyard parable, but by means of the rejection motif in Psalm 118 Jesus links it to the parable. The psalm citation reveals that the rejected stone is given the most important place of all the building blocks. The Lord has elevated the capstone to this exalted place.

Jesus deliberately intertwined the imagery of the vineyard and that of the stone by saying, "Therefore I tell you that the kingdom of God will be taken away from you and given to a people who will produce its fruit. He who falls on this stone will be broken to pieces, but he on whom it falls will be crushed" (Matt. 21:43, 44).[20] The kingdom of God has become the vineyard in which other people bring forth fruit. At the same time, the stone smashes and crushes the Son's opponents. "Vineyard" and "building stone" are metaphors that were readily understood by a theologically trained audience of religious leaders. From the prophecy of Isaiah they knew that "the vineyard of the LORD Almighty is the house of Israel, and the men of Judah are the garden of his delight" (Isa. 5:7). And from the same prophecy they knew that "the LORD Almighty . . . for both houses of Israel . . . will be a stone that causes men to stumble and a rock that makes them fall. . . . Many of them will stumble; they will fall and be broken" (Isa. 8:13–15).[21]

The point of the parable and the psalm citation did not escape the religious leaders. All three evangelists report that "they knew he had spoken the parable against them." They, in fact, would be crushed by the Son whom they had rejected but whom God had exalted.

Application

Obviously the parable was applied to the chief priests, the Pharisees, the teachers of the Law, and the elders. They were depicted as the wretched tenants as well as the biased builders. They opposed the owner of the vineyard, killed his son, and rejected the capstone. By choosing enmity against God and his Son, they met crushing defeat and sudden death.

What is the point of the parable? Jesus teaches that seemingly endless patience of God is extended toward those who oppose him. But when this patience ends at the rejection of his Son, God's swift retribution is sure to follow.

The passage proclaims a message of assurance and confidence to the faithful follower of Jesus. Even though the church may experience adverse times, Jesus Christ is the eternal King whose victory is certain. In the words of a confession from the sixteenth century:

> This church has existed
> from the beginning of the world
> and will last until the end.
> That appears from the fact
> that Christ is the eternal King,
> from which it follows
> that he cannot be without subjects.
>
> And this holy church is preserved by God
> against the rage of the whole world.
> It shall never be destroyed
> even though for a while
> it may appear very small
> and may even seem to be
> snuffed out.[22]

15 Wedding Banquet

Matthew 22:1–14

¹Jesus spoke to them again in parables, saying: ²"The kingdom of heaven is like a king who prepared a wedding banquet for his son. ³He sent his servants to those who had been invited to the banquet to tell them to come, but they refused to come.

⁴"Then he sent some more servants and said, 'Tell those who have been invited that I have prepared my dinner: My oxen and fattened cattle have been butchered, and everything is ready. Come to the wedding banquet.'

⁵"But they paid no attention and went off—one to his field, another to his business. ⁶The rest seized his servants, mistreated them and killed them. ⁷The king was enraged. He sent his army and destroyed those murderers and burned their city.

⁸"Then he said to his servants. 'The wedding banquet is ready, but those I invited did not deserve to come. ⁹Go to the street corners and invite to the banquet anyone you find.' ¹⁰So the servants went out into the streets and gathered all the people they could find, both good and bad, and the wedding hall was filled with guests.

¹¹"But when the king came in to see the guests, he noticed a man there who was not wearing wedding clothes. ¹²'Friend,' he asked, 'how did you get in here without wedding clothes?' The man was speechless.

¹³"Then the king told the attendants, 'Tie him hand and foot, and throw him outside, into the darkness, where there will be weeping and gnashing of teeth.'

¹⁴"For many are invited, but few are chosen."

Just as the parable of the great supper is peculiar to Luke, so the parable of the wedding banquet belongs to the Gospel of Matthew. There may be some resemblance and the two parables may have a common theme, but the differences are so fundamental that it is well to speak of two distinct parables.

THE PARABLE

Jesus told the story of a king who prepared a wedding banquet for his son. The king—not his wife, not his son, but the king—made all the arrangements. For this joyful occasion of his son's marriage the king planned an elaborate feast. He wanted to have all the important dignitaries in his kingdom present at the wedding. He sent out the wedding announcements.

As was the custom in those days, invitations were hand-delivered and guests were given a reminder on the day of the wedding. But as the servants of the king delivered the announcements, they met ill-will. The dignitaries and members of nobility made it known to the servants that they wanted nothing to do with the forthcoming wedding. They expressed bitterness and opposition. Even though they knew that a royal invitation was equivalent to a royal command, they refused to acknowledge the king's announcement.

A shadow fell across the royal palace. High-ranking people openly snubbed the king. They refused to honor him with their presence at the wedding of the crown prince. The king, nevertheless, continued to make preparations for the wedding. When the day came for his son to be married, he sent out his servants to remind the dignitaries throughout the land that they were invited to the banquet. Everything was ready.

Unfortunately, the king's action met reaction. The king might have known the kind of response his servants would receive when they were sent out a second time. Already they had received hostile, negative replies. They certainly would experience the same bitterness and resentment, if not worse. The servants went forth with the king's message: "My oxen and fattened cattle have been butchered and everything is ready. Come to the wedding banquet."[1] But the invited guests paid no attention to the royal invitation. They acted in open defiance: one went to his field, another to his business. And when the king's servants lingered a bit too long at one individual's residence, they were mistreated. Some of them were even killed.

The king in righteous wrath sent out his soldiers to punish the murderers and burn their city. He vented his anger by taking punitive action; but at the same time he wanted people to come and celebrate his son's wedding with him. Thus he told his servants to go out to the street corners and to invite anyone who wished to come to the banquet. Both good and bad people came in great numbers, so that the hall was filled with guests.

However, one of the guests had refused to put on the wedding garment offered to him when he entered the hall. Because of his clothes, he was very conspicuous. The moment for the king's arrival in the banquet hall had come. The king surveyed the array of guests, nodding his approval, until he spotted the person who had refused to put on the appropriate garment. In amazement, the king exclaimed, "Friend, how did you get in here without wedding clothes?" The man was tongue-tied. He could not very well tell the king in front of all the guests that he had refused to take the garment offered to him when he entered the hall. He remained silent. The king instructed his servants to take this obstinate guest, tie him up, and throw him out into the nightly darkness.

EXPLANATION

The parable of the wedding banquet is the third in a series of three, and forms the climax to the parables of the two sons and of the tenants.[2] These three kingdom parables were uttered during Jesus' last week on earth, when he experienced concealed hostility from Pharisees, chief priests, and elders, as they laid their traps to catch him in his teaching. Undaunted, Jesus taught the parable of the wedding banquet that was clearly directed against his opponents. This parable, therefore, should be read and understood against the historical background of the closing events in Jesus' ministry.

The introductory line of the parable strikes a note of joy and happiness. The king prepares an elaborate banquet to celebrate his son's wedding. In order to celebrate, he invites worthy guests to the banquet. The joyful partaking of food and drink genuinely expresses the bond of peace and unity of host and guests.[3] Obviously, a banquet is not merely for the purpose of satisfying one's appetite. When host and guests eat together, they engage in table talk and become better acquainted. Uneasiness disappears and a spirit of understanding and affinity takes its place. At banquets peace and harmony prevail.

The guests invited by the king refuse to come. In the East, as elsewhere, it is expected that invited guests will accept a royal invitation as a matter of duty. It is also expected that wedding guests will come with appropriate gifts. And because the guests in the parable cannot reciprocate by inviting the king and his family to a similar feast, the gifts must be expensive—especially since it is the wedding of the king's son.[4] Refusal to attend the wedding has far-reaching implications that may result in trouble and hostility. It conveys the message that the king's son is not worthy of a gift, that the guests do not approve of the marriage, and that they no longer render allegiance to the king.[5] The king is obligated to take measures to assert his authority. He does this by sending his servants out a second time, but now with the urgent appeal to come immediately. He takes no other course of action for the moment. The king hopes that the guests have changed their minds and will now accept his invitation.

The invited guests, however, have had no change of heart. They go about their own business, ignoring the king's messengers. When the messengers press home the urgency of the royal invitation, they shower them with contempt and ridicule and do not hesitate even to kill them.[6]

Jesus is relating Israel's history, and his audience understands that he refers to the prophets sent by God with an urgent message of repentance. But Israel, instead of accepting God's call to repentance, treated the prophets shamefully and killed some of them (Matt. 23:35).[7] Jesus reminds his audience of a black page in their history books. The Pharisees, teachers of the Law, priests, and elders recognize that the indirect reference to this history page involves them.

Jesus continues the story and pictures an angry king who sends out his army to destroy the murderers and to burn their city. The king, having reminded the guests a second time by means of his servants, and seeing that his messengers are scorned and some even killed, realizes the political consequences of their detestable act. It is of paramount importance to the king to meet the rebellious opposition to his rule. He orders his militia to destroy the murderers and to burn their city.[8] Whether this happened on the very day of the wedding or immediately afterward is inconsequential. What is significant is that the king exerts his authority; he rules and demands obedience.

Although the reference to the burning of a city may be an allusion to the destruction of Jerusalem in A.D. 70, it is more realistic to think that the people listening to Jesus were well acquainted with historical accounts of kings dispatching armies to destroy opponents and to set fire to their cities.[9] Jesus' audience may have seen the figure of the angry king as a personification of God. They knew that "the Lord . . . God is a consuming fire, a jealous God" (Deut. 4:24). God's patience is not everlasting, and when his mercy is not matched by repentance, the result is judgment.

Invitations to banquets among prominent Jews and Gentiles were usually extended to family members, close friends, and intimate acquaintances, who were expected to invite the host in turn (compare Luke 14:12). Poor people were not seated at banquet tables; those that were there served the guests.

Now the king bids the good and the bad to come and fill the empty seats. He invites the people of the city and surrounding countryside to come to the festive wedding hall. They come from far and near; those who are either good or bad; they fill the places left vacant by unworthy guests. The king is a picture of benevolence and thus portrays the mercy and love of God extended to sinners.[10] People from all walks of life receive the invitation and respond affirmatively.

The king's servants welcome these people when they enter the palace and tell each guest to put on wedding clothes made for the occasion. The king invites the people, and he expects them to put on the clothes he provides. By wearing the wedding garment furnished by the king, no one reveals poverty or misery. Every guest can hide his social and economic status behind the clothes received from the king.[11] The clothes are clean and white, which in an Eastern culture signifies joy and happiness.[12] In this culture a host would not eat with the guests at a formal banquet; rather, he would make his appearance during the meal.[13]

May everybody come to the wedding of the king's son? The answer is that everyone is welcome provided they wear wedding clothes. When the king enters the wedding hall and notices that one of the guests is not dressed in appropriate clothes, he considers it a deliberate insult. He cannot tolerate obstinacy, contempt, or refusal. He wants his guest to accept whatever he has to offer. Anyone who chooses to decline the king's offer evokes his wrath, and must suffer the consequences. The one guest who appeared at the banquet in his own clothes is summarily removed and thrown outside into the darkness of the night. Filled with remorse, there he weeps and gnashes his teeth and realizes that not everyone can remain in the wedding hall. Only those may stay who accept the king's invitation and enter the place on his terms.

It is especially the Book of Revelation that speaks of the righteous wearing white clothes or fine linen that is bright and clean.[14] God provides these garments that represent the righteousness God gives to his people. God gives them a garment of righteousness as a symbol that the wearer of this garment has been forgiven, sins have been covered, and that he or she is a member of the household of God through Christ. When the father welcomed home the prodigal son he had him put on the best robe, by which he signified that the son's past was forgiven (Luke 15:22).[15] As the king in the parable wanted all the guests to put on the wedding clothes he made available, so God wants sinners to come to the feast of his son and put on the white clothes that symbolize repentance, forgiveness, and righteousness.

The guest who did not have wedding clothes at the royal banquet unmistakably represents the self-righteous sinner. He wants to make it known that he does not need the sacrificial death and atoning blood of Jesus to enter heaven. He does not listen to Jesus' word, "No one comes to the Father except through me" (John 14:6), and thus he appears before God and is thrown out. It is an utter impossibility to appear before God without the protective clothing offered by Jesus Christ.

The paragraph ends with the words, "For many are invited, but few are chosen." Both the first and the last clauses of the parable refer to people who have been invited. Those who refuse to come, as well as the guest without the wedding clothes, do not belong to the ones who have been chosen. Although the invitation is universal and is extended to all people, only the few who accept it in faith and repentance are appointed to eternal life (Acts 13:48).

God takes no pleasure in the death of the wicked man; he wants him to live (Ezek. 18:23; 33:11). God does not want "anyone to perish, but everyone to come to repentance" (2 Peter 3:9). But if people make it known that they have no need for Jesus, they thereby refuse the righteousness Jesus imparts. They have to come to repentance realizing that in their own condition they are totally unworthy to enter the presence of God. They need the clothes of righteousness that Jesus provides. It takes "a broken and a contrite heart" (Ps. 51:17) to accept these clothes willingly and readily.

The invitation of the gospel is proclaimed throughout the world, but relatively few people respond to the offer of salvation. And even among those who accept the invitation there are many who are content with a mere profession of faith. But a profession of faith must demonstrate newness of life.[16] Believers must put their words into deeds. And although God elects without regard to works, election comes to full expression when the elect live a life of obedience to God.[17]

Election involves the Triune God. The elect are "chosen according to the foreknowledge of God the Father." They are chosen "through the sanctifying work of the Spirit, for obedience to Jesus Christ and sprinkling by his blood" (1 Peter 1:2). God elects, and believers respond. Divine election represents the one side of the picture; human responsibility of accepting God's invitation in true faith is the other side.[18] The words, "For many are invited, but few are chosen," form the counterpart of, "But small is the gate and narrow the road that leads to life, and only a few find it" (Matt. 7:14).

16 Fig Tree

Matthew 24:32–35

³²"Now learn this lesson from the fig tree: As soon as its twigs get tender and its leaves come out, you know that summer is near. ³³Even so, when you see all these things, you know that it is near, right at the door. ³⁴I tell you the truth, this generation will certainly not pass away until all these things have happened. ³⁵Heaven and earth will pass away, but my words will never pass away."

Mark 13:28–31

²⁸"Now learn this lesson from the fig tree: As soon as its twigs get tender and its leaves come out, you know that summer is near. ²⁹Even so, when you see these things happening, you know that it is near, right at the door. ³⁰I tell you the truth, this generation will certainly not pass away until all these things have happened. ³¹Heaven and earth will pass away, but my words will never pass away."

Luke 21:29–33

²⁹He told them this parable: "Look at the fig tree and all the trees. ³⁰When they sprout leaves, you can see for yourselves and know that summer is near. ³¹Even so, when you see these things happening, you know that the kingdom of God is near.

³²"I tell you the truth, this generation will certainly not pass away until all these things have happened. ³³Heaven and earth will pass away, but my words will never pass away."

The Gospels reveal that Jesus was an astute observer of nature. His teaching touches on the environment that surrounded him and his listeners. The parables are no exception, for many times they touch the life of the farmer, the fisherman, and the shepherd. Jesus' audience lived closer to nature than most of us do now, and had no difficulty understanding the meaning of his message.

In biblical times the fig tree was a fruit tree common throughout Israel, especially near Jerusalem where Bethphage ("house of figs") was located. In Israel, the saying that had reference to the peaceful reign of Solomon—each man lived in safety "under his own vine and fig tree" (1 Kings 4:25; Micah 4:4)—was well known.

During the summer, the fig tree with its large green leaves provides ample shade. But unlike such trees as the olive, the cedar, and the palm, the fig tree loses its leaves with the approach of winter. While other deciduous trees begin to show signs of life early in the spring—for example, the blossoming almond tree—the fig tree continues to thrust its bare branches heavenward until the warm season has made its initial debut. Then the sap begins to flow, the buds swell, and within a matter of days the tender leaves appear. Nature proclaims the message that the danger of the killing night frost is past and summertime has come.

Jesus may have taught the parable of the budding fig tree during the first week of April, just at the time when the tree begins to show its first signs of life. "As soon as its twigs get tender and its leaves come out, you know that summer[1] is near." This was language his audience understood.

The question, however, was whether the people would be able to interpret this sign theologically and spiritually. The people had come to Jesus repeatedly asking for a sign, but Jesus was not in the habit of giving signs. At one time he told the Pharisees that no sign would be given except the sign of the prophet Jonah (Matt. 12:39); at another time he rebuked them for being able to interpret the appearance of the sky but not the signs of the times (Matt. 16:2, 3). Would his disciples know how to read the sign of the budding fig tree? "Even so, when you see all these things, you know that it is near."[2]

The point of the illustration is rather obvious: when the trees begin to show tender leaves, you know that summer is approaching. Luke has added the words, "all the trees."[3] He generalizes by writing, "Look at the fig tree and all the trees, when they sprout leaves, you can see for yourselves that summer is near." Luke places less emphasis on the fig tree and more stress on the persons looking at the trees: they can see the evidence for themselves.

What, then, is the comparison? The evangelists differ in their wording of the point of comparison. Matthew is all-inclusive. He writes, "Even so, when you see all these things, you know that it is near, right at the door." Mark varies slightly, reading "when you see these things happening," which is identical to Luke's version. But Luke has a different ending: "you know that the kingdom of God is near." He omits the phrase, "right at the door."[4]

The expression, "when you see," occurs in the earlier part of the eschatological discourse of Jesus: "when you see 'the abomination that causes desolation' standing where it does not belong" (Matt. 24:15; Mark 13:14; Luke 21:20). Undeniably, the words, "these things," or "all these things," must refer to the predictions outlined earlier in the discourse. Jesus' disciples ask, "Tell us, when will these things happen?" (Mark 13:4). The entire discourse on the end of the age (Mark 13:5–23 and parallels), and especially the section on the siege of Jerusalem and the appearance of false christs and false prophets, are denoted by the phrase "these things" or "all these things."[5] Among other things, it refers back to "the abomination of desolation" that is predicted to come to the temple in Jerusalem. "When you see Jerusalem being surrounded by armies, you will know that its desolation is near" (Luke 21:20).

Jesus applies this truth directly to his contemporaries. "I tell you the truth," he tells his disciples, "this generation will certainly not pass away until all these things have happened" (Mark 13:30). Once more, he uses the expression "all these things." Certainly, the disciples will be able to ascertain the approaching desecration and destruction of the temple much the same as they determine the arrival of summer by looking at the fig tree. But the text reads, "this generation will not pass away until all these things have happened." And all these things predicted in the discourse on the end of the age go far beyond the time of Jesus' contemporaries.[6] However, the Qumran scrolls have shed significant light on the meaning of "the last generation." The expression indicates that its duration is not limited to one life span, and should not be taken literally.[7] It refers to people who persist, and are faithful to the end. It includes, therefore, the disciples who heard the words from Jesus' lips, the people who witnessed the fall of Jerusalem, and the believers throughout the centuries who have steadfastly looked forward to the fulfillment of the prophecies relating to the end of the age.

The image of the budding fig tree is usually associated with a period of blessing (Joel 2:22) and hardly with destruction and calamity. The parable as such should not be seen primarily in relation to the calamities predicted in the discourse.[8] Rather, the emphasis should remain on redemption evident in the coming of the kingdom of God. Although Matthew and Mark say of such calamities as famines and earthquakes that "all these are the beginning of birth pains" (Matt. 24:8; Mark 13:8), Luke omits this sentence. He presents the words of Jesus in a frame of joyful expectation. "When these things begin to take place, stand up and lift up your heads, because redemption is drawing near" (Luke 21:28). Luke uses nearly identical language in the application of the parable of the budding fig tree: "Even so, when you see these things happening, you know that the kingdom of God is near" (Luke 21:31). Of course, the terms *redemption* and *kingdom of God* in this context refer to the future consummation of salvation.[9] They allude to the ultimate coming of the

kingdom of God in which the people of God will be released from afflic-
tion. Then also "creation itself will be liberated from its bondage to decay
and brought into the glorious freedom of the children of God" (Rom.
8:21).

The parable concludes with the saying, "Heaven and earth will pass
away, but my words will never pass away." That which passes away has
become part of the past and is no longer significant for the present.[10]
The meaning of the parable is that the words of Jesus do not lose their
impact when a particular prediction has been fulfilled in time. Rather,
Jesus' words are as valid today as when they were first spoken.

What is the message of the parable? Until the day of Christ's return
when the kingdom of God comes in all its fullness, no generation is exempt
from calamities. But Christians ought not to be dismayed or disheartened.
They ought to observe the signs of the times very carefully, much the same
as they look at the budding fig tree, and know that the events occurring
around them are ushering in a new age. The parable, therefore, urges
believers to persevere in watchfulness. The adversities they encounter
ought not to diminish their endurance and undermine their confidence.
Rather, adversities ought to confirm expectations of the approaching glorious finale of which these adversities are harbingers. And even though
believers throughout the ages have suffered afflictions and have coped
with disaster, the Christian today, more than ever before, is encouraged
by the timely words of Paul, "And do this, understanding the present time.
The hour has come for you to wake up from your slumber, because our
salvation is nearer now than when we first believed. The night is nearly
over; the day is almost here" (Rom. 13:11, 12).

17 Watchful Servant

> ### Mark 13:32–37
> [32]"No one knows about that day or hour, not even the angels in heaven, nor the Son, but only the Father. [33]Be on guard! Be alert! You do not know when that time will come. [34]It's like a man going away: He leaves his house and puts his servants in charge, each with his assigned task, and tells the one at the door to keep watch.
> [35]"Therefore keep watch because you do not know when the owner of the house will come back—whether in the evening, or at midnight, or when the rooster crows, or at dawn. [36]If he comes suddenly, do not let him find you sleeping. [37]What I say to you, I say to everyone: 'Watch!'"
>
> ### Luke 12:35–38
> [35]"Be dressed ready for service and keep your lamps burning, [36]like men waiting for their master to return from a wedding banquet, so that when he comes and knocks they can immediately open the door for him. [37]It will be good for those servants whose master finds them watching when he comes. I tell you the truth, he will dress himself to serve, will have them recline at the table and will come and wait on them. [38]It will be good for those servants whose master finds them ready, even if he comes in the second or third watch of the night."

The title of this chapter is much more applicable to the parable recorded in the Gospel of Mark than that in Luke. In Mark, all the servants receive a specific assignment from the master of the house, who is ready to leave. The doorkeeper is told to keep watch. The audience, however, is included because the universal command is given in the plural, "Therefore keep watch because you [plural] do not know when the owner of the house will come back" (Mark 13:35).[1]

In Luke's parable, all the servants are expected to be ready to open the door when the master of the house returns from a wedding banquet during a particular night. Also, the general admonition given (in the plu-

ral) to everyone hearing these words is, "Be dressed ready for service
and keep your lamps burning" (Luke 12:35). An appropriate title for
Luke's parable is "The Waiting Servants."

The two parables, in Mark 13 and Luke 12, are not at all identical in
wording. They show no parallel sentences or phrases. Yet the basic teaching of the two accounts is the same. Both present the message of watchfulness for servants awaiting the arrival of their master. In the parable
of Mark, the master goes away, presumably to another country,[2] and in
Luke's Gospel the master is attending a wedding. In Mark's parable, the
servants do not know when the master will return except that all indi-
cations point to his coming home during the night, "whether in the
evening, or at midnight, or when the rooster crows, or at dawn." Luke
has a similar list of time divisions. "It will be good for those servants
whose master finds them ready even if he comes in the second or third
watch of the night." Mark reflects the Roman custom of dividing the
night into four watches, each three hours in length.[3] Luke, however,
divides the night into three watches.[4]

MARK 13:33−37

The time of Jesus' return is unknown to all. The angels in heaven lack
the information, and even the Son is not informed. Only the Father
knows. "Be on guard! Be alert![5] You do not know when that time will
come." How does the believer watch?

It is like a man who has a number of servants and one of them is the
night watchman. As the owner of the house prepares to leave for an
indefinite period of time, he gives each of his servants a suitable task.
The watchman, for example, is to watch the entrance to the estate.
Houses in Israel were often separated from the road or street by a high
wall surrounding the property. The house itself was located, together
with other dwellings, away from the gate. Near the entrance the little
house of the doorkeeper was found. Ultimate security for the people living inside the walled property rested with the doorkeeper.[6] He was
expected to be on duty at night and enjoy his rest during the day. To
sleep on the job was a grave offense, contrary to the explicit instructions
that the owner of the house had given the night watchman (Mark 13:34,
36).

Somehow the tasks assigned to the other servants do not seem as
important as that of the watchman, and the servants are not commanded
to assist the doorkeeper in his task. The emphasis of the parable has
shifted. The disciples of Jesus are exhorted to keep watch. Jesus applies
the parable directly to his followers with the intention that they under-

stand the exhortation spiritually.[7] It becomes apparent that the owner of the house personifies the Son of Man who, at the time known only to the Father, will come "with great power and glory" (Mark 13:26). Jesus' followers are exhorted to be vigilant, not to fall asleep, to await his return. As the watchman patiently and expectantly awaits the return of the owner of the house during any of the four watches of the night, so the followers of Jesus must be alert, wide awake, and responsive to his coming.

The owner of the house could not be precise in determining the exact time of his arrival at the gates. It could be any time, early or late. Likewise, no one is able to ascertain the exact time of Jesus' return. It may be any time. Just like the doorkeeper could not say that his master would be back during the fourth watch just before daybreak,[8] so the followers of Jesus cannot say that Jesus will return when the night of adversities is past. The return of Jesus takes place suddenly (Mark 13:36). Therefore, Jesus exhorts not only his immediate audience, but he addresses all people: "What I say to you, I say to everyone: Watch!"

Throughout the parable the note of watchfulness is repeatedly sounded, for in every verse the idea is expressed either positively or negatively. Those who hear the parable must not be found sleeping. They are exhorted to keep watch, for they do not know when Jesus will come back.[9]

LUKE 12:35–38

The parable of the waiting servants is akin to that of the doorkeeper. It is commonly asserted that both parables are derived from a parable originally taught by Jesus.[10] By implication, the early Christian community or the evangelist created the present reading in the Gospels. However, the two accounts of the doorkeeper and the waiting servants are so diverse in wording and sentence structure that it is impossible to assume one original parable. It is much simpler to say that both parables come from the lips of Jesus. Mark reported one and Luke the other.

In Luke's account, the parable is introduced as a comparison. After an exhortation to watchfulness, Jesus compares the state of readiness to "men waiting for their master to return from a wedding banquet, so that when he comes and knocks they can immediately open the door for him." Jesus tells his disciples to be ready for service and to keep their lamps burning. Clearly, the message Jesus conveys must be understood spiritually. In the doorkeeper parable, even though all the servants were given tasks to do in the absence of their master, the watchman had to keep awake and answer the knock on the door when the owner of the house returned during the course of the night. In Luke's parable all the servants wait for their master to return. They are the ones who open the door for him when he knocks. Although they cannot be certain when that knock will be heard—anytime from ten in the evening to six in the morning—they know that during that particular night their master will come home from a wedding banquet. But why must all the servants stay awake? And why must all the servants open the door?[11] The answer to these questions is that Jesus wanted to portray the close relationship between the master and his servants. In this short parable the clause, "it will be good for those servants" (Luke 12:37, 38), occurs twice. Also, by way of comparison, Jesus points to the bond of fellowship that exists between himself and the disciples.

The disciples are told to be dressed and ready for service[12] and to keep their lamps burning. The burning lamps suggest a period of the night during which the disciples must stay awake, ready to serve Jesus[13] when he returns. The parable pictures the master standing outside the door of his own house, knocking and waiting for the servants to open the door and admit him to his own house. The image is repeated in the letter addressed to the church in Laodicea, "Here I am! I stand at the door and knock. If anyone hears my voice and opens the door, I will come in and eat with him, and he with me" (Rev. 3:20).

The parable continues with a word of commendation. "It will be good for those servants whose master finds them watching when he comes." The sequel, of course, would be that the servants, after opening the door, are busy serving their master. However, an unexpected turn of events occurs: the master becomes the servant.

He dresses himself for service, he has the servants recline at the table, and he waits on them.[14] This indeed is contrary to the normal custom, which is aptly described in the parable of the servant's reward (Luke 17:7–10). However, this reversal of roles is completely in harmony with the teaching and conduct of Jesus. He taught the servant role most vividly in the upper room when he washed his disciples' feet.[15] In short, within the context of the parable of the waiting servants Jesus furnishes a concealed reference to himself.

Once more the servants who have waited for their master to return are commended. The servants have fulfilled that which was expected of them: to wait for their master's return. Likewise, all believers, not just the disciples of Jesus, are told to be ready, to watch for and await their Lord's return. If they are dressed and ready for service with their lamps burning brightly in the dark night, the Lord will not withhold his reward when he comes.

18 Burglar

> **Matthew 24:42–44**
> [42]"Therefore keep watch, because you do not know on what day your Lord will come. [43]But understand this: If the owner of the house had known at what time of night the thief was coming, he would have kept watch and would not have let his house be broken into. [44]So you also must be ready, because the Son of Man will come at an hour when you do not expect him."
>
> **Luke 12:39, 40**
> [39]"But understand this: If the owner of the house had known at what hour the thief was coming, he would not have let his house be broken into. [40]You also must be ready, because the Son of Man will come at an hour when you do not expect him."

The parable of the burglar follows that of the waiting servants in Luke's Gospel. Because of its brevity it is considered to be a parabolic saying rather than a parable as such. And, while the parable of the waiting servants showed a promise turned into a reward, the parable of the thief at night constitutes a warning. The one describes a joyful event, the other impending disaster.

The teaching of this parabolic saying is rather simple. While the owner of the house slept, thieves came to his dwelling. They dug a hole in a wall made of brick, broke into the house, and stole the owner's valuables. If the owner had known what hour the thief was planning to come, he would have kept watch to prevent the burglary.

The parabolic saying is based on the reality of life, for burglaries take place frequently, especially in times of economic distress. The image of the thief in the night is applied to the coming day of the Lord in the Epistles and Revelation. Paul uses the image for the return of the Lord:

You know very well that the day of the Lord will come like a thief in the night. While people are saying, "Peace and safety," destruction will come on them suddenly, as labor pains on a pregnant woman, and they will not escape. But you, brothers, are not in darkness so that this day should surprise you like a thief.

1 Thessalonians 5:2–4

Peter paints a similar picture: "But the day of the Lord will come like a thief. The heavens will disappear with a roar; the elements will be destroyed by fire, and the earth and everything in it will be laid bare" (2 Peter 3:10). In the Book of Revelation, John records the letter addressed to the church at Sardis. The risen and exalted Lord says, "Remember, therefore, what you have received and heard; obey it, and repent. But if you do not wake up, I will come like a thief, and you will not know at what time I will come to you" (Rev. 3:3). And once again he says, "Behold, I come like a thief! Blessed is he who stays awake and keeps his clothes with him, so that he may not go naked and be shamefully exposed" (Rev. 16:15).[1]

Jesus predicts his own return in the context of his discourse on the last things. He instructs his followers to be aware of the suddenness of his coming. He compares the time of his coming to the days of Noah.

For in the days before the flood, people were eating and drinking, marrying and giving in marriage, up to the day Noah entered the ark; and they knew nothing about what would happen until the flood came and took them all away. That is how it will be at the coming of the Son of Man.

Matthew 24:38, 39

In the parable of the thief at night Jesus repeats the same warning, "So you also must be ready because the Son of Man will come at an hour when you do not expect him."[2]

Does Jesus warn his own disciples of imminent danger? We expect the followers of Jesus to look forward to a joyful occasion at the time of his return. Those who listen attentively to and in obedience act upon Jesus' words will be prepared when he comes. For them his return will be a joyous event. But for those people, even for those who were Jesus' immediate followers, a word of warning against falling away is in place. After all, among the twelve disciples were Peter who denied his Lord and Judas who betrayed him.[3]

The parable addresses itself to those who wait for Jesus' glorious return and to those who are ignoring Jesus' instructions. While the image of the coming of the Son of Man evokes joyful expectation among the faithful, the image of the prowling burglar creates anxiety and worry in those who are not prepared.

What does the parable teach? In the days before the coming of the Lord, many people live in total disregard of impending judgment. His coming occurs without advance notice. The suddenness of this event for those who fail to pay attention may be compared to the unexpected moment when a burglar strikes and robs. Those who prepare themselves and are ready will not be surprised when Jesus returns.

19 Servant Entrusted with Authority

> ### Matthew 24:45–51
> [45] "Who then is the faithful and wise servant, whom the master has put in charge of the servants in his household to give them their food at the proper time? [46]It will be good for that servant whose master finds him doing so when he returns. [47]I tell you the truth, he will put him in charge of all his possessions. [48]But suppose that servant is wicked and says to himself, 'My master is staying away a long time,' [49]and he then begins to beat his fellow servants and to eat and drink with drunkards. [50]The master of that servant will come on a day when he does not expect him and at an hour he is not aware of. [51]He will cut him to pieces and assign him a place with the hypocrites, where there will be weeping and gnashing of teeth."
>
> ### Luke 12:41–46
> [41]Peter asked, "Lord, are you telling this parable to us, or to everyone?"
> [42]The Lord answered, "Who then is the faithful and wise manager, whom the master puts in charge of his servants to give them their food allowance at the proper time? [43]It will be good for that servant whom the master finds doing so when he returns. [44]I tell you the truth, he will put him in charge of all his possessions. [45]But suppose the servant says to himself, 'My master is taking a long time in coming,' and he then begins to beat the menservants and maidservants and to eat and drink and get drunk. [46]The master of that servant will come on a day when he does not expect him and at an hour he is not aware of. He will cut him to pieces and assign him a place with the unbelievers."

The parable of the servant in authority is one of the parables in which Jesus teaches the necessity of watchfulness. Besides emphasizing watchfulness, Jesus also stresses faithfulness. In brief, the parable concerns a servant who is entrusted with the responsibility of managing the household in the absence of his master. If he proves to be faithful and wise, the master will reward him generously upon his return. But if he is lazy, mean, and careless, the master will come back unexpectedly and inflict severe physical punishment.

THE FAITHFUL SERVANT

Both Matthew and Luke show that Jesus addressed his disciples (Matt. 24:1; Luke 12:22). As Jesus was teaching his disciples, Peter interrupted Jesus with the question of whether the parable was meant for the disciples or for everyone.[1] That is, was Jesus' teaching to be specifically applied only to his disciples? Or was it to be applied to others as well? It was Peter, the spokesman for the twelve disciples, who had to ask the question. He as always was ready to ask (Matt. 15:15), "Lord, are you telling this parable[2] to us, or to everyone?" Jesus answered Peter's question by telling another parable: the story about the faithful servant.

A master of a number of servants has to leave his household for an undetermined length of time. He makes the necessary plans for his departure and calls in one of his servants who, in the master's opinion, is able to manage the day-to-day duties of the household.[3] It is the servant's duty to be in charge of his fellow servants, to give them their food at the proper time, and to prove his faithfulness and prudence in his master's absence. If the master finds everything in order upon his return, he intends to promote the servant to be the manager of his possessions.

The servant demonstrates two indispensable characteristics: faithfulness and prudence. He is dependable because his yes is yes and his no is no. His fellow servants know that he does not break his word. They can trust him. He is also shrewd, for he has a canny way of anticipating problems, of being fully prepared to meet them skillfully and to solve them effectively. With apparent ease he seems to be in full control of every situation.

When the master returns from his journey, he makes an inspection tour and finds everything in good order. He is pleased with the glowing reports he hears about the servant. As a reward for his faithfulness, the master promotes the servant to the position of manager over all his possessions. He knows now that the servant has stood the test of efficiently managing his household. He awards him by placing him second in command.

The Unfaithful Servant

When a master places someone in charge of his household, he appoints a trustworthy servant whom he expects to do well. The master wants to leave his house in dependable hands. But human nature is not always dependable, and the master may make a serious error in appointing a particular servant in whom he has put his confidence. In other words, the master can never be absolutely certain that the servant will live up to his expectations.

The servant may have put up a facade before he received the appointment. Now that his master has left, he reveals his true character. He is sly, cruel, and intemperate. On the basis of other journeys his master has taken, the servant calculates that he will stay a long time. In the master's absence, the servant begins to beat his fellow servants. He feels quite safe in doing so, thinking that the time of his master's return is in the distant future. He spends his time in the company of drunkards with whom he indulges in excesses of food and drink.[4]

His master hurries home, and appears suddenly and unexpectedly. What is the master going to do with this servant who has been irresponsible and unfaithful? The master hears the stories about his behavior, his parties, his slothfulness. Nothing escapes him and everything becomes known to him. The master is now the judge and the law enforcer. He must pronounce the verdict and declare the offender guilty. Then he must administer appropriate punishment.

Jesus said, "He will cut him to pieces and assign him a place with the hypocrites, where there will be weeping and gnashing of teeth" (Matt. 24:51). The text presents some difficulty in understanding the phrase "cut to pieces." If the phrase is taken literally, how can he be given a place among the hypocrites? It is possible that the text contains an idiom that should be understood metaphorically,[5] much the same as the expression "skin him alive." From the Qumran literature, new light has been shed on this text.[6] The phrase "cut him to pieces" is a more literal translation of "to cut him off" from the midst of his people. This wording harmonizes with the teaching of Psalm 37, in which the righteous will inherit the land, but the wicked will be cut off.[7] The servant who failed his master receives the opposite reward of the responsible, trustworthy, and faithful servant. He is separated, cast out, and cut off from his people.

Interpretation

The account of the parable is identical in the Gospels of Matthew and Luke except for the difference in wording.[8] For example, the faithful and wise servant in Matthew's Gospel is a faithful and wise manager in Luke's Gospel, even though Luke refers to him as "servant" in the rest of the parable. Matthew writes that the wicked servant begins to beat his fellow servants, but Luke says that he begins to beat the menservants and the maidservants. And this servant is assigned a place with the hypocrites, according to Matthew, and a place with the unbelievers, according to Luke.

A number of minor differences can be shown, but how significant are they? Guided by the Holy Spirit, the apostle Matthew was reminded of everything Jesus had told him (John 14:26). As a companion of Paul, Luke relied on the report handed down to him by eyewitnesses and servants of the Word (Luke 1:2).[9] Both writers were inspired by the Spirit of God when they wrote their Gospel accounts, yet each reflects his own style and purpose. Matthew as a Jew sought to bring the gospel to his Jewish contemporaries. Luke the Hellenist wrote his Gospel for the Greek-speaking world of his day.

By using the term *manager* at the beginning of his parable, Luke wants to focus attention on a chief servant. This servant supervised his master's household consisting of menservants and maidservants.[10] And because he uses the word *servant* throughout the remainder of the parable, Luke clearly shows that he views the managerial setting much the same as Matthew except perhaps on a somewhat larger scale. The difference in wording, therefore, may be ascribed to the style characterizing the individual writer. This is especially true in respect to the word *hypocrites*, which occurs rather frequently in Matthew's Gospel.[11] Luke, on the other hand, uses the term *unbelievers*, which in context does not differ in meaning from Matthew's wording because a hypocrite is in fact an unbeliever.[12]

The point of the parable is to call attention to the responsibility given to the follower of Jesus. Some followers receive greater privileges than others, but they also are charged with greater responsibilities. Because each one has his or her own duty in the service of the Lord,[13] no one is excluded or exempt. In Matthew's sequence this parable serves as an introduction to the parables of the ten virgins and of the talents. Everyone is accountable to Jesus.

The master of the household representing Jesus leaves with the promise of his return. In Jesus' absence, his followers have privileges and responsibilities. If believers are faithful and wise in the discharge of their duties, Jesus will reward them abundantly upon his return.[14] But if they are unfaithful and behave irresponsibly, at Jesus' return they face complete separation from the people of God along with dreadful punishment.

Whereas Matthew concludes the parable with the familiar saying "where there will be weeping and gnashing of teeth" (Matt. 24:51),[15] Luke finishes the sequence of three parables on watchfulness (the doorkeeper, the burglar, and the servant entrusted with authority) with a conclusive word of Jesus, recorded only by Luke:

> That servant who knows his master's will and does not get ready or does not do what his master wants will be beaten with many blows. But the one who does not know and does things deserving punishment will be beaten with few blows. From everyone who has been given much, much will be demanded; and from the one who has been entrusted with much, much more will be asked.
>
> Luke 12:47, 48

20 Ten Virgins

> **Matthew 25:1–13**
>
> ¹"At that time the kingdom of heaven will be like ten virgins who took their lamps and went out to meet the bridegroom. ²Five of them were foolish and five were wise. ³The foolish ones took their lamps but did not take any oil with them. ⁴The wise, however, took oil in jars along with their lamps. ⁵The bridegroom was a long time in coming, and they all became drowsy and fell asleep.
>
> ⁶"At midnight the cry rang out: 'Here's the bridegroom! Come out to meet him!'
>
> ⁷"Then all the virgins woke up and trimmed their lamps. ⁸The foolish ones said to the wise, 'Give us some of your oil; our lamps are going out.'
>
> ⁹"'No,' they replied, 'there may not be enough for both us and you. Instead, go to those who sell oil and buy some for yourselves.'
>
> ¹⁰"But while they were on their way to buy the oil, the bridegroom arrived. The virgins who were ready went in with him to the wedding banquet. And the door was shut.
>
> ¹¹"Later the others also came. 'Sir! Sir!' they said. 'Open the door for us!'
>
> ¹²"But he replied, 'I tell you the truth, I don't know you.'
>
> ¹³"Therefore keep watch, because you do not know the day or the hour."

Only Matthew has recorded the parable of the ten virgins. He has skillfully placed it after Jesus' discourse on the end of the age. In the last part of that discourse Jesus speaks of a division between those who are chosen, alert, and faithful, and those who are not. "Two men will be in the field; one will be taken and the other left. Two women will be grinding with a hand mill; one will be taken and the other left" (Matt. 24:40, 41). The faithful and wise servant is placed in charge of all his master's possessions, but the wicked servant is assigned a place with the hypocrites (Matt. 24:45–51). Thus in the parable of the ten virgins, five enter the bridegroom's house; the other five find the door locked. This theme of separating the good from the bad is continued in the parable of the talents (Matt. 25:14–30) and the description of a shepherd separating the sheep from the goats (Matt. 25:31–33).

The Wedding

Jesus tells a story of ten bridesmaids, who prepared themselves for the arrival of the bridegroom; they observed the local wedding customs of that day. It is an interesting story, intended to teach the pointed lesson of being prepared.

Although detailed information is varied and sketchy, it appears that in Jesus' day marriage generally took place at an early age. Because sexual maturity is reached in teenage years, marriages in Israel were contracted when individuals were in their mid-teens.[1] It was customary for a bride to be surrounded by ten bridesmaids,[2] who most likely were her special friends and of the same age as the bride.

The introductory sentence, "At that time the kingdom of heaven will be like ten virgins who took their lamps and went to meet the bridegroom," sets the stage.[3] That is, ten teenage girls took their lamps and went to the bride's home for the purpose of preparing her to meet the bridegroom. The introductory sentence, understandably, does not refer to the actual meeting of the bridegroom and the virgins, for that takes place later as the story develops (Matt. 25:10).

These young girls should not be thought of as sitting somewhere along the road in the middle of the night, overcome by sleep, while their lamps begin to flicker for lack of oil. It is better to see these girls busy at the home of the bride, adorning her and caring for last-minute preparations. It is uncertain if the text refers to the bride as well, as footnotes in many Bible versions indicate.[4] It is a fact, however, that the parable is not concerned with the bride. It focuses attention on the bridesmaids, and especially the five foolish ones.[5] These ten girls were to accompany the bride to the house of the bridegroom or his parents, where, according to established custom, the wedding would be held.[6]

Five of the girls were foolish; five were wise. The foolish ones had taken their lamps, but had neglected to take oil along. What type of lamps were these that needed frequent replenishing in order to keep burning? Small oil lamps used in the home would not be suitable for an outdoor procession because the wind would extinguish the flame. The lamps of the wedding procession were torches—long poles with oil-drenched rags at the top. When lit, these torches would burn brightly, illuminating the festive procession on the way to the bridegroom's house. However, because of the brightly burning flame, the oil content was soon depleted. Within fifteen minutes, additional olive oil had to be poured on the rags to keep the torch burning.[7] Torchbearers, therefore, had to have a ready supply of oil available to keep the torches burning, especially if the bridesmaids were expected to perform torchlight dances upon their arrival.

The five foolish bridesmaids had arrived at the home of the bride completely unprepared; they had neglected to take extra oil along. Because they would not need their torches until the procession started, they were, unfortunately, unaware of their negligence.

The bridegroom was delayed in coming for the bride. The problem of settling the dowry may have caused this delay. This ancient custom, mentioned frequently in Scripture,[8] consists of the giving of gifts by the family of the bridegroom to that of the bride. Discussion of the dowry could take considerable time and lead to protracted arguments.[9] When everything was duly signed and the parties were in full agreement, the wedding feast could begin. The bridegroom could not go to his bride until the bride-price was paid and the marriage contract signed.[10]

Meanwhile the bridesmaids waited, became drowsy, and fell asleep. Both the wise and the foolish girls slept, thus passing the time quickly. But suddenly at midnight the cry was heard, "Here's the bridegroom! Come out to meet him!"[11] The bridegroom and his attendants were joyfully approaching the home of the bride. Inside the bridesmaids quickly awoke, got up, checked their appearance, and put their lamps in order.[12] All ten had their torches brightly burning, but five of them realized that without extra oil their torches would be completely out even before the procession started. They tried to acquaint the other girls with their problem. They said, "Give us some of your oil; our lamps are going out." But the five girls who had taken oil jars along knew that every fifteen minutes they would have to replenish their own torches, and also that they had to keep their torches burning during the procession as well as during a torchlight dance upon arrival. Common sense told them that the oil they had taken along in the jars would be sufficient for five torches but not for ten. They politely refused to share their oil. Instead, they advised the five girls to go to oil merchants to buy extra oil.

The five girls who had spent their time waiting and sleeping now had to rush to a merchant, wake him, and buy the needed oil. In the meantime the bridegroom arrived and the procession started. All went to the home of the bridegroom, and were participating in the festivities. They closed the entrance to the wedding hall at the groom's house, and anyone who had not been part of the procession was not permitted to enter. That was a customary procedure among the rich in the culture of the day.[13]

The parable ends with the scene of the five girls who came to the closed door, calling out, "Sir! Sir! open the door for us!" Their insistent call eventually brought the bridegroom to the door, who told the girls that he did not wish to have anything to do with them.[14] They were too late.

MEANING

The conclusion Jesus gives to the parable is simple and to the point: "Therefore keep watch, because you do not know the day or the hour." He obviously refers to himself and in this parable is teaching about his own return. He is the bridegroom; he is the one who is coming. Repeatedly during his teaching ministry he makes reference to the bridegroom. To the question of why his disciples do not fast, Jesus replies, "How can the guests of the bridegroom mourn while he is with them? The time will come when the bridegroom will be taken from them; then they will fast" (Matt. 9:15). Moreover, the ending of the parable of the ten virgins is a clear echo of Jesus' teaching recorded in Matthew 7:21–23:[15]

> Not everyone who says to me, "Lord, Lord," will enter the kingdom of heaven, but only he who does the will of my Father who is in heaven. Many will say to me on that day, "Lord, Lord, did we not prophesy in your name, and in your name drive out demons and perform many miracles?" Then I will tell them plainly, "I never knew you. Away from me, you evildoers!"

The obvious teaching is that Jesus excludes from the kingdom of heaven all those who fail to do the will of God the Father. In the day of Jesus' return they may call him by name and point to their religious deeds, but because of their failure to do the Father's will they have no part in the kingdom.

Five of the virgins in the parable are called wise. They are the ones who come prepared. They are wise because they throw themselves completely into the situation and follow the customary instructions carefully.[16] The Scriptures teach that a wise person has true insight into the will of God.

The five girls who are called foolish and who occupy the center of attention in the parable do not seem to be guilty of anything evil. They come with the best intentions and wish the bride and the groom years of matrimonial happiness. But they fail to do the wishes of the bride and bridegroom, for they neglect to take the necessary oil along. "Does a maiden forget her jewelry, a bride her wedding ornaments?" (Jer. 2:32). The answer is, of course not. Yet these five girls forget to make adequate preparations for their appointed task. They come unprepared and for that reason are excluded from the wedding hall.[17]

Nothing in the parable indicates that the ten girls were expected to stay awake. The wise as well as the foolish girls fell asleep while they were waiting. Watchfulness is therefore not the outstanding characteristic that is taught in this parable. Rather, it is the quality of preparedness that is predominant.

As the bridegroom in the time and culture of Jesus' day might come at any time during the long hours of the night, so Jesus will come suddenly on the day of his return.

INTERPRETATIONS

The parable of the ten virgins has been interpreted allegorically in numerous ways from the early church to the present. In such interpretations, Jesus is the bridegroom and the ten virgins the church. The church consists of the good and the bad, the elect and the reprobate, the wise and the foolish. The lamps the virgins carry are good works, because Christians are exhorted to let their works shine before men. The oil is the Holy Spirit, for when Samuel anointed David with oil the Holy Spirit came upon him. The oil merchants are Moses and the prophets. And the call, "Here's the bridegroom!" is the trumpet call of God at the return of Christ.

This type of interpretation leads to confusion and frequently ends in nonsense. Some interpreters understand oil to mean joy or love, while others see it as good works or giving help to the needy. Still others consider oil to be the word of teaching.[18] Moreover, the uncharitable attitude of the wise girls toward the five needy girls could be questioned. And the negative reply—"I don't know you"—of the bridegroom would need critical evaluation. But the handing down of allegorical interpretations or the questioning of the parable's detailed parts goes contrary to the spirit of Jesus' teaching.[19] In the parable of the ten virgins, the interpreter should not lose sight of the forest because of the proverbial trees. He must find the central meaning of the parable.

When the prophet Nathan came to King David and told him the story of the rich man who took the ewe lamb that belonged to a poor man, David reacted instantaneously and wanted to punish the main figure of the story, the rich man. Then Nathan pointed to David and said, "You are the man" (2 Sam. 12:1–10). Nathan conveyed the central message of the parable most effectively, for he elicited an immediate response from David. If, on the other hand, the parable is interpreted allegorically, it loses its punch. Then the rich man is David and the poor man Uriah; the ewe lamb becomes Bathsheba, but the visiting traveler somehow does not fit the allegory. In short, interpreting the details of a parable allegorically robs the story of its direction and often results in absurdity.

The central message of the parable of the ten virgins is directed at the followers of Jesus. The wise who are constantly seeking to do the will of God are the ones who fervently pray, "Maranatha," that is, "Come, Lord Jesus, come quickly." But the foolish ones seem to pay no attention to the imminent return of the Lord. The parable is directed at them to elicit from their mouths the words: How foolish can you be!

The parable of the ten virgins must be seen in the broader context of Jesus' teaching on his return. The concluding statement, "Therefore keep watch, because you do not know the day or the hour" (Matt. 25:13), is a repetition of the preceding verses, "No one knows about that day or hour" (Matt. 24:36) and "Therefore keep watch, because you do not know on what day your Lord will come" (Matt. 24:42). It is Jesus who utters his familiar "I tell you the truth" (Matt. 25:12), thereby indicating that he speaks about his own return. This is a word of Jesus rather than that of a teenage bridegroom. That is, by means of the parable Jesus clearly teaches his followers to be prepared for his return. Those who are unprepared will be excluded forever from the kingdom when Jesus returns. They are the ones who hear Jesus say, "I tell you the truth, I don't know you." They are the fools who have eliminated thoughts of the return of Christ from their lifestyle.[20] But for them the day of the Lord will come unexpectedly while they are completely unprepared.[21] Then it will be too late to mend one's ways.

In the setting in which Jesus tells this parable, the theme of the return (coming) of the master (bridegroom) predominates. The master of the servant entrusted with authority returns at the appropriate time; the bridegroom comes at midnight; and, in the parable of the talents, the master returns after a long time (Matt. 25:19). In this context, the parable of the ten virgins enjoys its true dimensions.

Also, in the parable of the servant entrusted with authority, the servant is characterized as faithful and wise; the next parable describes five virgins as wise; and in the parable of the talents two of the servants are called good and faithful. In succession, the parable of the servant teaches faithfulness and wisdom; the parable of the virgins stresses wisdom; the parable of the talents communicates the virtue of faithfulness.[22]

21 Talents

Matthew 25:14–30

[14]"Again, it will be like a man going on a journey, who called his servants and entrusted his property to them. [15]To one he gave five talents of money, to another two talents, and to another one talent, each according to his ability. Then he went on his journey. [16]The man who had received the five talents went at once and put his money to work and gained five more. [17]So also, the one with the two talents gained two more. [18]But the man who had received the one talent went off, dug a hole in the ground and hid his master's money.

[19]"After a long time the master of those servants returned and settled accounts with them. [20]The man who had received the five talents brought the other five. 'Master,' he said, 'you entrusted me with five talents. See, I have gained five more.'

[21]"His master replied, 'Well done, good and faithful servant! You have been faithful with a few things; I will put you in charge of many things. Come and share your master's happiness!'

[22]"The man with the two talents also came. 'Master,' he said, 'you entrusted me with two talents; see, I have gained two more.'

[23]"His master replied, 'Well done, good and faithful servant! You have been faithful with a few things; I will put you in charge of many things. Come and share your master's happiness!'

[24]"Then the man who had received the one talent came. 'Master,' he said 'I knew that you are a hard man, harvesting where you have not sown and gathering where you have not scattered seed. [25]So I was afraid and went out and hid your talent in the ground. See, here is what belongs to you.'

[26]"His master replied, 'You wicked, lazy servant! So you knew that I harvest where I have not sown and gather where I have not scattered seed? [27]Well then, you should have put my money on deposit with the bankers, so that when I returned I would have received it back with interest.

[28]"'Take the talent from him and give it to the one who has the ten talents. [29]For everyone who has will be given more, and he will have an abundance. Whoever does not have, even what he has will be taken from him. [30]And throw the worthless servant outside, into the darkness, where there will be weeping and gnashing of teeth.'"

The parable of the talents teaches that the servants of the Lord must be faithful by promptly and efficiently administering what has been entrusted to them until the day of reckoning. As the bridesmaids are expected to wait for the coming of the bridegroom, so the servants await the return of their master. Although the parable of the virgins does not speak about work during the nightly vigil, the parable of the talents teaches that the servants must always be busy in their master's absence.[1] Both parables show that women as well as men ought to be alert while they wait for the return of the Lord.

According to Matthew, Jesus addressed the discourse on the end of time (chapter 24) to his disciples and followed it with a few parables related to his eventual return. All this took place two or three days before the celebration of the Passover feast (Matt. 26:2). On the other hand, Luke (19:12–27) records that Jesus taught the parable of the ten pounds (minas) after he had left Jericho and was approaching Jerusalem, just before or on Palm Sunday. That parable is similar to the one of the talents, yet they are not identical.[2] On the basis of the setting and historical framework given by the evangelists, in addition to the scope of the parables, we believe that Jesus taught these two parables on two different occasions.[3]

The parable of the talents is the longest parable in the Gospel of Matthew. It relates in rather detailed form the conversations between the master and his servants. And it has a somewhat lengthy conclusion that ties it to other parables.

Entrusted Money

The word *talent* today points to a natural gift. Thus if a person has an artistic talent, he or she is very creative and, because of this talent, is greatly admired. But in the New Testament, the word *talent* refers to a currency unit representing a lot of money. In this parable we are to think in terms of a worker's annual wage. The amounts the master entrusted to his servants were large but not phenomenal.

A well-to-do person called his servants together and told them that he would be out of the country for an extended period of time. He treated his servants not on a commercial basis but in oriental fashion as partners in his enterprise.[4] His available cash resources amounted to eight talents, which he entrusted to his three servants. The master knew his servants very well. He had learned to appreciate their capabilities and was confident that they could be trusted with his wealth. He expected them to put his money to work, so that upon his return he might honor them for increasing his financial assets. Thus he gave the first servant a total of five talents, the second servant two talents, and the third only one talent.

Undoubtedly contracts were drawn up setting forth the conditions to which the parties agreed. The capital, of course, belonged to the master.[5] In return, the master would award the servants accordingly and they could look forward to further shares in the partnership.

The first servant put the five talents to work and after some time doubled the amount. So did the servant who had received two talents. The man who had been given one talent, however, was afraid to put the money to use. Perhaps he felt slighted because the other servants had been entrusted with larger sums of money. He knew his master to be a hard man who demanded an increase. But the profit on the one talent would be small in comparison to that of the five talents and the two talents of the other servants. He did nothing with the money except bury it in the ground.[6] There it would be safe. Upon the return of his master he could give back the original sum of one talent.

Two Servants

Eventually, after a long period of time, the master returned and called his servants together to settle accounts.[7] The day of reckoning had come; the books were opened and each servant was asked to report on the money he had received in trust.

The first servant came not only with the five talents he had received but also with the five talents he had gained. He gave his master the capital sum and the profit, totaling ten talents. He handed his master a vast amount of money, proving unquestionably that he was worthy of the trust the master had placed in him. Without calling attention to himself, he merely asked his master to note the five additional talents.[8]

The response of the master matched the servant's faithfulness. He was generous in his praise and reward of the servant. First, he exclaimed "well done" in praise of the servant's excellent performance. Second, he called him "good and faithful." Third, he placed him in charge of many things. And fourth, he invited the servant to sit at the master's table and celebrate the outcome with a banquet.[9] Sitting at the master's table, of course, implies equality.

The second servant came before his master with the two talents and the additional two he had gained by putting the money to work. Also, this servant did not call attention to himself but to the talents he had gained. The master was no less generous with the second servant than with the first. As with the first servant, all the rewards more than matched the faithfulness he had shown. The master proved to be most generous.

ONE SERVANT

When it was the turn of the third servant to give an account, the scene changed. Instead of returning the entrusted money as the other servants had done, this servant gave a little speech. He did not praise the master for the generosity shown to the other two servants. Instead, he described his master as a hard man, who harvested where he had not sown and who gathered where he had not scattered seed. Because he was afraid to take a risk, he dug a hole in the ground and buried the money. He seemed to say to his master: "Why did you put so little confidence in me by giving me only one talent? What could I really do with it, considering that if there were any profit I would not see much of it? To get even with you I decided not to do anything with the money."[10]

His speech was marked by contradiction. He failed to understand the goodness of the master, but viewed him in the light of his own envious and selfish nature. He felt slighted, yet in his own words he said that he was afraid to put the money to work. He had not profitably used the talent, yet he seemed to wait for some word of commendation for merely keeping it safe.[11] He wanted to get the message across that he had not lost any of his master's money. He explicitly said that the talent belonged to his master. He had kept it safe.

Why did the servant not take the money to a bank where it could have accumulated interest? Possibly the servant did not trust the unscrupulous bankers who might alter or annul agreements.[12] Perhaps the servant was motivated by a desire for revenge against the master and therefore decided not to invest the money in a bank. Although investing the money involved some risk, he knew that the master had the ability to recover the talent with interest.[13] To keep the talent and bury it in the ground would deprive the master of accumulated interest. Then when his master returned, the servant could hand the one talent back to him.

THE MASTER

When the master handed the total sum of eight talents to his three servants, he himself became dependent upon their honesty and faithfulness. Should they lose the money in business transactions, he would be a ruined man. Understandably, he was extremely pleased when the first and second servants showed that they had doubled the money he had entrusted to them. He praised them for their diligence, and rewarded them liberally.

The appearance of the third servant with the one talent told the master that he had misjudged the character of this servant, that the trust he had placed in him had been mistaken, and that instead of rewarding him he had to inflict punishment.

The master's response to the servant's lame excuse for his slothfulness was the opposite of his response to the other two servants. First, words of praise could not be uttered. Next, the master called the servant wicked and lazy. Third, he chided him for his indolence and faithlessness. And last, he had the servant permanently removed from his presence.

With the words from his own mouth the servant was judged. He knew that his master was expecting the best efforts his servants could exert. In fact, the master wished to reap a harvest where he had not sown. When opportunity knocked, he was present. By setting these standards, he had become a hard man in the eyes of the lazy servant.

"Take the talent from him and give it to the one who has ten talents," said the master. Although the lazy servant had explicitly stated that the one talent belonged to the master, the saying constitutes a termination of the master-servant relationship.[14] The partnerships with the other two servants continued, whereas the third servant knew that he was no longer a partner. He was now regarded as a debtor who had to pay interest on the money that had been in his possession. If he had brought the talent to the bankers, the master would have demanded it back with interest. Now the master turned to the servant and sought to recover what rightfully belonged to him, that is, the expected increase. "Whoever does not have, even what he has will be taken from him."[15] The master, therefore, took the servant's own possessions. The servant was worthless to the master. He was cast out into the darkness, according to Jesus' familiar saying,[16] "where there is weeping and gnashing of teeth."

SIGNIFICANCE

The parable of the talents is set in the framework of Jesus' teaching on his return. Just as the bridesmaids waited, so the servants who received their master's money worked. The parable teaches that during the absence of Jesus, his followers are expected to work diligently with the gifts he has entrusted to them. His followers are responsible to him at his return. Because of such sayings as "share your master's happiness" and "throw that worthless servant outside, into the darkness where there will be weeping and gnashing of teeth," Jesus intimates that these

are not merely the words of the master. These are his own words referring to the day of judgment.

When the disciples initially heard the parable, they might have
thought it applied not to them but to their contemporaries. The Jews
had been entrusted with the very words of God, as Paul aptly stated in
later years.[17] They could see the parallel relationship of master and servants in God and Israel. God had given the Jewish people his Word and
he expected that they would make his revelation known everywhere. But
in Jesus' day a pious Jew could keep the Law of God in great detail and
yet neglect to share the riches of God's revelation. Jesus' disciples might
have seen the law-abiding Pharisee and the teacher of the Law personified in the servant who buried the one talent his master had given him.[18]
The religious leaders of Israel were entrusted with a sacred deposit;
many of them failed, however, to put it to proper use. They were content to return it to God, saying, "We have kept the Law." They kept the
deposit in themselves. By doing this they failed to put it to work. But
God, who had given them the sacred trust of his revelation, on the day
of reckoning would call them to give an account.

However, the parable of the talents was originally addressed to the
disciples of Jesus. They were the ones who had been entrusted with the
gospel; they were told to preach in Christ's name repentance and forgiveness of sins to all nations, beginning at Jerusalem (Luke 24:47). But
the teaching of the parable was not limited to the disciples. The author
of the Epistle to the Hebrews pointedly warned the Christians of his day
by asking, "how shall we escape if we ignore such a great salvation?"
(Heb. 2:3). And throughout the centuries the parable of the talents has
spoken and continues to speak to all Christians. They are to be the chan-
nel through which the message of God's Word flows to the world around
them.

CONCLUSION

The servant entrusted with the one talent kept the deposit safely in a
hidden place. He feared to put it to use, for he knew that his master
would demand the talent from him upon his return. Fear, therefore,
completely overshadowed love, trust, and faith.[19] Fear is the opposite of
confidence.

The Christian who puts faith to work will reap immense dividends.
He is not concerned about himself and his own interests, for whatever
he owns belongs to the Lord and whatever he does he does for the Lord.
No follower of Jesus can ever say that he lacks the gifts to be of service
simply because he is not a Paul, Luther, Calvin, or Knox. The parable

teaches that every servant has received gifts, "each according to his abil-ity." Jesus knows the capability of every Christian, and he expects an increase.

As with many other parables, specific details cannot and should not be stressed and applied. Rather, the central message of faithfulness is important. The parable of the talents teaches that every believer has been endowed with gifts differing according to ability, and that these gifts must be put to use in God's service. In the kingdom of God every-one is expected to employ fully the gifts he has received. In God's king-dom there simply is no room for drones—only for worker bees.

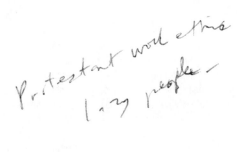

22 Last Judgment

> **Matthew 25:31–46**
>
> [31]"When the Son of Man comes in his glory, and all the angels with him, he will sit on his throne in heavenly glory. [32]All the nations will be gathered before him, and he will separate the people one from another as a shepherd separates the sheep from the goats. [33]He will put the sheep on his right and the goats on his left.
>
> [34]"Then the King will say to those on his right, 'Come, you who are blessed by my Father; take your inheritance, the kingdom prepared for you since the creation of the world. [35]For I was hungry and you gave me something to eat, I was thirsty and you gave me something to drink, I was a stranger and you invited me in, [36]I needed clothes and you clothed me, I was sick and you looked after me, I was in prison and you came to visit me.'
>
> [37]"Then the righteous will answer him, 'Lord, when did we see you hungry and feed you, or thirsty and give you something to drink? [38]When did we see you a stranger and invite you in, or needing clothes and clothe you? [39]When did we see you sick or in prison and go to visit you?'
>
> [40]"The king will reply, 'I tell you the truth, whatever you did for one of the least of these brothers of mine, you did for me.'
>
> [41]"Then he will say to those on his left, 'Depart from me, you who are cursed, into the eternal fire prepared for the devil and his angels. [42]For I was hungry and you gave me nothing to eat, I was thirsty and you gave me nothing to drink, [43]I was a stranger and you did not invite me in, I needed clothes and you did not clothe me, I was sick and in prison and you did not look after me.'
>
> [44]"They also will answer, 'Lord, when did we see you hungry or thirsty or a stranger or needing clothes or sick or in prison, and did not help you?'
>
> [45]"He will reply, 'I tell you the truth, whatever you did not do for one of the least of these, you did not do for me.'
>
> [46]"Then they will go away to eternal punishment, but the righteous to eternal life."

Strictly speaking, the passage on the last judgment is much more prophetic than parabolic. Only the part about the sheep and the goats is a parable. And yet this rather brief comparison eminently serves Jesus' purpose in teaching his followers the doctrine of the last judgment.[1] Jesus briefly refers to a common pastoral scene of his day. A shepherd herds a mixed flock of sheep and goats. In areas where grazing is sparse because of drought, goats tend to browse rather than graze.[2] They mingle with the sheep, but neither sheep nor goats seem to have been given a disposition to become intimately acquainted. When evening comes, sheep listen to the shepherd's voice, while goats may choose to ignore his call. At nightfall, sheep prefer the open air in contrast to the goats, which cannot take the cold and must be sheltered.[3]

The shepherd puts the sheep to the right and the goats to the left. He does not separate ewes and rams, but sheep and goats. He sets apart two species. Symbolically he puts the sheep on his right side and the goats on his left. Sheep are more valuable than goats,[4] and their white fleece, in distinction from the black-colored skin of the goat, stands out as a symbol of righteousness.[5] A goat has long been associated with evil. The Old Testament portrays the goat as a sin-bearing animal sent into the desert (Lev. 16:20–22). Even our own language contains the word *scapegoat*, recalling the passage in Leviticus. Moreover, the right side always denotes that which is good, while the left may refer to something sinister, shady, evil, and base.

All the nations of the world are compared to sheep and goats that are separated by the shepherd at the end of the day. The nations will be gathered before the Son of Man sitting on his throne in heavenly glory. By divine command the angels will go forth and gather the elect from the four directions of the wind and present them before the judgment throne (Matt. 13:41, 42; 24:31; 2 Thess. 1:7, 8; Rev. 14:17–20). All people will stand before the Judge. All the good and the bad, all the wicked and the righteous appear. No one is excluded. And the Judge separates the people one from the other as a shepherd divides his flock of sheep and goats after a day of grazing in the pasture.

THE RIGHT SIDE

Throughout the Gospel of Matthew the theme of separation and judgment unfolds. The wheat is gathered into the barn, but the chaff is burned up with unquenchable fire (Matt. 3:12); the weeds are separated from the wheat, tied into bundles, and burned, while the wheat is gathered into the barn (Matt. 13:30). Angels separate the righteous from the wicked, at the end of the age, and throw the wicked into the fiery furnace (Matt. 13:49, 50). Five wise bridesmaids enter the wedding hall, but the five foolish ones find the door locked and hear the bridegroom say, "I don't know you" (Matt. 25:12). The two diligent servants sit at the master's table, but the lazy servant who buried his one talent is thrown outside into the darkness (Matt. 25:30). And in the parable of the sheep and goats, the principle of separation and judgment is clearly applied.

The Son of Man, as Jesus calls himself, comes in his glory and sits on his throne in heavenly glory, surrounded by his angels. Scripture passages in both Old and New Testaments reiterate this truth, which unmistakably points to the last judgment as a universal judgment.[6] In the parable of the sheep and the goats, Jesus accepts all those brought before him who have been chosen from eternity. They are the ones who hear the King say, "Come, you who are blessed by my Father, take your inheritance, the kingdom prepared for you since the creation of the world." They are saved, therefore, because God the Father has blessed them and tells them to take possession of the kingdom that he has prepared beforehand.[7] Salvation for the righteous is rooted not in their good works but rather in the good pleasure of God the Father. The good works that the righteous perform are not the root but rather the fruit of grace.[8] Good works are not annulled by the Father's electing grace; they are expected from his blessed children as a natural outflow of their obedience and love.

Interestingly, without explanation, the evangelist shifts from the image of Son of Man to that of King. Why does Matthew use these two appellations? Certainly, the identification of Jesus as Son of Man with the human race is self-evident. The transition from Son of Man to King becomes meaningful, however, in the light of the prophecy of Daniel, where the person of the Son of Man comes with the clouds of heaven. "He was given authority, glory and sovereign power; all peoples, nations and men of every language worshiped him. His dominion is an everlasting dominion that will not pass away, and his kingdom is one that will never be destroyed" (Dan. 7:14). The Son of Man, indisputably, is King and in the judgment day speaks as sovereign judge.[9]

The deeds of the righteous are deeds of love and mercy unwittingly performed for Christ himself. Six times Jesus uses the first-person pronoun *I* compared to the selfless *you* in speaking to the righteous.

I was hungry	and you gave me something to eat,
I was thirsty	and you gave me something to drink.
I was a stranger	and you invited me in,
I needed clothes	and you clothed me.
I was sick	and you looked after me,
I was in prison	and you came to visit me.[10]

The righteous have shown human responsibility and genuine concern in all their deeds. They have proved to be worthy citizens of the kingdom of heaven. In the day of judgment they will be given the privilege of taking possession of that kingdom. In their daily activities they showed faithfulness and diligence. In the judgment day they will receive their reward. In the little things of life the righteous demonstrated their love and loyalty. In the last day God himself will honor them.

The people who are standing on the right of Jesus the King hear that they fed Jesus when he was hungry, and gave him something to drink when he was thirsty; they were the ones who invited him in, clothed him, looked after him, and visited him. They cared for the people with whom Christ identified himself. But who were these people who became recipients of the love and kindness of the righteous? This is the surprised question put to Jesus: "Lord, when did we see you hungry?" And the King's reply is, "Whatever you did for one of the least of these brothers of mine, you did for me." But who are these brothers of Christ?[11]

In the New Testament Christ identifies himself and is identified with his followers.[12] The most striking illustration of the bond between Christ and his followers is Paul's encounter with Jesus on the Damascus road. "Why do you persecute me?" Jesus asked. Paul was, in fact, persecuting his followers.[13] Jesus is one with his followers, for every believing Christian is a brother or sister of Christ. Thus, by persecuting the believers, Paul persecuted Jesus.[14]

In the Gospel of Matthew, the expression "little ones" is a synonym for the disciples of Jesus. When the twelve disciples are sent out two by two, Jesus says, "And if anyone gives a cup of cold water to one of these little ones because he is my disciple, I tell you the truth, he will certainly not lose his reward" (Matt. 10:42).[15] When he calls a little child and places him in the circle of the disciples, he exhorts the twelve to become like little children. The little ones who believe in Jesus belong to him (Matt. 18:5, 6, 10). Likewise, in Matthew 25:40 the term *little* is used in the superlative when Jesus says, "I tell you the truth, whatever you did for one of the least of these brothers of mine, you did for me." Favors expressed to one of Christ's followers, therefore, are done to Christ himself. Christians are highly exalted, because the world's giving or withholding of deeds of kindness will be judged with reference to them. They and Christ are one!

The follower of Jesus Christ is commissioned to be a living witness for him. He is a representative of the King, and has been given authority to testify in behalf of the Lord. A messenger always belongs to the one who sends him. And the one who is sent must always represent his sender.

Those who receive the messengers of the King, and treat them well
by providing food when they are hungry, drink when they are thirsty,
clothing when they are cold, and comfort when they are sick or imprisoned, are doing this in effect to the King himself. Denying these messengers love and mercy is in fact shutting out the one whom they represent (Matt. 10:40).

THE LEFT SIDE

Two of the pivotal texts in the passage on the last judgment are
Matthew 25:40 and Matthew 25:45. "I tell you the truth, whatever you
did for one of the least of these brothers of mine, you did for me"; and,
"I tell you the truth, whatever you did not do for one of the least of these,
you did not do for me." These are parallel verses with virtually the same
wording. The omission of the phrase "brothers of mine" in verse 45 may
be stylistic. The first of these texts is stated positively and is addressed
to the righteous; the second is directed to the unrighteous in negative
terms.

The wicked have not perpetrated any crime. They did not kill anyone; they did not commit adultery; they did not steal. Their sins are not
deeds of commission but of omission. What they have failed to do is
enumerated in the judgment day. The entire list of needs properly
responded to by the righteous is repeated, but now the glaring omis-
sions are highlighted.

I was hungry	and you gave me nothing to eat,
I was thirsty	and you gave me nothing to drink,
I was a stranger	and you did not invite me in,
I needed clothes	and you did not clothe me,
I was sick and in prison	and you did not look after me.

At the judgment, as depicted in this passage, no question is asked about
faith or repentance in Christ. Only questions about conduct are posed.[16]
To be sure, the list of deeds can be performed by anyone; one does not
need training in the Christian faith in order to qualify.

When the followers of Christ came in need to those who will be standing to the left of the King, they were rebuffed. Here then is the question
whether one is for or against Jesus. There is no neutrality when it concerns Jesus: one must choose. As Jesus succinctly put it, "He who is not
with me is against me, and he who does not gather with me scatters"
(Matt. 12:30). If a person refuses the claims of the gospel and rebuffs

the follower of Jesus, he or she rejects the Christ and chooses the side of the enemy.[17]

Are people who have never known Jesus included? They will be judged like all the others who in the judgment day appear before the Son of Man. The apostle Paul touched on this question when he wrote of God's righteous judgment: "All who sin apart from the law will also perish apart from the law" (Rom. 2:12). Only those who obey the Law of God are declared righteous.[18]

Because of their refusal to aid the followers of Christ, the unrighteous have placed themselves outside the sphere of God's blessings. They are under the curse. They hear the awful words, "Depart from me, you who are cursed, into the eternal fire prepared for the devil and his angels." They are condemned and given a place with Satan and his followers.[19] The unrighteous are forever separated from the Christ; they are sent to a place where they will spend eternity with Satan and his cohorts. It is a place Scripture describes as hell.[20]

In the courtroom, the people who will be to the left of the judge are surprised, and question the verdict: "Lord, when did we see you hungry or thirsty or a stranger or needing clothes or sick or in prison, and did not help you?" The answer to that question is that they refused to see the Christ when his followers asked for help. They closed their eyes and hardened their hearts when followers of Jesus were in need of the basic necessities of life. "Whatever you did not do for one of the least of these, you did not do for me." The phrase, "brothers of mine," although omitted, is implied. Jesus points to his followers, his brothers. They are the ones who believe in him and make up the church. When they are rejected, Christ is rejected. They represent Jesus.

Before the judgment throne all nations are gathered; the nations of the world appear before Christ. And although every person is judged individually, the nations also come before the judge collectively. Human beings are held responsible for their attitude and response toward Jesus, his Word, and his kingdom, and receive his verdict as individuals. But people are also part of their community and citizens in their nation. With their fellow countrymen they bear corporate responsibility for actions initiated and performed "against the LORD and against his Anointed" (Ps. 2:2). During his earthly ministry, Jesus denounced the cities of Chorazin, Bethsaida, and Capernaum, because they did not repent in spite of the miracles he had accomplished there (Matt. 11:20–24). In the day of judgment it will be more bearable for Tyre, Sidon, and Sodom than for the cities of northern Galilee that did not respond to Jesus' message. They will receive corporate judgment.

IMPLICATIONS

The parable of the sheep and the goats is introductory to a portrayal of the last judgment. As a shepherd separates his sheep from the goats, so Jesus divides the righteous from the wicked in the judgment day. In that day, all the nations of the world will stand before the Son of Man and will be judged on the basis of their reception or rejection of him when his messengers presented his claims.[21] The implication of this portrayal is that the judgment can take place only when the command of the Great Commission has been carried out fully. "Therefore, go and make disciples of all nations" (Matt. 28:19). When this command has been fulfilled, the end is near. The followers of Jesus must faithfully proclaim the message of the kingdom to all nations; and the end will come once this task is completed (Matt. 24:14).

Messengers of the gospel of Jesus experience hardships and endure hunger, thirst, cold, sickness, loneliness, and imprisonment. Paul relates his experiences and speaks of being hungry and thirsty, of being cold and naked, of being threatened by his own countrymen and by Gentiles, of being in prison, flogged, and exposed to death (2 Cor. 11:23–27).[22] The people who assisted him and cared for him in his trials and hardships demonstrated genuine love. Their deeds, as Paul says of the Philippians who sent him gifts, were "a fragrant offering, an acceptable sacrifice, pleasing to God" (Phil. 4:18). But when everyone forsook Paul when he was on trial, the Lord stood at his side and gave him strength. Of those who deserted him Paul writes, "May it not be held against them" (2 Tim. 4:16). He leaves the judgment to his Lord. Although he represents Jesus, he does not appropriate authority that belongs properly to his sender. Jesus is the judge, and he will hand down the verdict on the judgment day. Paul can only pray that the act of desertion may not be held against those who should have supported him.

Jesus' self-identification with his brothers does not include all the poor and needy in the world. To see in the passage on the last judgment a basis for Christian love for the poor, indiscriminately considered, because the poor represent Christ, is reading something into the text. To see the Christ in every rejected figure of a man along the Jericho road or of a Lazarus lying near the doorstep of the rich man's house is faulty exegesis.[23] The parable of the sheep and the goats and its subsequent portrayal of the judgment day accentuates the word *brother* (Matt. 25:40). For Matthew the term *brother* does not apply to everybody but only to those who acknowledge Jesus as their Lord and Savior.[24] In his Gospel, Matthew provides a Christian understanding for the word *brother*.[25] For him, the word means a disciple, a follower of Jesus. Therefore, the phrase "these brothers of mine" in Matthew 25:40 refers to those people who believe in Jesus. They are the members of his body, the church.

Of course, Jesus' words, "The poor you will always have with you, but you will not always have me" (Matt. 26:11; Mark 14:7; John 12:8), do not mean that in his absence Jesus is represented by the poor. His words are an exhortation to care for the poor, as God had told the Israelites: "There will always be poor people in the land. Therefore I command you to be openhanded toward your brothers and toward the poor and needy in the land" (Deut. 15:11). Paul was mindful of this same injunction, which came to him afresh when he engaged in Gentile missions. After he had received the right hand of fellowship from James, Peter, and John, he said: "All they asked was that we should continue to remember the poor" (Gal. 2:10).

No one may ever ignore the poor, because God's command, "Love your neighbor as yourself," is clear enough. The fulfillment of the Law is love, and he who keeps this royal Law is doing right (James 2:8). Christians are therefore under divine obligation to show genuine love and heartfelt concern to the needy and rejected regardless of race, origin, age, sex, or religion. Anyone qualifies as a neighbor and has a claim on love, but not everyone is called a brother or sister of Christ. Only those who believe in Christ and do the will of God are Christ's brothers and sisters (Matt. 12:48).

In the parable and presentation of the judgment scene, the following people appear individually and collectively: (1) the Son of Man, (2) all the nations, (3) a shepherd, (4) the King, (5) the King's Father, (6) the righteous, (7) the King's brothers, and (8) the unrighteous. It is obvious that God is the Father of the King; yet God is not the judge. The King is the judge who is compared to a shepherd who separates sheep from goats. Furthermore, the King is also known as the Son of Man, the self-designation of Jesus. Also, the King's brothers are present at the judgment. Who are they? Jesus tells his disciples that "at the renewal of all things, when the Son of Man sits on his glorious throne, you who have followed me will also sit on twelve thrones, judging the twelve tribes of Israel" (Matt. 19:28). The privilege of judging with Christ is not limited to the twelve disciples. The saints will judge the world, writes Paul to the Corinthian congregation (1 Cor. 6:2).[26] The judge is not alone but is the spokesman for his brothers. He does not pass judgment on his brothers; rather, all the nations appear before the throne and are separated into two groups: those to the right of the judge, because they helped the brothers, and those to the left, because they refused to help.

In this parable Jesus provides only one aspect of the last judgment scene. Other passages in Scripture provide additional insight on what will take place on that day.[27] The parable of the sheep and the goats describes a division between those who are placed on the right and those on the left. The portrayal of the judgment scene concludes with a reference to their permanent destinies. "Then they [those on the left] will go away to eternal punishment, but the righteous to eternal life" (Matt. 25:46). The conclusion indicates that the verdict for both parties is final and unalterable. The righteous enjoy the fullness of everlasting life, and the wicked endure the curse of everlasting punishment.

23 Two Debtors

Luke 7:36–50

36Now one of the Pharisees invited Jesus to have dinner with him, so he went to the Pharisee's house and reclined at the table. 37When a woman who had lived a sinful life in that town learned that Jesus was eating at the Pharisee's house, she brought an alabaster jar of perfume, 38and as she stood behind him at his feet weeping, she began to wet his feet with her tears. Then she wiped them with her hair, kissed them and poured perfume on them.

39When the Pharisee who had invited him saw this, he said to himself, "If this man were a prophet, he would know who is touching him and what kind of woman she is—that she is a sinner."

40Jesus answered him, "Simon, I have something to tell you."

"Tell me, teacher," he said.

41"Two men owed money to a certain moneylender. One owed him five hundred denarii, and the other fifty. 42Neither of them had the money to pay him back, so he canceled the debts of both. Now which of them will love him more?"

43Simon replied, "I suppose the one who had the bigger debt canceled."

"You have judged correctly," Jesus said.

44Then he turned toward the woman and said to Simon, "Do you see this woman? I came into your house. You did not give me any water for my feet, but she wet my feet with her tears and wiped them with her hair. 45You did not give me a kiss, but this woman, from the time I entered, has not stopped kissing my feet. 46You did not put oil on my head, but she has poured perfume on my feet. 47Therefore, I tell you, her many sins have been forgiven—for she loved much. But he who has been forgiven little loves little."

48Then Jesus said to her, "Your sins are forgiven."

49The other guests began to say among themselves, "Who is this who even forgives sins?"

50Jesus said to the woman, "Your faith has saved you; go in peace."

The parable of the two debtors is relatively short, consisting of only three verses (Luke 7:41–43). Its historical setting is the anointing of Jesus by a sinful woman in the home of Simon the Pharisee. The parable teaches the simple truth that the degree of thankfulness expressed by someone whose debt has been canceled stands in direct proportion to the amount of that canceled debt. A moneylender who cancels a sizable debt of a creditor will receive more appreciation and thanks from him than from someone whose canceled debt was insignificant. Jesus applied this truth in the home of Simon the Pharisee, who was visibly embarrassed by a woman of ill repute. But Simon learned a lesson.

THE SETTING

Perhaps the occasion was on a Sabbath day when Jesus had preached in the local synagogue worship service. Because it was considered meritorious to invite a guest preacher to dinner,[1] Simon the Pharisee asked Jesus to come to his house after the morning service and to enjoy the midday Sabbath meal with him and other invited guests.

The host, however, neglected to show the common courtesies of kissing Jesus, of washing his feet, and of pouring scented oil on his head.[2] Jesus reclined at the table and, like the other guests, took off his sandals.[3] In the typical style of the day, the guests reclined on divans around a table, leaning on their left arm, with their right hand free to partake of food and drink, and their feet extending away from the table. If the time of year was not winter, the dinner might have taken place in the courtyard, because Jews liked to eat in the open air.[4] While the meal was in progress, a woman who lived in that town arrived—a woman who was known to have a questionable moral life. She quickly walked up to Jesus, intending to give Jesus a present of an alabaster jar filled with perfume.

Because she knew Jesus, she wanted him to have the present of the costly perfume. She wished to express her thanks to him for helping her, presumably by teaching her the message of salvation. She could not control her emotions, however, and before she knew it her tears were flowing and falling on Jesus' feet. She had no towel to wipe the tears from his feet. She loosened her hair and wiped them dry. Then she kissed his feet, and took the bottle of perfume and poured it over them.

From Simon's point of view, this was a most embarrassing incident. If the woman had purchased the expensive perfume with money of her earnings from prostitution, the gift was tainted. According to Deuteronomy 23:18, God detested such earnings, which therefore might not be brought into his house. Gifts from immoral people were considered dirty and unacceptable by any respectable person. Furthermore, the woman loosed her hair in the company of men; by doing so she showed what kind of woman she was. It was contrary to all social graces for a woman to untie her hair in public.[5]

The Pharisee was amazed that Jesus permitted all this to happen to him. He began to look at Jesus through different eyes. If Jesus were a prophet,[6] he reasoned within himself, he should have known that this woman was a moral outcast, and that she and her gifts were tainted by sin. No self-respecting prophet would allow himself to be made unclean by a woman of ill repute. For the woman did not merely touch his feet—she continued to kiss them until, finally, she left. Did Jesus not understand?

THE PARABLE

Jesus preached the gospel of salvation and called the people to repentance and faith in God. Perhaps earlier that day the woman had been in his audience, and now responded positively to his word. Overcome by her guilt, yet knowing that God would forgive her, she came to Jesus. She was unable to stem a flood of tears expressing sorrow for sins committed and joy for grace received.[7]

But Simon the Pharisee could not see that this sinful woman experienced the joy of regeneration. It did not occur to him that she could be forgiven and be filled with happiness. "Jesus should never have allowed the woman to touch him," said Simon to himself.

Jesus knew Simon's thoughts and, in a gentle, corrective way, told him that he appreciated what the woman had done to him because she did what the host should have done for his guest. But before Jesus told the Pharisee what he saw in the woman, he asked him a question in the form of a parable. He introduced the parable by telling Simon that he had something to say. Simon was ready to listen.

Jesus told the little story of a moneylender who had two debtors. One owed him the total sum of five hundred denarii, and the other owed him fifty. A denarius in that day was the daily wage of a farmhand. Both debtors in Jesus' story lacked the funds to repay the moneylender. Then something unusual happened. The creditor canceled the debts of both debtors. "Now which of them will love him more?" Jesus asked Simon. And Simon, somewhat grudgingly, replied, "I suppose the one who had the bigger debt canceled." Suddenly he realized that the little parable involved him too. He knew that Jesus was not quite finished with his story. The application explaining the presence of the woman, Jesus' attitude toward her, and Simon's role as host would inevitably follow.

"Do you see this woman?" Jesus asked. Of course Simon saw the woman; but Jesus wanted him to see her in a spiritual dimension.

Simon's eyes were blinded because while he saw her as a sinner he
failed to see her as a forgiven sinner. His self-righteousness blocked his
vision. In his opinion, the woman was a sinner. Jesus, however, did not
rebuke him, did not scold him, but in a masterful way gave him a spiritual perspective.

"When I entered your house, Simon, you did not provide water to
wash my feet, did not greet me with a kiss, and did not give me any oil
for my head. But," said Jesus, "this woman with her tears washed my
feet and, because she lacked a towel, dried them with her hair. She
demonstrated her deepest respect for me by kissing my feet. Moreover,
she took a bottle of costly perfume and poured it on my feet."

Jesus saw the woman as a forgiven sinner. He did not specify her sins.
He only summed them up by saying that they were many. And because
her many sins were forgiven, she loved much.[8] She wanted to express
her gratitude to God and turned to Jesus who was sent by God. He
became the recipient of the woman's gift.[9]

THE WOMAN

The woman did not speak at all throughout her stay in Simon's house.
Yet her actions spoke louder than words. She burst into tears because
of her sins. Like the debtor who was told by his creditor that his debt
had been canceled, so the woman experienced the forgiving grace of
God. And because of this grace, she wanted to express her thankfulness
by giving Jesus a precious gift. That is, by showing her love to Jesus, she
proved that her sins had already been forgiven. It was not because she
demonstrated her love that she obtained forgiveness of sin,[10] for then
she would have earned her forgiveness. By means of the parable Jesus
taught that the debts of the two men were canceled without any work
on their part. So the woman, relieved of the burden of sin, could now
show her gratitude by kissing and anointing Jesus' feet.

"But he who has been forgiven little loves little." Did Jesus imply that
the sins of Simon the Pharisee were little and that because they were
forgiven he loved little? Hardly.

Simon had not expressed any love or thanks to Jesus apart from his
invitation to come for dinner. And he had not seen any need to ask for
forgiveness. The comparison nevertheless remained. Jesus did not elaborate, but by implication he asked Simon to come to a knowledge and
confession of his sin and thus experience the joy that accompanies the
cleansing power of God's grace.

Jesus asked Simon if he saw the woman. By means of the contrast exemplified in the parable, Jesus now intimated that Simon should look at his own spiritual life.

Scottish poet Robert Burns summed up his view of self-examination in pithy verse:

> O wad some Pow'r the giftie gie us
> To see oursels as others see us,
> It wad frae many a blunder free us
> And foolish notion.[11]

After Jesus had addressed Simon, he turned to the woman and said, "Your sins are forgiven." God had forgiven her sins. Now Jesus confirmed the woman's assurance that she was a forgiven sinner by telling her that she had been fully restored: "Your faith has saved you; go in peace." She had already professed this assurance by her deeds of love and gratitude. In faith she had come to express her thanks to Jesus. Her love, therefore, was the consequence and not the cause of her salvation.[12] With God's peace in her heart, the woman could face the world anew as a restored human being. With the words, "go in peace," Jesus gave her a parting blessing.

CONCLUSION

What does the parable in the historical context of the forgiven woman teach? Love for Jesus can only be genuine when we acknowledge him as the Savior in whom we receive forgiveness of sin. We can have the greatest respect for Jesus and can even serve him; but genuine love for him comes only when in Jesus we have experienced remission of sin and assurance of pardon. Then we have learned to know him as Savior; then our love is expressed to him in deeds of gratitude.

24 Good Samaritan

Luke 10:25–37

²⁵On one occasion an expert in the law stood up to test Jesus. "Teacher," he asked, "what must I do to inherit eternal life?"

²⁶"What is written in the Law?" he replied. "How do you read it?"

²⁷He answered: "'Love the Lord your God with all your heart and with all your soul and with all your strength and with all your mind'; and, 'Love your neighbor as yourself.'"

²⁸"You have answered correctly," Jesus replied. "Do this and you will live."

²⁹But he wanted to justify himself, so he asked Jesus, "And who is my neighbor?"

³⁰In reply Jesus said: "A man was going down from Jerusalem to Jericho, when he fell into the hands of robbers. They stripped him of his clothes, beat him and went away, leaving him half dead. ³¹A priest happened to be going down the same road, and when he saw the man, he passed by on the other side. ³²So too, a Levite, when he came to the place and saw him, passed by on the other side. ³³But a Samaritan, as he traveled, came where the man was; and when he saw him, he took pity on him. ³⁴He went to him and bandaged his wounds, pouring on oil and wine. Then he put the man on his own donkey, took him to an inn and took care of him. ³⁵The next day he took out two silver coins and gave them to the innkeeper. 'Look after him,' he said, 'and when I return, I will reimburse you for any extra expense you may have.'

³⁶"Which of these three do you think was a neighbor to the man who fell into the hands of robbers?"

³⁷The expert in the law replied, "The one who had mercy on him."

Jesus told him, "Go and do likewise."

The parable of the good Samaritan has become part of our culture and vocabulary. It is not uncommon to see hospitals and institutions of mercy bearing that name. The Jericho road has found its way into hymn and song, and today the tourist can find the Inn of the Good Samaritan halfway between Jerusalem and Jericho.

PLACE AND PEOPLE

On his way to Jerusalem, Jesus was asked by an expert in the Old Testament Scriptures the way to inherit life eternal. This theologian, of course, did not ask the question in ignorance, for he wanted to test Jesus and hear his explanation of the Scriptures. He addressed Jesus as "teacher," thereby acknowledging him as a person of authority in religious matters. He expected Jesus to provide an answer to a frequently asked question.[1]

Skillfully and at the same time gently, the Teacher instructed his theological student in the teachings and implications of the Word. He came with a counterquestion: "What is written in the Law?" In effect he asked, "How do you recite the Law in summary form when you worship in the synagogue?" The theologian responded by citing the two commands linked by the key word *love:* "Love the Lord your God" and "Love your neighbor as yourself."[2]

The theologian realized that Jesus was fully in control of the situation and that he knew the answer. To Jesus' compliment, "You have answered correctly.... Do this and you will live," he put the query, "And who is my neighbor?" That was the fundamental question.

The Jew lived in a circular world: he placed himself at the center, surrounded by his immediate relatives, then his kinsmen, and finally the circle of all those who claimed Jewish descent and who were converts to Judaism. The word *neighbor* has a reciprocal meaning: he is a brother to me and I to him.[3] Thus the circle is one of self-interest and ethnocentrism. The lines were carefully drawn to ensure the well-being of those who were inside and to deny help to those who were outside.

In Jesus' day there was a marked influx of non-Jews into Israel. The Samaritans separated the Jews in the north from those in the south. The Roman occupation forces were present everywhere, and Hellenist travelers visited Israel regularly. Israel functioned as a bridge of nations, and daily the Jew rubbed elbows with the foreigner. "Who is my neighbor?" was a common question.

The theologian did not see any problems in regard to the first and great commandment, "Love the Lord your God." But love for God cannot be expressed apart from the second commandment, "Love your neighbor as yourself." He saw a problem in this second commandment and asked the question, expecting Jesus to delineate the boundaries. But Jesus refused to answer directly. Instead, he applied the principle of the

Golden Rule, "Do to others as you would have them do to you" (Luke 6:31), and told the story of the good Samaritan. He wanted the theologian to ask, "Whom do *I* treat as my neighbor?"

The story Jesus told is so lifelike and true to fact that it may well refer to an actual account reported by a man who was robbed and lived to tell the event in great detail. Although no time and exact place are related, the incident may have happened that year not too far from Jerusalem.[4]

The road from Jerusalem to Jericho is only 27 kilometers (17 miles) long, and along that stretch it drops 1,200 meters (3,300 feet). The area is virtually uninhabited, without vegetation, and marked by limestone cliffs and gullies on both sides of the road. The road in Bible times had been given the name "the path [ascent] of blood," most probably because it was considered unsafe.[5] The route was heavily traveled by pilgrims and caravans. From time to time bandits hiding behind the limestone rocks robbed these people.[6]

According to the story Jesus told, a man was going down the Jericho road. Whether he was a rich man or a poor man is not said. He was robbed and, because he resisted, he was beaten. Stripped of his clothes, he was left half-dead alongside the road. Soon after the crime was committed a priest came by on his way home to Jericho.[7] He took one look at the wounded man, and passed by on the other side. If he were riding a donkey, he did not even bother to get off. He denied the man any help or hope. A little later, a Levite did exactly the same thing—one look and he went on.

Along came a merchant, whose clothes identified him as a Samaritan. He stopped and looked at the man, helpless and lying in his own blood. The Samaritan was filled with pity. If he had been in the wounded man's place, he too would have expected relief. He approached, and gently lifted his patient. He tore some linen into strips, applied oil and wine,[8] and cleansed and bound up the man's wounds.

Then the Samaritan went the second mile, so to speak. He placed the man on his own donkey and, steadying him, brought him to the nearest inn. There he nursed him for the rest of the day and night. With business pressing, he had to leave the wounded man the following day; but first he paid the innkeeper two silver coins and gave instructions to look after him.[9] And he told the innkeeper if more money was needed, he could simply charge it to the Samaritan, who would pay him on his return trip.

IMPLICATIONS

Jesus ended the story by asking, "Which of these three do you think was a neighbor to the man who fell into the hands of robbers?" The theologian had to say, "The one who had mercy on him." In other words, the Samaritan proved to be a brother to the wounded man. With the admonition, "Go and do likewise," Jesus dismissed the theologian.

In the parable, five people are portrayed (apart from the robbers). In succession they are: the man robbed and wounded; the priest; the Levite; the Samaritan; and the innkeeper. The focus is not so much on the man who was robbed and left half-dead beside the road, although he is the object of attention. After the robbery he is at first neglected but afterward lavished with kindness. Also, the subject of the story is really not the priest, Levite, or innkeeper. The focus is the Samaritan. He is the doer, the agent, the main character. Hence the parable is called the parable of the good Samaritan and not the parable of the man who was robbed and wounded. The wounded man is a faceless figure whose occupation, nationality, religion, or race is not given.[10] Perhaps the man without his clothes could not be identified by priest, Levite, and Samaritan. In short, the identity of the man does not count. He plays the part of the neighbor and that is enough—a low profile, no more.

The robbers come and go. They commit the crime and leave. It is therefore useless to speculate whether they belonged to the leftist Zealot party, whether they bore a grudge against the man (after all, the priest, Levite, and Samaritan are not attacked), or whether they were local residents who made a living by robbing a hapless wayfarer.

The priest and presumably the Levite were on their way home from temple service in Jerusalem. By law, they were not allowed to touch a corpse.[11] Should they transgress the injunction, they would inconvenience themselves socially (by being unclean), financially (by paying burial costs), and professionally (by being barred from priestly and Levitical services).[12]

Of course, the robbed and wounded man was not quite dead. But would a priest or a Levite get off his donkey, take a stick, poke at the victim to see whether he is alive, and then finally administer first aid? Hardly. In the story, the man *was* alive and thus the members of the clergy could not very well excuse themselves. Whether they were afraid of being ambushed, were hard-hearted, believed they might interfere in God's judgment that had struck a wayward sinner, or were too conceited as religious leaders to stoop down and help a hapless victim, we will never know.[13] The fact is that both priest and Levite showed no mercy.

The Samaritan as depicted finds a warm spot in everyone's heart. He is the favorite in the story. He knows what to do and he does it well. Race, religion, and class distinctions are unimportant to him. He sees a fellow human being in need and he is the man to help.

Samaritans, to be sure, were not the most lovable people. Their hatred toward the Jews had erupted in numerous ways. For example, some time between 9 and 6 B.C. they had desecrated the temple area to prevent the Jews from celebrating the Passover feast. They did this by scattering human bones all across the courts of the temple.[14] In the eyes of the Jews, Samaritans were half-breeds. They had settled the land of Israel during the Jewish exile and their Bible consisted only of the five books of Moses. They had built their own temple on Mount Gerizim (John 4:20); the Jews destroyed this in 128 B.C. Because of profound hatred, the Jews did not associate with the Samaritans.[15] Two centuries before the birth of Christ, Ben Sirach expressed his extreme dislike of Samaritans in these words:

> Two nations I detest,
> and a third is no nation at all:
> the inhabitants of Mount Seir, the Philistines,
> and the senseless folk that live at Shechem.
>
> Ecclesiasticus 50:25, 26 REB

Yet this traveler, known by clothes, speech, and manners as a Samaritan, stopped his donkey, stooped down in kindness, and helped his fellowman. He did not ask whether the wounded victim was a Jew, Roman, Greek, or Syrian. For him, the person naked, wounded, and half-dead was a brother in need of help. He readily paid the innkeeper the necessary money to keep the man at the inn for a few days. Most likely he provided clothes as well.

The Samaritan did not do this work of love and charity on a reciprocal basis. He could have asked that the patient upon recovering repay the amount the Samaritan had spent on him. He did not even know whether the patient would express gratitude after learning who treated him. The Samaritan's actions represented a genuine sacrifice of money, possessions, risk of health and safety, and many hours of loving, watchful care.[16] He fulfilled the Golden Rule and went the proverbial second mile. By taking care of the wounded man and staying with him in the inn, the Samaritan ran the ominous risk of being regarded as the perpetrator of the crime. "The stranger who involves himself in the accident is often considered partially, if not totally, responsible for the accident."[17]

The last person mentioned in the parable, the innkeeper, receives little attention. The innkeeper must have known the Samaritan because of frequent visits. A relationship of trust and mutual confidence had developed between them, which is an eloquent testimony to the moral conduct of the Samaritan. He was a man the innkeeper could depend on. "Look after him," said the Samaritan, "and when I return, I will reimburse you for any extra expense you may have." His word was as good as gold.

OLD TESTAMENT PARALLELS

Although the story may have referred to an actual, recent incident, Jesus is the originator of the parable. In teaching the parable of the good Samaritan, he alerts his theologically educated listener to at least two Old Testament parallels. The theologian must have recognized allusions to these familiar passages in Scripture. First, there is the account recorded in 2 Chronicles 28:5–15. It tells of the people in Jerusalem and Judah during the reign of King Ahaz in 734 B.C., who were led captive to Samaria. The account closes with these words:

> The men designated by name took the prisoners, and from the plunder they clothed all who were naked. They provided them with clothes and sandals, food and drink, and healing balm. All those who were weak they put on donkeys. So they took them back to their fellow countrymen at Jericho, the City of Palms, and returned to Samaria.
>
> 2 Chronicles 28:15

Numerous key words, of course, crop up in the parable of the good Samaritan.[18]

A second reference is the text in Hosea 6:9: "As marauders lie in ambush for a man, so do bands of priests; they murder on the road to Shechem, committing shameful crimes."[19]

By teaching the parable that echoes familiar words of Scripture, Jesus demonstrates that his words are a continuation of the Scripture and an explanation of the Law and the Prophets. Thus, his skillful exposition of the second great commandment, "Love your neighbor as yourself," receives a deeper perspective. Jesus appears as the interpreter of the Law.[20] He says to the theologian, "Do this and you will live."[21]

APPLICATION

During his earthly ministry, Jesus teaches the far-reaching demands of the Law, "Love your neighbor as yourself." In the Sermon on the Mount, the command does not stop with the neighbor but includes the enemy as well: "Love your enemies" (Matt. 5:44; Luke 6:27).

In the case of the priest and the Levite depicted in the parable, the word *neighbor* referred to a Jew who could be clearly identified. But an unidentified person, robbed, beaten, unclothed, and half-dead, simply did not qualify.

For the theologian questioning Jesus, it was a matter of knowing where to draw the line. He wanted to know if love has limits. He wanted to justify himself and to ascertain whether he had fulfilled the demands of the Law.

If the Law could be used as a protective hedge, a person could live peacefully in its shelter, where everything is spelled out and familiar.[22] But when the Law is open-ended—"Love your neighbor," which includes "Love your enemy"—a whole new world stands out in full view making claims on that Law.

Jesus did not teach a story about a Jew who found an injured Samaritan along the road and helped him by taking him to a nearby inn.[23] Such a story might cause an adverse reaction, because the Jew would be considered a traitor to the Jewish cause. Likewise, if Jesus had used the triad of priest, Levite, and Israelite, the effect would have been entirely different. It would have created a contrast between the clergy and the laity with a decidedly anticlerical bias. Because Jesus introduced a Samaritan at the proper junction, the listener is pleasantly surprised and unable to raise objections. The Samaritan demonstrates how one should love his neighbor and be a brother to him.

If the theologian had any theological objections, they wilted as the story developed. Jesus could have referred to the foreigner who lived among the Jews and was treated as a native.[24] And he could have mentioned the Jewish converts and the so-called God-fearers who regularly attended the synagogue worship services. But these people were able to repay the kindness given them. Moreover, they were considered friends and in some cases even members of the Jewish faith.

Jesus, however, puts the spotlight not on the neighbor—"Who is my neighbor?"—but on the one who showed love and compassion. The neighbor is not an attractive person. In the parable he is shown covered with blood, naked, and half-dead. He is unable to return the labor of love, the money, and the clothes. He needs help and cannot repay. To bypass this neighbor is to incur divine wrath, for it constitutes not only the transgression of the second great commandment but the undoing of the first as well.

The parable of the good Samaritan is timeless. Substitute today's occupations, nationalities, and races, and nothing has changed since the day Jesus taught the parable. Therefore, the parable is not a story of someone who did a good deed as if he were a member of the Boy

Scouts. It is an indictment against anyone who has raised protective barriers in order to live a sheltered life.[25]

"Love your neighbor as yourself" is a command that reaches out beyond the circle of friends and fellow Christians we meet on a regular basis. It is a call to show mercy to all the unfortunate people lying beside the Jericho road of human life. And it is a cry to affluent nations to alleviate the suffering and poverty countless people experience in underdeveloped countries.

Exegetes from early patristic times to the present have sought to interpret the parable symbolically. Variations are numerous and sometimes humorous. Augustine's interpretation is classic: the man who was robbed and beaten is Adam, the robbers are the devil and his angels, the priest and Levite are the priesthood and ministry of the Old Testament, the Samaritan is Jesus, the oil is comfort and the wine an exhortation to work, the inn is the church, the two coins are the commands to love God and to love the neighbor, and the innkeeper is the apostle Paul.[26]

It is rather common to see Jesus as the good Samaritan who is the friend and brother of people from all walks of life, from any nation, and from every race. However, even though Luke himself may have thought this when he recorded the parable, he does not give us the least indication that Jesus intended to convey that message. The context and text do not support that interpretation.[27]

The message Jesus teaches by means of the parable is summarized in the pithy word addressed to the theologian who evoked the story: "Go and do likewise." In the language of James, "Do not merely listen to the word, and so deceive yourselves. Do what it says" (James 1:22).

25 Friend at Midnight

Luke 11:5–8
⁵Then he said to them, "Suppose one of you has a friend, and he goes to him at midnight and says, 'Friend, lend me three loaves of bread, ⁶because a friend of mine on a journey has come to me, and I have nothing to set before him.'
⁷"Then the one inside answers, 'Don't bother me. The door is already locked, and my children are with me in bed. I can't get up and give you anything.' ⁸I tell you, though he will not get up and give him the bread because he is his friend, yet because of the man's boldness he will get up and give him as much as he needs."

Luke records the Lord's Prayer in a shorter form than that found in Matthew's Gospel. He does not follow the prayer with an exhortation that people ought to forgive one another, but instead he writes a parable in which Jesus teaches the petitioner to be persistent. The teaching of the parable of the friend at midnight is concisely echoed by the apostle in his injunction "pray continually" (1 Thess. 5:17). Only Luke records the parable of the friend at midnight. In just a few, colorful words he paints the picture of a man who was out of bread—he probably had the last bite for supper—and then received a traveler who arrived at midnight.[1] The village was small and bread could not be had unless a neighbor was willing to lend a few loaves.

The traveler arrived at midnight, perhaps to avoid the heat of the day.[2] Tired and hungry, he looked to his host for hospitality. But, by his coming at an unusual hour, he placed his host in a predicament of either refusing hospitality, because he was out of bread, or by going to his neighbor to ask for a few loaves. An impossible situation! If he would refuse to feed his traveler friend, he would break the established norm

148

of hospitality and bring shame on himself and the village. If he would go to his neighbor and wake him, he would incur his displeasure.

The story told by Jesus may be based on an actual event, and belongs to those classified as "Have you ever heard?" It brought discreet smiles to all who heard the story because it was so true to life. Everyone was eager to hear how the story ended.

Houses in Israel, especially in rural areas, were small, consisting of one room used as sitting room, dining room, and bedroom.[3] A house had one door, which was left open throughout the day. But in the evening when the sun had set, the head of the family would close the door and slide a wooden bar through rings on both door and wall to keep out intruders.[4] Mats were spread out and were used as beds on which the family slept all in a row. In such circumstances it was rather difficult to get up in the dark and find a needed article.

The host, wishing to abide by the rules of hospitality, walked to his neighbor's house and called him out of his sleep: "Friend, lend me three loaves, because a friend of mine on a journey has come to me, and I have nothing to set before him." He addressed his neighbor as "friend," possibly to discourage anger, even though it was not a friendly gesture to wake him in the middle of the night. The question is whether the obliging neighbor was more of a friend than the one who woke him. Who deserves the name "friend"?

A loaf of bread in those days was no bigger than the size of a stone that could be held in one's hand. (Thus, Matthew in the parallel context records, "Which of you, if his son asks for bread, will give him a stone?" [Matt. 7:9].) And three of these loaves made up a meal for one person. The borrower's lengthy explanation was an attempt to describe his predicament to his neighbor, and it expressed the hope that the neighbor would understand. Naturally, the host was fully aware of the difficulty his request would cause. Nevertheless he asked, knowing that was the only way bread could be had to feed his weary and hungry friend.

Providing bread to a neighbor whose supply had run out was a custom in Israel. In the morning hours when fresh bread was baked the borrowed amount was repaid. Thus it was not the amount borrowed that mattered to the neighbor. It was a matter of timing.

The neighbor's voice was far from pleasant. In an all-too-human reaction of one disturbed in sleep, he said, "Don't bother me. The door is already locked and my children are with me in bed. I can't get up and give you anything." He expressed unwillingness, not inability, to grant the request. He would have to get up, arouse his children by lighting a lamp, find the bread, and open the door by removing the wooden bar. It would have been much easier if his next-door neighbor had disappeared in the dark.

But the next-door neighbor did not give him rest and sleep. He could not return home empty-handed, where his friend was waiting. He kept on asking for the bread until the neighbor got up, lit the lamp, removed the wooden bar, opened the door, and gave him the bread. In addition to bread he gave what was eaten with it, including olives, grape-molasses, and cheese "as much as he needs" (v. 8).[5] His neighbor did not do this because of friendship but because of the persistence of the one who asked.

The word *persistence* is the key word in the conclusion of the parable.[6] It portrays the attitude of a man who is obligated to show hospitality to a friend who came to him at midnight. In the context of his culture, he goes out of his way to provide for the physical needs of his visiting friend. He is willing to sacrifice friendship with his neighbor in order to be an accommodating host. He persists. He knows that his request will be honored even in adverse circumstances.

In this parable, Jesus clearly applies the Jewish rule of contrasts.[7] It is a rule that points up the greater by teaching the lesser. In this instance, by drawing attention to the persistence of the host, who knows that his neighbor will supply the three loaves of bread, Jesus teaches that we may go to God in prayer knowing that he will answer. "I tell you . . . because of the man's boldness he will get up and give him as much as he needs. So I say to you: Ask and it will be given to you; seek and you will find; knock and the door will be opened to you" (Luke 11:8, 9). If the neighbor awakens at midnight and gets up to give his friend three loaves of bread, how much more will God the Father answer the prayer of his child who comes to him in need![8]

What does the parable teach? It does *not* teach that, like the neighbor aroused from sleep, God does not wish to be disturbed. Rather, it conveys the idea that as the host continued to ask, knowing that his neighbor would open the door and give him bread, so the Christian must continue diligently in prayer. The parable of the unjust judge teaches the same message (Luke 18:1–8).[9] In faith he knows that God will answer his petitions and give him as much as he needs. God answers prayer in response to the faith the believer expresses. Thus the Christian concludes his prayer with the word *amen*. In the words of a sixteenth-century catechism on the Lord's Prayer,

> *Amen* means,
> This is sure to be!
> It is even more sure
> that God listens to my prayer,
> than that I really desire
> what I pray for.[10]

26 Rich Fool

Luke 12:13–21

[13]Someone in the crowd said to him, "Teacher, tell my brother to divide the inheritance with me."

[14]Jesus replied, "Man, who appointed me a judge or an arbiter between you?" [15]Then he said to them, "Watch out! Be on your guard against all kinds of greed; a man's life does not consist in the abundance of his possessions."

[16]And he told them this parable: "The ground of a certain rich man produced a good crop. [17]He thought to himself, 'What shall I do? I have no place to store my crops.'

[18]"Then he said, 'This is what I'll do. I will tear down my barns and build bigger ones, and there I will store all my grain and my goods. [19]And I'll say to myself, "You have plenty of good things laid up for many years. Take life easy; eat, drink and be merry."'

[20]"But God said to him, 'You fool! This very night your life will be demanded from you. Then who will get what you have prepared for yourself?'

[21]"This is how it will be with anyone who stores things up for himself but is not rich toward God."

"Do not judge, or you will be judged," said Jesus in the Sermon on the Mount. He was fully aware of the meaning of this saying when surrounded by a crowd of people. Someone asked him to become a judge in a family dispute. Two brothers had been quarreling about their inheritance. The father had died and the elder brother, in the opinion of the younger, did not fulfill the stipulations spelled out in the will. Perhaps the reason for not dividing the inheritance was based on religious grounds.[1] But the younger brother objected to the course of action and appealed to Jesus. He addressed him as "teacher," that is, "rabbi."[2]

151

Jesus, however, refused to be involved in a quarrel and serve as judge and arbiter. He refused to become another Moses, who took sides in a dispute and as a result had to leave the country.[3] He refused to be used by someone who acted out of selfish motives.

The brother who asked Jesus to intervene seems to have come to him alone. We have no indication that the elder brother had agreed to have a third party evaluate the situation. Also, nothing is said about the details of the claim. What is evident is that the person addressing Jesus wanted to use him as a lawyer, judge, and arbiter. In brief, he desired to employ him as a servant. He failed to see Jesus as a teacher. And because rabbis, schooled in the Law, served in the dual capacity of teacher and lawyer, the brother simply did not see a distinction.

For this reason Jesus, after addressing the man rather pointedly, proceeded to teach the crowd a spiritual lesson by way of a general saying and a parable. "Watch out! Be on your guard against all kinds of greed; a man's life does not consist in the abundance of his possessions." As teacher, Jesus warned the people against the spiritual danger of greed. Greed is idolatry.[4] It is the worship of the creature in place of the Creator. Jesus went straight to the root of the man's problem. He uncovered the source of the error that caused the man to ask Jesus to be his lawyer. He warned him and the crowd of the danger of greed. Greedy persons do not inherit the kingdom of God.[5]

Jesus' words are elaborated in Paul's first letter to Timothy: "For we brought nothing into this world, and we can take nothing out of it. But if we have food and clothing, we will be content with that" (1 Tim. 6:7, 8). Food, clothing, and shelter constitute the necessities of life. Anything above these is abundance and is to be shared with the poor.

THE PARABLE

The parable of the rich fool points out that life in the true sense of the word does not depend on earthly riches. Some years ago, definitions of happiness were much in vogue: "Happiness is. . . ." But among all these definitions, none mentioned wealth. Wealth does not bring happiness. Rather, it is often the cause of ruin and destruction.

In Jesus' parable, a wealthy farmer had an exceptional summer, and at harvesttime he gathered a bumper crop. The farmer talked to himself, considering what to do with the harvest and where to store it. He made up his mind and said: "I will tear down my barns and build bigger ones, and there I will store all my grain and my goods." By talking to himself and by using the words *I* and *my* repeatedly, he reveals his utter selfishness.[6] God had promised to fill man's barns with plenty if man would honor him with the firstfruits of all the produce.[7] But this man had no regard for God's promise. In fact, he showed contempt by tearing down his barns and building bigger ones.[8] He wanted to be in complete control of the situation. For him there was no trust in and dependence on God. Moreover, helping the poor never entered his mind. Instead, he thought about his own ease, pleasure, and security. He demonstrated an utter disregard for the basic summary of God's Law: "Love the Lord your God with all your heart, with all your soul and with all your mind. And love your neighbor as yourself." God and neighbor did not exist for him. He only thought about himself.

"And I'll say to myself, 'You have plenty of good things laid up for many years. Take life easy; eat, drink and be merry.'" The rich man engaged strictly in self-indulgence;[9] enrichment of his own life was not even considered. Self-indulgence is really compounded selfishness. The circle of his life had been reduced to a dot. His life was not character-ized by sins of commission but by sins of omission. He failed to thank God for riches received, and he neglected to care for his needy neigh-bor. Without God and neighbor his life was centered on himself alone. Alone, without reference to God, he wanted to secure his future. James, in his Epistle, addresses such people who say, "Today or tomorrow we will go to this or that city, spend a year there, carry on business and make money." Retorts James, "Why, you do not even know what will happen tomorrow. What is your life? You are a mist that appears for a little while and then vanishes" (James 4:13, 14).

God intervened by calling the rich man a fool,[10] and by telling him that his life would come to an end that night.[11] He would lose his life and all his riches. God called him to give an account of all his wealth. God wanted a bank balance of his earthly and his spiritual possessions.

The rich farmer had piled up his produce in barns and had accumu-lated sufficient wealth to last for a number of years. But because he had not shared his goods with his fellowman and had never reckoned with God, his spiritual bank account registered zero. When God called the man, the accounts were closed and could not be altered.[12]

"This very night your life will be demanded from you. Then who will get what you have prepared for yourself?" The question is rhetorical and implies that man's riches in effect belong to God. He gives and he takes at the appointed time.

CONCLUSION

Jesus did not say that man should shun earthly riches, pleasure, and ease. Nor did he try to tell the younger brother who had come with a complaint about his portion of the inheritance to disregard material goods. Man must realize that God is the owner of his great creation, and that God has placed man as a steward in this created world.[13] As a steward, man must give periodic accounts to God. When man fails to do this and acts as if he is the owner of his possessions, he transgresses the Law of God and stands condemned as a fool. Whenever man lives for himself, he is spiritually dead.

In the presence of God we stand empty-handed, "For we brought nothing into the world, and we can take nothing out of it" (1 Tim. 6:7). Only that which we have given to God and to our neighbor will last. Death cannot take our gifts of love and gratitude from us, because they have spiritual value.

> Only one life, 'twill soon be past;
> Only what is done for Christ will last.

Jesus concluded his parable by urging man to store up treasure in heaven and to be rich toward God. This is as Jesus taught in his Sermon on the Mount: "For where your treasure is, there your heart will be also" (Matt. 6:21).[14]

27 Barren Fig Tree

> **Luke 13:6–9**
>
> [6]Then he told this parable: "A man had a fig tree, planted in his vineyard, and he went to look for fruit on it, but did not find any. [7]So he said to the man who took care of the vineyard, 'For three years now I've been coming to look for fruit on this fig tree and haven't found any. Cut it down! Why should it use up the soil?'
>
> [8]"'Sir,' the man replied, 'leave it alone for one more year, and I'll dig around it and fertilize it. [9]If it bears fruit next year, fine! If not, then cut it down.'"

The owner of the vineyard is simply called "someone." Whether the man was rich or not is unimportant. Not what he is but what he says and does counts. This person had a fig tree in his vineyard—something rather common in Israel. After it had been planted, he had to wait at least three years before the tree began to bear fruit. And after that, according to the Law of Moses (Lev. 19:23), he would have to wait another three years before the fruit was considered clean. The owner had come to the tree after the first three years had passed. Year after year he came to look for fruit but found none. The tree was barren.

Because of its location, the tree had been well treated. It occupied a parcel of ground that could have been used for vines. In other words, every year the tree remained barren was a loss to the owner. It took moisture and nutrients away from the nearby vines. The fig tree was a debt and became increasingly so as the years went by. Another tree or vine could be planted and within a few years yield its fruit. There is an end to the patience of a fruit farmer. Enough is enough!

The fruit farmer instructed the man who took care of the vineyard to cut the fig tree down. But the man intervened with a plea for patience. He wanted to give the tree one more year, during which he would loosen the soil around it and add fertilizer. "If it bears fruit next year, fine! If not, then cut it down."

The fig tree played a dominant role in the life of the Israelite. He knew that God used the fig tree to indicate Israel's prosperity—with everyone living in security under his own vine and under his own fig tree.[1] But the contrary was also true. When God was displeased with his people because of their unfaithfulness, he would make it known by referring to the lack of fruit on vine and fig tree.[2] Israel as a nation was often symbolized by a fig tree. She had received a choice spot in God's vineyard and therefore was highly privileged. But with the privilege came responsibility. Israel, however, failed to match privilege with duty.[3] God's judgment could no longer be postponed, and the falling of figs from the fig tree was symbolic of God's displeasure.[4]

The parable Jesus taught shows an implied contrast. If the man who was in charge of the vineyard lavished special care on one fig tree for an extra year, how much more love and consideration will God shower upon man, and certainly upon his own people.[5] Although the parable does not indicate whether the owner reaped figs the following year or whether the tree was cut down, the point of the story is that patience is delimited by time—one year and that is all. God's mercy is great, but in the end the day of judgment comes. The time of grace that God grants sinners must be used to repent and to turn to him.

Jesus taught the parable of the barren fig tree in the historical context of Pilate's gruesome deed of mixing the blood of Galileans with their sacrifices (Luke 13:1–5). Were these slain Galileans sinners who had met divine punishment? The answer Jesus gave was negative. Repent, said Jesus to his audience, or you too will perish. Do you think that the eighteen people who were killed in the catastrophe of the falling tower of Siloam were greater sinners than the others living in Jerusalem? Again, the answer Jesus gave was, no. Once more he called the audience to repentance and followed that call with the parable of the barren fig tree.

What, then, does the parable teach? In the context of the calamities that had come to the Galileans and the eighteen inhabitants of Jerusalem, Jesus told his audience that God's patience eventuates in judgment if the sinner does not repent. To whom much has been entrusted, from him much will be required. The author of the Epistle to the Hebrews echoes the same sentiment when he warns Christians in the second half of the first century to pay close attention to the gospel. "For if the message spoken by angels was binding, and every violation and disobedience received its just punishment, how shall we escape if we ignore such a great salvation?" (2:2, 3).

The point of the parable is that when the allotted time for one's repentance has expired, God's judgment is finalized. The time God allots is a period of grace, reflecting his mercy toward human beings. God does not merely go the second mile. He will go a third mile and, if need be, a fourth in order to save a sinner. But when his patience is exhausted and God's call for one's repentance has gone unheeded, then judgment is unavoidable.[6]

Our prayers to God in behalf of unrepentant sinners should be pleas for extra time. As the gardener in the parable asked the owner for one more year, so we ought to petition for a little more patience. Likewise, in his concern for his countrymen, Paul constantly pleaded with God for their salvation: "Brothers, my heart's desire and prayer to God for the Israelites is that they may be saved" (Rom. 10:1). Our concern is for man's eternal interest[7] and thus we implore God to exercise patience and grant grace.

28 Places of Honor at the Table

> **Luke 14:7–14**
> [7]When he noticed how the guests picked the places of honor at the table, he told them this parable: [8]"When someone invites you to a wedding feast, do not take the place of honor, for a person more distinguished than you may have been invited. [9]If so, the host who invited both of you will come and say to you, 'Give this man your seat.' Then, humiliated, you will have to take the least important place. [10]But when you are invited, take the lowest place, so that when your host comes, he will say to you, 'Friend, move up to a better place.' Then you will be honored in the presence of all your fellow guests. [11]For everyone who exalts himself will be humbled, and he who humbles himself will be exalted."
> [12]Then Jesus said to his host, "When you give a luncheon or dinner, do not invite your friends, your brothers or relatives, or your rich neighbors; if you do, they may invite you back and so you will be repaid. [13]But when you give a banquet, invite the poor, the crippled, the lame, the blind, [14]and you will be blessed. Although they cannot repay you, you will be repaid at the resurrection of the righteous."

After the synagogue service on the Sabbath, Jews would eat a substantial meal to which quite often a number of guests were invited.[1] A leading Pharisee had invited Jesus to such a noon meal with the purpose of trapping him. There, right in front of Jesus, was a man with dropsy. Would Jesus heal on the Sabbath, or would he wait until evening when the Sabbath ended?

Jesus healed the man and sent him home, because the Pharisees refused to answer his question whether it was lawful to heal on the Sabbath or not. He put a further question to them and thus appealed to their sense of compassion and mercy. "If your son or your ox falls into a well on the Sabbath, what would you do?" asked Jesus. Even to that question, which came close to home, the Pharisees would not reply.

In this less than congenial atmosphere, where guests had selfishly picked the best seats at the table, Jesus taught the parable of the arrogant guests—a lesson in humility. He used the setting of a wedding feast to which a number of guests had been invited. Couches at a wedding feast were arranged in the shape of an elongated horseshoe consisting of a number of tables. The man receiving the highest honor was at the head table, with second and third places to the left and right of this person.[2] Every couch accommodated three people, with the middle man receiving the highest honor. The couch to the left of the head table was next in order of priority, and after that the couch to the right. Consequently, Jewish guests were governed by the social etiquette of the day to find the correct place at the table. However, if the privilege of choosing seats was given to the invited guests, they could very well display selfishness, conceit, and pride. And this was exactly what happened at the house of the prominent Pharisee to which Jesus was invited. Pharisees and experts in the Law had created a climate of haughtiness and arrogance devoid of love and humility. In this setting Jesus taught a lesson of self-abasement.

The parable is only found in the Gospel of Luke, although the sentiment expressed occurs in other places in the Gospels and Epistles.[3] Of course we are immediately reminded of the footwashing scene in the upper room on the night of Jesus' betrayal.

The Example

The Pharisees and experts in the Law were acquainted with the Proverbs of Solomon. They knew the passage, "Do not exalt yourself in the king's presence, and do not claim a place among great men; it is better for him to say to you, 'Come up here,' than for him to humiliate you before a nobleman" (Prov. 25:6, 7). Jesus artfully alluded to this passage when he pictured a hall filled with wedding guests seated at the table. An honorable guest arrived after all the choice seats at the table had been taken.[4] The host could not permit his worthy guest to take the lowest place. That would be an unpardonable breach of etiquette. In such a case the host had only one choice: inform the person occupying a seat of honor to which he was not entitled to take the lowest place, and then invite the distinguished visitor to come to the seat of honor. The humiliated guest learned a lesson he would not soon forget.

Would it not be wiser upon arrival to take the lowest place at the table? Should the host find that the seat you had taken was too lowly a place, you would hear him say to you, "Friend, move up to a better place." Consequently, you would be honored in the presence of all the guests.

Start at the bottom and end up at the top. The words of Jesus, "For every-one who exalts himself will be humbled, and he who humbles himself will be exalted," were rather familiar in that time. A contemporary of Jesus, Rabbi Hillel, uttered a similar Jewish proverb: "My self-abase-ment is my exaltation, my self-exaltation is my abasement."[5]

Jesus did not merely teach the Pharisees and theologians a few nec-essary table manners; he did not dispense some worldly wisdom. He taught a lesson of humility and love by addressing the guests at the table as well as the host who invited them. Jesus told the host that he should not invite guests on a reciprocal basis: "If you love those who love you, what reward will you get?" (Matt. 5:46). If the host invites his relatives, friends, and acquaintances to a meal with the understanding that they in turn will invite him, he can calculate his reward. But if he invites peo-ple who are financially and socially unable to return the invitation, his reward will be paid by God himself at the time of the resurrection.

Who would arrange a banquet and invite the lowest class of society: the poor, the crippled, the lame, and the blind? The poor are financially dependent on the rich, and those who are crippled, lame, or blind most often need the help of the physically able. These people simply do not have the means and the strength to repay favors.

To extend an invitation to people who are deprived of the dining plea-sures enjoyed by the rich is to deserve the commendation of being blessed. Of course, Jesus does not imply that a host should never invite anyone but the downtrodden. He teaches that our deeds should be performed without a thought of reciprocity. They should be performed in a spirit of unselfish love and humility. Such deeds gain divine approval, for "what-ever you did for one of the least of these brothers of mine, you did for me" (Matt. 25:40). This universal teaching is not limited to giving ban-quets but includes all deeds that cannot be repaid by the recipient.

29 Great Supper

Luke 14:15–24

[15]When one of those at the table with him heard this, he said to Jesus, "Blessed is the man who will eat at the feast in the kingdom of God."

[16]Jesus replied: "A certain man was preparing a great banquet and invited many guests. [17]At the time of the banquet he sent his servant to tell those who had been invited, 'Come, for everything is now ready.'

[18]"But they all alike began to make excuses. The first said, 'I have just bought a field, and I must go and see it. Please excuse me.'

[19]"Another said, 'I have just bought five yoke of oxen, and I'm on my way to try them out. Please excuse me.'

[20]"Still another said, 'I just got married, so I can't come.'

[21]"The servant came back and reported this to his master. Then the owner of the house became angry and ordered his servant, 'Go out quickly into the streets and alleys of the town and bring in the poor, the crippled, the blind and the lame.'

[22]"'Sir,' the servant said, 'what you ordered has been done, but there is still room.'

[23]"Then the master told his servant, 'Go out to the roads and country lanes and make them come in, so that my house will be full. [24]I tell you, not one of those men who were invited will get a taste of my banquet.'"

Jesus' teaching in the home of a prominent Pharisee elicited a response from one of the guests in the Pharisee's dining room. He said, "Blessed is the man who will eat at the feast in the kingdom of God." The speaker implied that, come what may, he would be present at the heavenly festivities. But should the invitation to celebrate this feast in the kingdom of God eventually come, would he readily accept it? Jesus wanted to test the man's sincerity and told the parable of the great banquet.

THE STORY

A well-to-do person in a certain town made elaborate preparations for a banquet. He had been in touch with numerous friends who responded favorably to his suggestion of hosting a banquet. They told him that when he was ready all he had to do was say the word and they would come.

The day of the banquet came, and the host instructed his servant to make the rounds and tell the guests to come to the banquet.[1] He arrived at the home of the first guest and said: "Come, for everything is now ready." Unfortunately, the guest had a conflict of interest, and regretfully, he had to decline the invitation. He told the servant, "I have just bought a field, and I must go and see it." In effect he said, "I am sorry, but I am unable to attend the banquet. Business comes before pleasure, you know. Please excuse me." He conveyed his kindest regards to the host and trusted that the host would understand.

The servant went on to the second guest and invited him to the banquet, for the host was waiting: "Come, for everything is now ready." The invited guest looked perplexed when he heard the invitation. He was in the midst of a business deal. He had just paid out a sizable amount of money for five yoke of oxen and was on his way to try them out. It was impossible to leave because all the oxen drivers depended on him. He was the one to make decisions; he was the key figure. To walk away from his farm at this moment in order to attend a banquet would be highly irresponsible. He expressed deep regret and asked the servant to send warm greetings to the host. He was sure that the host would understand his predicament.

The servant continued on his way. He knocked at the door of guest number three. By now he was prepared to receive negative replies to his host's invitation. When he had acquainted the guest with the invitation to the banquet, he heard that during that week the guest had gotten married. If there was ever a conflict of interest, it was now. The guest had his own festivities. In fact, he did not even have to excuse himself. No one in his right mind would think ill of the bridegroom for being at the side of his bride.

When the servant had contacted all the invited guests, he returned to the host and conveyed their sincere regrets and kind regards. Understandably, the host was not at all happy. Instead, he was angry. He could not let the food go to waste. He had no choice but to fill his house with other guests. And thus he ordered the servant to go into the streets and alleys and tell the beggars, the crippled, the blind, and the lame to come to his banquet. The servant did so, but when all the guests were seated there was still room. His master sent him once more to go to the outcasts of society. This time he had to find them out of town along the roads and country lanes. The host wanted to have every seat in the banquet hall filled; if an earlier invited guest planned to come late, he would be turned back for lack of room.

INTERPRETATION

One of the guests in the home of the prominent Pharisee had said, "Blessed is the man who will eat at the feast in the kingdom of God." He visualized heaven as the place where there is no more death, mourning, crying, or pain (Rev. 21:4), where blind people can see and the lame can walk. What a blessing to sit at the table of God as his child and to enjoy the heavenly feast and fellowship reserved for him!

Jesus teaches the parable of the great supper in order to indicate that although we may have the best intentions of honoring our obligations to God, when the cares and concerns of this earthly life make their demands we put them first and offer our excuses to God. We have made a promise to God to love him with all our heart, soul, and mind. But this promise readily becomes hollow when the interests of this life demand our undivided attention. Then we make our excuses and say that God should understand that we have to take our responsibilities seriously, that our lives are taken up in numerous relationships, that opportunity knocks infrequently.[2] Our obligations, connections, and expediencies frequently go contrary to our promise to love and serve God. We honor our own interests and hope that God will give us a second chance.

The excuses offered by the guests simply do not stand the test. They touch on business and family commitments that could easily take a second place to the invitation earlier accepted. The field would still be there for inspection the following day, the oxen could rest for an afternoon and evening, and the newlyweds should make allowances for an occasional separation.

The sequence of excuses builds up to the punch line. In the after-dinner speech of Jesus we detect a note of humor. First, the example of the man who had bought a field exhibits irrelevancy—a buyer inspects a field before he makes the purchase, not afterward. Likewise, the second excuse does not convince—five yoke of oxen could easily be put to work the following day.[3] Moreover, if the farmer had not tried them out before he bought them, he demonstrated the height of foolishness. The third example was the climax of the illustrations. A newlywed husband unable to leave his wife for an evening of feasting provides excellent material for numerous jokes.[4]

The objective of enumerating these excuses was to show their insufficiency and flimsiness. No one could take them seriously. They simply did not stand up. Besides, everyone in Jesus' day knew the prevailing custom of honoring an invitation to a banquet. To refuse a second invitation constituted an outright insult to the host—to such a degree that among Arab tribes it was the equivalent of a declaration of war.[5] The invitation had to be honored as if it were a command.

Jesus' immediate audience in the Pharisee's home realized that the parable was addressed to all who listened. Host and guests were invited to God's banquet to which they originally had consented to come. Would they come, or should God turn to others because the invited guests refused to come? Jesus told the Pharisees and experts in the Law that God's banquet is not some event to be celebrated at the end of time. Rather, the feast is ready and God is calling them to respond now.[6] As a reply to the person who said, "Blessed is the man who will eat at the feast in the kingdom of God," Jesus said, "Yes, the time for this feast has come. You who have been invited, *come now*. Hereafter it will be too late." The religious establishment in Jesus' day was not ready to accept the coming of the kingdom, even though the signs and wonders Jesus performed were there for all to see.

By means of the parable, Jesus intimated that God's kingdom would not lack citizens. If the religious leaders of Israel rejected God's invitation to enter the kingdom, he would extend it to the social outcasts, that is, the tax collectors, the waywards, and the Gentiles.[7]

The message of salvation was not accepted by the religious rulers of Jesus' day. It often met contempt and generally was disregarded. But the common people accepted it eagerly (Mark 12:37). They were the social and moral outcasts. They were the uneducated. They were the Samaritans and the Gentiles who came readily to Jesus.

SETTING

The parable of the great supper was told as an after-dinner speech on a certain Sabbath after the morning worship service. By contrast, Jesus taught the parable of the wedding banquet in the last few days of his earthly life (Matt. 22:1–14). The two parables share a common theme, but the setting is entirely different. In Luke the parable is addressed *to* Pharisees and experts in the Law. In Matthew the parable of the wedding banquet is leveled *against* the religious leaders.[8] That is, the account in Matthew relates the harsh reality of a king provoked to anger who metes out swift retribution. In the Gospel of Luke, the picture is presented of a snubbed host who gives vent to his emotions by inviting the riffraff of society.

The four Gospels repeatedly show that Jesus taught in the rabbinic fashion of his day. For him to teach meant to repeat.[9] Thus he taught the parable of the great supper at the time he was invited to a Sabbath noon meal in the home of a Pharisee; and he taught the parable of the wedding banquet a few days before his death.[10]

When Jesus told the parable of the great supper, the theologically educated religious class of that day must have caught the allusion to two passages in Deuteronomy:

> The officers shall say to the army: "Has anyone built a new house and not dedicated it? Let him go home, or he may die in battle and someone else may dedicate it. Has anyone planted a vineyard and not begun to enjoy it? Let him go home, or he may die in battle and someone else enjoy it. Has anyone become pledged to a woman and not married her? Let him go home, or he may die in battle and someone else marry her."
>
> Deuteronomy 20:5–7

> If a man has recently married, he must not be sent to war or have any other duty laid on him. For one year he is to be free to stay at home and bring happiness to the wife he has married.
>
> Deuteronomy 24:5

The theologians knew that these passages were valid only in regard to war and military service and were not meant to excuse someone from social obligations.[11]

They also knew the prevailing customs. Excuses to a host could be made when the first invitation to a banquet was given. To decline the second invitation when all the preparations were made was not merely breaking a promise but insulting the host. Clearly, the parable was addressed and applied to the Pharisees and teachers of the Law. Unless they accepted the invitation to be Jesus' guests in the kingdom of God, they would be bypassed and others, for whom they had no respect, would take their place.

APPLICATION

The host is sometimes portrayed as a victim of circumstance. Whereas one of the invited guests may have declined the invitation, the host now learns that all of them have refused to come.[12] Perhaps it is more accurate to see a deliberate snubbing in the making when all the guests—and we do not have to stop with the three examples—refused to come. Although they may not have conspired to make it uniform, the effect nevertheless was the same. As such, the invited guests reflected the attitude of the religious hierarchy.

Jesus involves himself in the conclusion when he says, "I tell you, not one of those men who were invited will get a taste of my banquet." The speaker is no longer the host addressing the servant. Jesus is the central figure who talks about "my" banquet and says that none of those contemptuous guests will get a taste of his food.[13] Jesus is the host, who by means of his servants sends out invitations calling people to the feast in the kingdom of God. When the call goes forth from Jesus via his servants to the people, it is not to be understood as an invitation that people may accept or reject at will. The call is equivalent to a command that expects compliance.[14] God's people, who are part and parcel of the church, receive this call to obedient service. They have responded to the initial invitation. Now the call to service is sounded. Will God's people respond to the command to love God heartily and the neighbor unselfishly?[15] The man who eats at the feast in the kingdom of God is called blessed because he obeys the laws of the kingdom and fulfills the commands of the King.

The lesson of the parable is clear. Jesus is sending his servants forth with the message that God's kingdom has come. Those who hear the message are invited to share in this kingdom. They should not make excuses and delay, because Jesus will not keep a place for them.[16] Instead, he will fill his kingdom with others, who come from hither and yon. He wants his house to be full. He says, "Make them come in."

The parable obviously has missionary overtones. Jesus gathers his own people from the streets and alleys of the town and from the roads and country lanes abroad. He is not ashamed to call the poor, the crippled, the blind, and the lame his brothers (Heb. 2:11). They are made holy and belong to the family of God. In an age in which many people belonging to the church offer flimsy excuses for nonparticipation in the continued work of God's kingdom, God's faithful servants must go out into life's streets and lanes with the invitation to come to Jesus Christ, the Savior of the world. And while those who refuse to acknowledge the call of Jesus are bypassed and lose their citizenship in the kingdom, aliens to the kingdom are now persuaded to respond to Christ's call in faith.

In the preceding context Jesus noted that the Jews who had been invited but refused to come would be denied a place at the dinner table. He said, "People will come from east and west and north and south, and

will take their places at the feast in the kingdom of God" (Luke 13:29).
Paul adhered to the rule "first for the Jew, then for the Gentile" (Rom.
1:16; and see Matt. 10:5). He and Barnabas brought the gospel to the
Jews in Pisidian Antioch, but when those people rejected the offer of
salvation, the apostles turned to the Gentiles (Acts 13:46).[17]

Accepting the invitation required faith on the part of the guests. When
the servant came with the message of the host, "Come, for everything is
now ready," the invited guests saw only a man.[18] When a minister of
God's Word proclaims the message of salvation, many people hearing
that Word see only a preacher. It takes faith to see and hear behind the
preacher the Savior Jesus Christ, who offers salvation full and free. The
Philippian jailer came to Paul and Barnabas and was told, "Believe in
the Lord Jesus and you will be saved—you and your household" (Acts
16:31).

30 Tower Builder and Warring King

> **Luke 14:28–33**
>
> [28]"Suppose one of you wants to build a tower. Will he not first sit down and estimate the cost to see if he has enough money to complete it? [29]For if he lays the foundation and is not able to finish it, everyone who sees it will ridicule him, [30]saying, 'This fellow began to build and was not able to finish.'
>
> [31]"Or suppose a king is about to go to war against another king. Will he not first sit down and consider whether he is able with ten thousand men to oppose the one coming against him with twenty thousand? [32]If he is not able, he will send a delegation while the other is still a long way off and will ask for terms of peace. [33]In the same way, any of you who does not give up everything he has cannot be my disciple."

The twin parables of the man who wanted to build a tower and the king who wanted to go to war are found only in the Gospel of Luke. The historical setting in which they were told was during the time large crowds accompanied Jesus on the way from Galilee to Jerusalem. The people mistakenly saw in Jesus an earthly ruler who was on his way to Jerusalem to establish his kingdom, and they wanted to be there with him and his disciples. But in Jerusalem Jesus would not ascend an earthly throne. Instead, he would be apprehended, tried, and executed. His followers would have to count the cost of discipleship before they made up their minds to throw in their lot with Jesus.[1] They should know that anyone who does not hate his own immediate relatives, and even his own life, cannot be Jesus' disciple (Luke 14:25–27).

In Semitic terms, to hate means to love less than someone or something else. It means that someone or something does not receive priority but is relegated to second or third place. Whoever does not say, "Jesus is first and foremost in my life," cannot be Jesus' disciple. But being Jesus' disciple implies carrying one's own cross and following Jesus wherever he leads. The one who said, "Come to me, all you who are weary and burdened" (Matt. 11:28), also said, "Anyone who does not carry his cross and follow me cannot be my disciple" (Luke 14:27). "No one who puts his hand to the plow and looks back is fit for service in the kingdom of God" (Luke 9:62). Discipleship is a wholehearted commitment to Jesus. "Count the cost," Jesus tells the crowd accompanying him, "and consider what following me really means."

PARABLES

To illustrate his point Jesus teaches two relatively short parables. The first is taken from the agricultural world of that day, the second from the political scene. Both parables teach the same lesson and, in their simplicity, do not fail to make the point.

Suppose, says Jesus, that a farmer decides to build a tower on his farm. He needs a place to keep his implements and produce. He wants to safeguard his property from possible intruders and would-be thieves. If he builds the tower, he will gain respect in the community, and his property will rise in value. He establishes the necessity for the building,[2] but he fails to sit down and count the cost involved in materials and labor. He begins the construction of the tower by laying a foundation. When he is busy with the superstructure, he runs out of money and has to abandon the project. There it stands, unfinished and, in a sense, worthless. The farmer has lost his money by investing it in a building he cannot use in its unfinished state. He has lost his prestige in the community, for everyone who sees the incomplete structure ridicules him openly: "This fellow began to build and was not able to finish." He has become the laughingstock of the village.

Jesus moves from the farm to the palace. Suppose, he says, that a king must go to war with another king. A territorial dispute has arisen, passions run high, words of revenge and retaliation are heard. The king must provide leadership and decide whether or not to go to war. The king would be utterly foolish to commit his army of ten thousand soldiers to war and find them outnumbered two to one on the battlefield. Rather, he sits down with his military advisors and calculates the risks of waging war against an enemy of superior strength. If he is wise, he will commission a few delegates to discuss terms of peace with the enemy and thus avert bloodshed.[3]

In the two parables the emphasis is the same, although the details vary. In that of the tower builder the message is: count the cost before you begin to build. And in that of the warring king: consider the chances of success before you send your soldiers into battle; be ready and willing to surrender. "In the same way," Jesus says, "any of you who does not give up everything he has cannot be my disciple."

CONCLUSION

At first sight, the teaching of the parables seems to go contrary to the message of the gospel of Christ to make disciples of all nations (Matt. 28:19). Upon reflection, however, no one can say that the parables intend to discourage prospective disciples. On the whole, the two examples Jesus taught instruct them how to be truly committed disciples. Jesus simply does not want and does not need any halfhearted followers. Such followers are like the seed that falls on rocky places. They hear the Word and at once receive it with joy. But because they have no root, they do not last. In trouble and persecution, which the Word brings about, they wither away (Matt. 13:20, 21).

The parables stress two main points: (1) the disciple of Jesus must think things out very carefully, and (2) he must be willing to give things up for Jesus.[4] Discipleship is not based on sham emotions and shallow enthusiasm. These come and go. But genuine commitment is the basis on which the disciple of Jesus builds. He has carefully counted the cost and analyzed the risks of following Jesus. He readily renounces relationships and possessions in the interest of taking up his cross and following Jesus.

Three times in succession Jesus repeats the refrain "cannot be my disciple" (Luke 14:26, 27, 33). Positively, only those who have counted the cost and are willing to renounce all for the sake of Christ are committed disciples.

or actually
do renounce

Are we just "playing church"

31 Lost Sheep

Matthew 18:12–14

[12]"What do you think? If a man owns a hundred sheep, and one of them wanders away, will he not leave the ninety-nine on the hills and go to look for the one that wandered off? [13]And if he finds it, I tell you the truth, he is happier about that one sheep than about the ninety-nine that did not wander off. [14]In the same way your Father in heaven is not willing that any of these little ones should be lost."

Luke 15:4–7

[4]"Suppose one of you has a hundred sheep and loses one of them. Does he not leave the ninety-nine in the open country and go after the lost sheep until he finds it? [5]And when he finds it, he joyfully puts it on his shoulders [6]and goes home. Then he calls his friends and neighbors together and says, 'Rejoice with me; I have found my lost sheep.' [7]I tell you that in the same way there is more rejoicing in heaven over one sinner who repents than over ninety-nine righteous persons who do not need to repent."

Among the parables Jesus taught, the parable of the lost sheep has been one that appeals to children. They visualize the wandering sheep, the love and concern of the shepherd, and the joy and happiness when sheep and shepherd are reunited. Many songs and hymns have been written about this parable.

Both Matthew and Luke have incorporated the parable of the lost sheep. Substantially, the two accounts in Matthew and Luke show an identical outline, although the details vary. It is not at all unlikely that Jesus told the parable twice but in two different settings.[1] Moreover, stories about sheep and shepherds had particular interest and meaning for the agricultural people of his day.

In Matthew as well as in Luke, Jesus begins the parable by asking a rhetorical question, which in Luke even involves the audience ("one of you"): "If a man owns a hundred sheep . . . will he not leave the ninety-nine . . . ?" A person who owned a hundred sheep was a man of considerable means who employed a shepherd and assistants to care for his sheep. The shepherd knew them all by name, and counted them at least once a day.[2]

When the shepherd's attention was temporarily diverted, one of the sheep wandered off, nibbling here and there, until it was completely by itself. The shepherd left the rest of the sheep on the hills (Matthew) or in the open country (Luke).[3] Although the parable merely states that the shepherd left the ninety-nine sheep, it does not say that they were unprotected; more than one shepherd took care of an extended flock and led them back to the village.[4] Moreover, the focus of the parable is not on the ninety-nine but on the one sheep that was lost. Sheep are very social animals; they stay and live together as a flock. When a sheep is cut off from the flock, it becomes bewildered.[5] It lies down, unwilling to move, waiting for the shepherd. When the shepherd at last finds it, he puts it on his shoulders and carries it, in order to cover the distance back to the flock more quickly. This onerous task of carrying a seventy-pound animal for an extended distance can be tiresome.[6] But soon shepherd, sheep, and flock are together again.

This could have been the end of the story, but it is not. The story has a climactic ending because the shepherd is filled with happiness. Says Jesus, "I tell you the truth, he is happier about that one sheep than about the ninety-nine that did not wander off" (Matt. 18:13). Happiness must be shared to be genuine. The shepherd goes home, calls his friends and neighbors together, and invites them to share his joy because, says the shepherd, "I have found my lost sheep" (Luke 15:6). The tension the shepherd had experienced while searching for the lost sheep has been released and has turned into joy.[7] He celebrates with friends and neighbors.

APPLICATION

The accounts of Matthew and Luke differ in application obviously because of the historical settings in which Jesus told the parable. In Matthew's Gospel, Jesus asked the question, "Who is the greatest in the kingdom of heaven?" His answer was given pointed meaning when he put a child among the disciples and said to them, "Unless you change and become like little children, you will never enter the kingdom of heaven" (Matt. 18:3). He followed it up with the warning not to lead "these little ones who believe in me" (Matt. 18:6) to sin, or to despise them. In this context Jesus told the parable of the lost sheep and applied it to the children. "In the same way your Father in heaven is not willing that any of these little ones should be lost."

The reference in context is to the children. But in view of the visual demonstration Jesus gave by placing a child among the disciples, the expression "these little ones" has taken on a spiritual meaning. Jesus is referring to those believers whose faith is characterized by childlike simplicity.[8] As a shepherd watches over his sheep, and even goes out to find one that wanders away, so God takes care of believers, especially those who are babes in the faith.[9] Should one of them wander off, God will recover him because he does not wish "that any of these little ones be lost."

The Gospel of Luke relates that Jesus was surrounded by tax collectors and "sinners" who had come to listen to him.[10] The Pharisees and teachers of the Law took offense at this by muttering, "This man welcomes sinners and eats with them" (Luke 15:2). Thus surrounded by spiritual infants, Jesus told the parable of the lost sheep and concluded by saying, "I tell you that in the same way there is more rejoicing in heaven over one sinner who repents than over ninety-nine righteous persons who do not need to repent." Jesus compared the tax collectors and the immoral people to a sheep that was lost. The sheep, when it was lost, did not respond anymore to the shepherd's call. It refused to move. When the shepherd found it, he had to lift it up and put it on his shoulders to take it back to the flock.

Tax collectors were Jewish people in the employ of the Roman government. In the mind of the people, they were traitors who had alienated themselves from society. They were in the same class as the moral outcasts. A Jew was not to have any contact with such men and women, and especially not table-fellowship. Barriers between the Jew and the "sinner" had been erected, but these did not prevent Jesus from teaching the outcasts the message of salvation. He bridged the gap and brought the sinner back to God.

God rejoices more over one of these moral outcasts who repents than over ninety-nine righteous persons who do not need to repent.[11] He is genuinely interested in the salvation of the sinner. As a shepherd he searches out the man who is unable to do anything for himself. God goes out to man, not man to God. In this respect, Christianity differs from other world religions.[12] God finds man who is lost in sin. When he has found him, heaven rejoices. Of course, there is joy over those who do God's will, but when a sinner turns to God in repentance and faith, it is time to celebrate together. God's child who was lost has been found.

32 Lost Coin

> **Luke 15:8–10**
>
> [8]"Or suppose a woman has ten silver coins and loses one. Does she not light a lamp, sweep the house and search carefully until she finds it? [9]And when she finds it, she calls her friends and neighbors together and says, 'Rejoice with me; I have found my lost coin.' [10]In the same way, I tell you, there is rejoicing in the presence of the angels of God over one sinner who repents."

Luke often presents his material in pairs. When he mentions a man, he most likely will also note a woman. In chapter 1 of his Gospel, Zacharias and Elizabeth are presented, and in the following chapter, Joseph and Mary, and Simeon and Anna. In succeeding chapters, he refers to the widow of Zarephath and Naaman the Syrian. In the parables, he places the man with the mustard seed next to the woman mixing yeast in her flour. The parable of the shepherd who found his lost sheep is followed by the parable of the woman who found one of her silver coins.[1] These two parables form a pair and teach virtually the same message. Thus Jesus makes his point in addressing the Pharisees and teachers of the Law.

This story, because of its brevity, sparkles with beauty. It reveals all the emotions of anxiety, worry, elation, and joy in only a sentence or two. Yet the story is complete.

Jesus portrays a woman who had ten silver coins. These coins were part of her dowry and were worn as ornamental decorations on her head-dress. The modern equivalent may be a woman's engagement ring and wedding band with studded diamonds. The loss of one of these diamonds causes dismay, anxiety, and worry. When the woman realized that one coin was missing, she knew that it must have become detached

174

and fallen off. It was unthinkable that someone might have stolen it.[2]
The place to look for the coin was in her own home.

Houses of the poorer class were constructed without windows. Near
the ceiling, perhaps, a few stones were left out of the wall to provide
some ventilation. But this opening, together with the entrance, did not
give the inside of the house much light. Even in the middle of the day it
was dark in the house. The woman would have to light a candle in order
to search for the coin that was somewhere on the stone floor.[3] Animals
were frequently kept inside rural homes, although in a somewhat separate part of the family dwelling.[4] Besides, the house served as a place
where the poor owner stored his goods.

Somewhere in the house was the coin the woman had lost. She took a
broom and, with the light of the candle illuminating the room, she swept
the house carefully. Every place where she might have been was searched,
until at last she caught sight of a gleam of metal or heard the tinkle of the
coin upon the hard floor. Her anxiety and worry suddenly disappeared
and gave way to joy and jubilation. Friends and neighbors had to share
her happiness. She called them together and said, "Rejoice with me; I have
found my lost coin." Congratulations were exchanged, and when the husband returned from the field, he too shared his wife's happiness.

"In the same way," said Jesus, "I tell you, there is rejoicing in the presence of the angels of God over one sinner who repents." As the house of
the woman was filled with happiness and laughter because that which
was lost had been found, so heaven rejoices when a sinner repents and
turns to God in faith. As the woman rejoices before her friends and neighbors, so God rejoices before his angels.[5] As the coin belonged to the
woman who diligently searched for it while it was lost, so the sinner
who repents belongs to God. Besides, God's love is directed toward his
erring child. "God demonstrates his own love for us in this: While we
were yet sinners, Christ died for us" (Rom. 5:8).

Jesus showed God's love to the "sinners" of his day. He taught the
publicans and moral outcasts, he entered their homes, he ate and drank
with them, and he was given the name "friend of sinners" (Matt. 11:19).
Because of this, the Pharisees considered even Jesus to be a sinner.

The two parables of the sheep and the coin have a definite evangelistic thrust. The church, known as the body of Christ, is called to extend
love and concern to the men, women, and children who are spiritually
lost in this world. Members of the church are called to seek that which
is lost and to tell those who live in sin that "Christ died for the ungodly"
(Rom. 5:6). The fervor Jesus displayed in associating with the so-called
sinners of his day must glow in every member of the church, radiating
the warmth of evangelistic zeal, and rejoicing with "the angels of God
over one sinner who repents."

33 Lost Son

Luke 15:11–32

[11]Jesus continued: "There was a man who had two sons. [12]The younger one said to his father, 'Father, give me my share of the estate.' So he divided his property between them.

[13]"Not long after that, the younger son got together all he had, set off for a distant country and there squandered his wealth in wild living. [14]After he had spent everything, there was a severe famine in that whole country, and he began to be in need. [15]So he went and hired himself out to a citizen of that country, who sent him to his fields to feed pigs. [16]He longed to fill his stomach with the pods that the pigs were eating, but no one gave him anything.

[17]"When he came to his senses, he said, 'How many of my father's hired men have food to spare, and here I am starving to death! [18]I will set out and go back to my father and say to him: Father, I have sinned against heaven and against you. [19]I am no longer worthy to be called your son; make me like one of your hired men.' [20]So he got up and went to his father.

"But while he was still a long way off, his father saw him and was filled with compassion for him; he ran to his son, threw his arms around him and kissed him.

[21]"The son said to him, 'Father, I have sinned against heaven and against you. I am no longer worthy to be called your son.'

[22]"But the father said to his servants, 'Quick! Bring the best robe and put it on him. Put a ring on his finger and sandals on his feet. [23]Bring the fattened calf and kill it. Let's have a feast and celebrate. [24]For this son of mine was dead and is alive again; he was lost and is found.' So they began to celebrate.

[25]"Meanwhile, the older son was in the field. When he came near the house, he heard music and dancing. [26]So he called one of the servants and asked him what was going on. [27]'Your brother has come,' he replied, 'and your father has killed the fattened calf because he has him back safe and sound.'

> [28]"The older brother became angry and refused to go in. So his father went out and pleaded with him. [29]But he answered his father, 'Look! All these years I've been slaving for you and never disobeyed your orders. Yet you never gave me even a young goat so I could celebrate with my friends. [30]But when this son of yours who has squandered your property with prostitutes comes home, you kill the fattened calf for him!'
>
> [31]"'My son,' the father said, 'you are always with me, and everything I have is yours. [32]But we had to celebrate and be glad, because this brother of yours was dead and is alive again; he was lost and is found.'"

HISTORICAL SETTING

Jesus was teaching the tax collectors and the moral outcasts spiritual truths concerning God's kingdom when the religious teachers of that day voiced their displeasure. They muttered, "This man welcomes sinners and eats with them." In the eyes of the Pharisees and teachers of the Law, publicans, who had sold themselves to the Roman government, and prostitutes, because of moral sin, had cut themselves off from Israel's religious community and were spiritually dead. Although they sought to gain converts, the teachers of the Law and the Pharisees were not interested in bringing such converts into meaningful relationship with God (Matt. 23:15). They were unable and unwilling to understand that God desired repentance, which, when shown, caused immense joy in heaven.

Jesus taught the parable of the prodigal son. Perhaps it would be better to speak of the two sons and their father. By means of these three characters, Jesus reflected the composition of his audience. Each person listening to Jesus had to look into the parabolic mirror and say, "That's me." The prodigal son portrayed the moral and social outcast, his brother the self-righteous Jew, and the father God.[1] Jesus addressed the members of his audience directly. He called the sinner to repentance and called the righteous to accept the sinner and to rejoice in his salvation.

The parable vividly depicts God's love toward his children, the wayward and the obedient. Jesus' contemporaries were fully acquainted with the fatherhood of God.[2] And from the prophecy of Jeremiah they knew that Israel had been the wayward son. Ephraim said,

Restore me, and I will return, because you are the LORD my God. After I strayed, I repented; after I came to understand, I beat my breast. I was ashamed and humiliated because I bore the disgrace of my youth.[3]

Jeremiah 31:18, 19

The Younger Son

Jesus told the story of a wealthy father who had two sons, presumably in their late teens. Both sons worked with their father on the family farm, but the younger of the two sons became restless and wanted to get away from parental supervision. He wanted to be free, to go to another country, and to live as he pleased.[4] His father had noticed the son's yearning to go abroad but had not said anything. He could have pointed to the son's position in life—he and his brother would inherit the entire farm someday. The son eventually would manage the farm, the servants, and the hired men. Instead, the father waited for the son to make his decision.

One day the younger son approached his father and said, "Father, give me my share of the estate." Of course, he could not ask for a division of the property because the family estate would remain intact as long as the father was alive. By asking for his share, the younger son confessed that he could not get along with his father, that he loathed the daily routine of work, and that he wanted to use the money he thought he was entitled to as he saw fit. The request was a mark of utter disrespect to the father whose death he implicitly desired. The younger son wanted his part of the inheritance before his father had died. And this was extremely unusual, although a landowner was free to give his children financial gifts at any time.[5] The father gave his son a share, possibly something like two-ninths of the total sum.[6] He would have received one-third of the inheritance at the time of his father's death (Deut. 21:17). But by receiving his share in advance, the son forfeited his claim to the estate when the inheritance provisions went into effect. And in addition he lost his name, standing, and prestige in the community in which he was raised. He was completely cut off and regarded as dead.[7] The father, although dividing the property, continued to manage the farm. Not the older son but the father was in control of the family estate.[8]

The younger son received his share and "got together all that he had." He was now on his own and free to go. His slogan was, "Have money; will travel." He could go to Babylon in the east, Asia Minor in the north, Greece and Italy in the west, or Egypt and Africa in the south. The world beckoned.

A number of factors emerged that had a profound influence on the future of the younger son. His youthful idealism, his inexperience and lack of discretion, his move from the farm to the urban areas, his possessions in ready cash available—all these played a significant role. His intentions to be on his own were soon thwarted when false friends surrounded him. Principles of life and conduct he had learned at home were put aside and forgotten. He was carefree and a spendthrift.[9] The older brother's remark—"this son of yours . . . squandered your property with prostitutes"—must be taken not as a truthful statement but as a slanderous accusation (v. 30). We have no proof that the younger son spent his days in immoral living. Transgression of economic as well as spiritual laws could not continue. He had to pay the price. And in a relatively short period of time he had spent everything. He had come to the end of the road.

The news of a crop failure made "headlines" in that country. Inflation caused prices to soar, jobs were at a premium, and the entire economy indicated that hard times had arrived. The wild-living youth was not only without money; he did not have a single friend to help him. In dire need he scoured city streets and countryside for employment, but all he could find was the lowly job of feeding pigs. He had now sunk to the very depth of degradation, for ever since early childhood days he had been taught as a Jew that a pig is an unclean animal (Lev. 11:7).[10] He was in the employ of a Gentile and thus had to forego any observance of the Sabbath. In this sad situation, he was cut off from the religion of his spiritual fathers.[11] He was desperate. His employer made him feel that pigs were of greater value than a lowly employee. He longed for human contact and consideration, but no one was concerned about him. Because of the famine, his daily food was insufficient to stave off the hunger pangs. He even longed to satisfy his needs by sharing the food given to the pigs, pods of the carob tree.[12] Lack of human concern for a hungry herdsman was more than the young man could take. For him it was the turning point. He had looked for human kindness and found none.

The news about the famine had trickled back to his homeland. He began to think about home. Would he return? When the thought first entered his mind he discarded it. The servants and the hired men would hardly be able to conceal their ridicule. His older brother would not take it at all kindly if he came home to an inheritance in which he no longer had a share. His father would see his second son barefoot and dressed in the simple clothes of a hired man; should he return home, he would be a picture of abject poverty. And last, in the community he would be mocked and scorned.

The son began to think about his father—how he had grieved him, how his father had provided him with the inheritance that he had squandered. He began to talk to himself. He said, "How many of my father's hired men have food to spare, and here I am starving to death!" He compared himself, not to the servants who were in steady employ but to the temporary help. Hired men, such as he was to his present employer, were living royally at his father's farm.

He knew that his father's love extended to all who belonged to the broad circle of his household. He also realized that he had transgressed the command, "Honor your father and your mother, so that you may live long in the land the Lord your God is giving you" (Exod. 20:12).[13] He had sinned against God.

When he came to his senses, he was ready to go home. He was ready to confess his sin to God and to his father. He said to himself, "I am going home and say to my father, 'I have sinned against God and against you.'"[14] He knew that he had transgressed God's commands and that by doing so he had wronged and grieved his father. He wanted to make amends. He was going to say to him, "Father, I am no longer worthy to be called your son; make me like one of your hired men." All he dared to ask for was to be employed as temporary help.[15] He yearned for reconciliation without seeking restoration. He got up and went home.

THE FATHER

Jesus introduced the parable by saying, "There was a man who had two sons." But as he continued, he showed that this man had an extraordinary relation to his sons: he loved them dearly, not possessively but wisely. We could have expected a father who was still relatively young to object vigorously to the younger son's outrageous request for a division of the property. The father could have refused to grant the request because no son would dare to ask his father to liquidate part of the parental estate and grant him his share of the inheritance. No argument took place, however. The father acknowledged the son's desire to be independent and, although it deeply offended him to yield to his son's importunity, he wisely kept this to himself.[16]

We may assume that the father had tried to find out where the son settled and what he was doing abroad. News about the famine certainly had reached him. He must have learned about the wretched conditions in which his son lived and which brought about his son's return, because he constantly looked down the road along which he expected him to return.

The question may be asked why the immediate relatives of the younger son had not contacted him when poverty degraded him. At the family farm they enjoyed affluence. It would have been thoughtful of them to send a care package to the son to alleviate his need. And the father could have sent a message inviting the son to return home. That would have been an expression of parental love.

But here is the contrast. The father did not seek out his son to bring him home. In the other two parables, the shepherd combed the hills to find the lost sheep, and the woman swept the floor to look for the lost coin. But the father stayed home. There is a difference between a sheep and a coin on the one hand and a son on the other. The only way for the shepherd to reclaim his sheep is to go out into the hills to find it. The only way for the woman to recover her coin is to sweep the floor. The father, however, has more than one option. The first is to visit the son and invite him to come home; but he has no guarantee that the son will accept the invitation. The second is to wait patiently and wisely for the son to come to his senses, so that he will confess his sin of his own accord and seek reconciliation. Then the father-son relationship is restored. Then the lost is found.[17]

Not the son but the father was in full control of the situation. The father looked in the direction from which he expected his son to return, and when he saw him his heart went out to him. Laying aside all dignity and decorum, he ran to meet his barefoot son dressed in rags. In oriental cultures it is a lack of self-respect for an affluent landowner to run, especially when this occurs in public view of the villagers. The son's parental home was not part of the farmland but was located in the village itself. Thus, when the son approached the community, he literally had to run the gauntlet of derision and denunciation. And if anyone could shield him from verbal and perhaps physical abuse, it was his father, who rushed toward him and provided protection.

The father threw his arms around his son and kissed him.[18] He accepted him as a member of the family before the son could so much as fall before him as a slave and kiss his feet, or bend the knee and kiss his father's hand. By embracing and kissing him, the father made it known to his son that he considered him his son. Therefore, when the young man wanted to utter his prepared speech and say that he would like to be employed as a hired man on his father's farm, he no longer could do so.[19] The father had ruled that out by kissing him and acknowledging him as his son. The son confessed his sin, "Father, I have sinned against heaven and against you. I am no longer worthy to be called your son." The young man spoke the truth. He was no longer worthy because of his past. He had forfeited every right to sonship. The father's love forces the son to let go of his carefully rehearsed plan to work for him as a hired man. The father accepted him as son, and this ended any thought of working on the farm as temporary help. The father determined that.

The long period of waiting had come to an end. The father had his son back. So it was time to celebrate. The father instructed the servants to bring the best robe and to put it on the son. They had to put a ring on his finger and sandals on his feet.[20] The son was highly honored by his father, for the best robe was always kept for very special guests. And the ring signified authority, so everyone could see that he was reinstated.[21] Of course, sandals were given him to indicate that he was a freeman. Slaves and the poor went barefoot. "Bring the fattened calf," said the father, "and kill it. Let's have a feast and celebrate." As the shepherd had called friends and neighbors together to celebrate the finding of the sheep, and the woman celebrated the recovery of her coin with friends and neighbors, so the father had the people make music and dance. All the members of his extended family, the servants, neighbors, friends, and acquaintances were invited to this festal occasion. Not a sheep but a fattened calf was slaughtered, which was sufficient to feed the entire community. It was time to celebrate and be happy. The purpose for the festivity was to reconcile the prodigal to all the villagers.[22]

"For this son of mine was dead and is alive again; he was lost and is found." The father referred to the fact that the son, by leaving the family estate and by terminating his material and moral obligations to his father, had cut himself off from the community. For all practical purposes, the son was dead.[23] In fact, he no longer had any claim to the property upon the death of his father. "Yet this son of mine," said the father, "returned home; he is alive again."

The parable does not teach how the legal aspects of inheritance rights were solved.[24] That is not the point. Of importance is the return of the young man, who is fully accepted as the father's son.

The Older Son

The parable of the prodigal son could have concluded with the words, "So they began to celebrate."[25] But then the introductory sentence, "There was a man who had two sons," would have had little or no significance. The story would be incomplete without further reference to the older son.

The father was not only the father of the younger son but also of the older. His firstborn had been a faithful son who took a personal interest in the farm. Of course, the son knew that he was the heir. He was out in the field when everyone else on the farm celebrated the return of his brother. He served his father well. And his father appreciated his son's diligence. As a father, he also knew the manifestations of envy, and that because of this envy the older son's attitude toward his brother was warped.

Why the older son was the last one to learn about his brother's return is not explained.[26] It could be that on that day he had gone to inspect the piece of land that was farthest from the home and that would cause him to return late in the evening. When he returned and heard the music and dancing, he asked one of the servants, "What's going on?" Within seconds he learned that his younger brother had come home and that his father had killed the fattened calf because he had his son back safe and sound.

If the older brother should enter the home, he would have to assume the role of the master of ceremonies according to the cultural rules of the time. This implied that he would have to mingle with the guests, monitor the supplies of food and beverages, and keep the celebration going throughout the evening and into the night.

The elder son refused to enter the house, because he simply could not understand why his father had to be so happy about the return of his good-for-nothing son.[27] And by repudiating cultural mores, he rebuffed his father and insulted him publicly. As the prodigal had insulted the father by asking him for the inheritance, so the older son offended him by staying away from the feast.

The elder son grumbled that no one ever expressed joy and happiness about him as the firstborn; no one ever had a party for the one who stayed home and served his father. So he would have nothing to do with his irresponsible brother, who upon his return had everybody running for him.

The father had gone out of the house to meet one son; he left the house again to meet the other. The first one received a welcome home, but so did the second. He treated both alike. However, the elder brother did not want equal treatment; he took it out on his father, humiliated him in public, even though the father continued to plead with him. The self-righteous son saw himself as a servant and not as a son. "All these years I've been slaving for you and never disobeyed your orders," he told his father. He did not understand what sonship meant and thus failed to see what fatherhood implied.[28] He accused his father of never giving him so much as a young goat in order to have a feast with his friends. For his spendthrift brother, by contrast, the fattened calf was killed. His words were sharp and bitter; he refused to address his father as "father" and to refer to his brother as "brother." Contemptuously he said, "This son of yours who has squandered your property with prostitutes comes home." Note, first, the absence of the title *father* in the address is meant as a deliberate affront. Next, to call his brother *this son of yours* is both a continuation of the offense to his father and a definitive break in family relations. Then he accuses his brother of squandering his father's property, but the misused money was inherited and rightfully belonged to his brother. And last, to denigrate his brother he imputes sexual immorality to him. With these words he grieved his father just as much as the prodigal son had done by his wild living. The elder brother separated himself just as far from the father as the younger had done. The one had come home; the father pleaded with the other to do likewise.

Both the elder and the younger were sons of the father, and the father addressed the elder son as tenderly as he had addressed the younger son. Said the father: "My son, you are always with me, and everything I have is yours."[29] The father taught his son the significance of sonship: to be always in the presence of the father as heir. The father, moreover, showed him the family relations of father to son and brother to brother. He was telling him, "Because you are my child, I am your father; and because the prodigal is my child, he is your brother."[30] As a family, said the father, "we had to celebrate and be glad, because this brother of yours was dead and is alive again; he was lost and is found."[31] The question of filial relationship was posed. Would the elder son, who had faithfully worked with his father on the family farm, stay with the father when he celebrated the return of the younger son? That was the question.

The parable ends on a refrain: "because this brother of yours was dead and is alive again, he was lost and is found." These words echo the words used at the conclusion of the section focusing on the younger son. The words link the brothers inseparably to each other and to the father.

Jesus did not say what the outcome was. He stopped purposely where he did. Had he shown the refusal of the elder son to enter the house, he would have closed the door. By leaving the story unfinished, he indicated that the door stood wide open. The father invited the son to participate in the festivities; the son had to decide. It was up to him.

APPLICATION

It was Jesus' intention to describe the attitude of the Pharisees and teachers of the Law toward tax collectors and prostitutes. He had been accused of welcoming such sinners and eating with them. He was made to understand that, should he associate with moral outcasts, he himself would be cut off. Jesus told this parable in which the father had the fattened calf killed and said, "Let's have a feast and celebrate." He wanted to show the Pharisees and teachers of the Law why he ate with tax collectors and prostitutes.

In the person of the prodigal son, Jesus' audience saw a picture of the moral outcasts of their day. The tax collectors and the "sinners" were Jews by nationality but, because of their occupation, the religious community had ostracized them. They were spiritually dead in the eyes of the law-abiding Jew. The prodigal son worked for a Gentile employer; so did the tax collector. The prodigal, however, came to his senses and returned to his parental home. Could the tax collector do likewise and return? The question Jesus put to his audience was this: "What happens when a tax collector or moral outcast repents?"

Jesus portrayed the love of the father for his sons in order to make it abundantly clear that God's love is infinite. His listeners recognized God in the person of the father. They knew that sin is always sin against God first and against fellowman second. How does God forgive a sinner and restore him as a member of his family? The father's attitude in the parable is representative of God's forgiving love toward a sinner who repents. As the father said to his servants, "Let's have a feast and celebrate," so God with his angels rejoices over one sinner who repents. And as in the parables of the lost sheep and the lost coin, all the friends and neighbors came together to celebrate, so in the parable of the prodigal son the elder brother is invited to celebrate and be glad.

The Pharisees and teachers of the Law could not escape the intended identification. Jesus pointed his finger at them through the character of the elder brother. However, Jesus did not accuse them in any way. By means of the parable he showed God's genuine love and care, not only toward the repentant sinner but also toward his obedient child. He asked the religious teachers of his day to celebrate and be glad when a moral and social outcast repents. He asked them to accept such a person in brotherly and sisterly love and to restore him or her to the religious community. Jesus presented the invitation, and the Pharisees and teachers of the Law had to make the decision.

The parable of the prodigal son proclaims the good news of the gospel. All those who have turned their backs on God, who consider the church old-fashioned and a permissive society up-to-date, will find a loving heavenly Father waiting for them the moment they return. There is a homecoming for them, because God is home.[32] Although repentance is a mystery, the Christian who has loved and obeyed God must rejoice and be glad when a sinner repents. For him are the words, "Child, you are always with me, and everything I have is yours." That is the message for righteous people who have fought battles for the Lord, who have toiled in the heat of the day, and who have kept the faith.

From an economic point of view, modern prodigals waste millions. Today's prodigals squander time and talents as if they are worthless. No wonder the righteous say, "Suppose these resources could have been used in spreading the gospel and the building of God's kingdom." No one can dispute this. But God is not interested in wasted time, talent, and energy—although he does not condone misuse and loss. God is interested in the salvation of human beings. And when a modern prodigal comes to his senses and turns to God, there is joy in heaven. As heaven rejoices, so the church must celebrate and be glad when the spiritually dead come to life and the lost are found. Proclaiming the gospel of salvation and seeing sinners come to a saving knowledge of Christ must be an endless celebration of life for believers.

Is this a story in which only the grace of God is revealed? Is the parable a story of Christianity without Christ?[33] The answer to these questions is that the parable must be seen in the context of Scripture. The Bible from beginning to end, from Adam and Eve's disobedience to the description of the multitudes surrounding the throne of the Lamb, is a running commentary on this parable.[34] It is Jesus who speaks of the Father's love, who opens the way to the Father's house, and who invites the sinners to come home. Jesus, who ate with social and moral outcasts (v. 1), welcomes repentant sinners to his Father's table and home.

34 Shrewd Manager

Luke 16:1–9

[1]Jesus told his disciples: "There was a rich man whose manager was accused of wasting his possessions. [2]So he called him in and asked him, 'What is this I hear about you? Give me an account of your management, because you cannot be manager any longer.'

[3]"The manager said to himself, 'What shall I do now? My master is taking away my job. I'm not strong enough to dig, and I'm ashamed to beg—[4]I know what I'll do so that, when I lose my job here, people will welcome me into their houses.'

[5]"So he called in each one of his master's debtors. He asked the first, 'How much do you owe my master?'

[6]"'Eight hundred gallons of olive oil,' he replied.

"The manager told him, 'Take your bill, sit down quickly, and make it four hundred.'

[7]"Then he asked the second, 'And how much do you owe?'

"'A thousand bushels of wheat,' he replied.

"He told him, 'Take your bill and make it eight hundred.'

[8]"The master commended the dishonest manager because he had acted shrewdly. For the people of this world are more shrewd in dealing with their own kind than are the people of the light. [9]I tell you, use worldly wealth to gain friends for yourselves, so that when it is gone, you will be welcomed into eternal dwellings."

Of all the parables Jesus taught, the parable of the shrewd manager is the most puzzling. For that reason, numerous interpretations have been given.[1] Each one is trying to explain the teaching of the parable in the light of its ethical implications. Questions that are asked include these: Did the lowering of the amounts the debtors owed reveal dishonesty, or was the manager dishonest all along, resulting in his dismissal? Should the parable end at verse 8a or at verse 9? Is Jesus condoning unethical

business practices? Some scholars explain the parable within a typical
Jewish setting that reflects Jewish practices. Thus the setting with all
its points must be reconstructed in order to gain a clear picture of the
teaching of the parable.[2] Others disagree and point out that the steward
was dishonest throughout his career. His master praised him for his
wisdom regarding his dishonesty. That is, the manager provided probable support for himself in view of his dismissal.[3] While discussing these
views, let us notice that their advocates must rely on suppositions to
explain this parable. But when hypotheses are used, obvious weaknesses
appear and inevitably diminish the weight of an interpretation. Let us
begin by looking at the setting and afterward consider the critique.

SETTING

Some scholars interpret the parable in the light of strict Jewish legal-
ism with respect to usury. They contend that an Israelite was repeatedly
told by God not to charge his Jewish fellowman interest on money, food,
or anything else that could earn interest. "If you lend money to one of
my people among you who is needy, do not be like a moneylender; charge
him no interest" (Exod. 22:25; also see Lev. 25:36; Deut. 15:8; 23:19).
God taught his people social responsibility and forbade usury. The implication was that a usurer was considered a robber.

Human nature being what it is, practices developed in the course of
time that were aimed at circumventing the Law of God. Rich people, for
example, would appoint a trustworthy person as a manager. Such a
manager was given full power to act in the name of his master. He was
responsible to his employer, but should he resort to usury, not the master but the manager could be brought to trial. At all times, a rich person stood to gain from the usurious transactions his manager negoti-
ated. Should such transactions be contested in court, the rich would go
free while the manager would have to pay the penalty.

The manager, however, was given ways to protect himself that even
the Pharisees and teachers of the Law condoned, and against which the
magistrate could do nothing except recognize them as necessary evils.
The manager and a borrower drew up a statement in which the debt
and interest were listed in one total figure. According to the religious
leaders, the following note revealed usury, and he who practiced it could
be brought to court: "I will pay Reuben 10 *kor* of wheat on the 1st day
of Nisan and if I do not, then I will pay 4 *kor* of wheat annually in addition."[4] But this note was considered legal: "I owe Reuben 14 *kor* of
wheat." What the note did not say was that the borrower had received
only 10 *kor* and had to pay the balance in interest.[5] For instance, in A.D.

33–34, Herod Agrippa I faced near bankruptcy and instructed his freedman Marsyas to borrow money from someone. Marsyas went to a banker who forced him to draw up a bond stating that he had received twenty thousand Attic drachmas. In reality, however, he received two thousand five hundred drachmas less.[6] The interest was added to the principal sum, and the borrower would have to pay the full amount even though he had received a considerably smaller amount.[7] The bond itself did not provide details.

Interest rates for borrowed wheat went as high as 20 percent, with an additional 5 percent for insurance against price fluctuations and depreciation of the value of the product. If the commodity happened to be olive oil, the interest rate was 80 percent plus 20 percent insurance cost, totaling 100 percent. The risk in lending olive oil was great. Olive crops are rather unpredictable and the value of olive oil, because of the size and quality of the olives, varies from year to year. Also, cheap oils extracted from other sources could be added to olive oil, and methods to determine its purity were inefficient.[8]

A manager was given a position of trust and confidence. He controlled his master's assets and was considered a member of his household. He represented his master and was given full authority to deal with debtors as he saw fit. Debtors, therefore, had to abide by the stipulations laid down by the manager. They were responsible to him alone.

Should the manager exhibit incompetence, inefficiency, or untrustworthiness, the master would summon him to give an account and afterward summarily dismiss him. The manager had no recourse to outside help. He would have to leave his master's employ with no possessions of his own, and he would not be welcomed by colleagues.[9]

Jesus related a story, which actually could have occurred, of a rich man who had appointed a manager to look after his business. He had placed complete confidence in this manager, but when he learned that the manager was wasting his possessions, he called him in and told him to get his books audited and to find other employment.

The manager knew that the charges brought against him were true, that he had abused his master's trust, and that he could not plead for mercy.[10] He knew that a successor would take his place. What did the future hold for the manager? He had to depend on his own ingenuity. He was not physically strong enough to do manual labor, and begging was out of the question.[11] He talked to himself, considering possibilities and alternatives. Suddenly he called out, "I've got it!" He knew what to do. He would make his master's debtors indebted to him, so that upon his departure they would welcome him into their homes.

He called in the debtors one by one. Two examples are given. The first came and the manager asked him how much he owed the master. He answered, "One hundred measures of oil." That was a sizable quantity of oil, amounting to 868 gallons or 3,946 liters.[12] One olive tree bears about 120 kilograms of olives or 25 liters of olive oil.[13] The amount of olive oil owed by the debtor would come from an orchard with some 150 trees or more. The manager told the debtor to take the bill, which stated the amount owed, and to reduce it by half.

The next debtor was asked the same question, "How much do you owe?" And his answer was, "One hundred measures of wheat." This is the equivalent of a thousand bushels, which corresponds to what one hundred acres yielded in that day.[14] The manager told him to take his bill and to reduce the amount by twenty measures. The rates between oil and grain fluctuated because of their respective values.

In both instances large sums of money were involved. Yet on the authority of the manager, who already had received notice of dismissal, they changed the figures on the bills. We may assume that other debtors did the same.

The debtors wrote out the amounts because they knew that the interest rate for borrowed olive oil was 100 percent and for borrowed wheat 25 percent. They gladly changed the totals to the amounts they actually owed the master. They did not falsify figures; rather, in their own handwriting they indicated how much they had to pay. In short, because the usurious rates were lifted, honesty prevailed.

When the manager presented the books to his master, who subsequently learned about the altered transactions, he was praised because he had acted shrewdly.[15] The manager was in control of the situation, not the master. Words of praise were conveyed because the manager had assured himself the hospitality and generosity of the debtors, and had paved the way for his successor by removing any ill will on the part of the debtors. And he had given his master an opportunity to praise him for removing the usurious rates and to show himself as a religious and law-abiding citizen. The manager must have placed the master in a most favorable light if he spoke words of praise.[16]

CRITIQUE

Scholars favoring the view that the manager had been dishonest all along object to the above-mentioned interpretation of the word *dishonest*. They say that if the term describes the manager's actions toward the debtors, the clause "because he had acted shrewdly" would then be a contradiction.[17] The rebuttal is that this term characterizes the manager's earlier life when he squandered his master's possessions. The characterization is the same as that for the unjust judge, who in the course of time had established a reputation for being unjust. When he spoke justice in behalf of the widow, he certainly did not do her an injustice.[18] Likewise the manager, because of his previous career of shady deals, is called dishonest, even though the instructions he later gave the debtors were honorable and praiseworthy in the eyes of the public. The master could not go to the debtors and apply the usurious rates earlier transacted by the manager, for then he would be a usurer who could be brought to justice. The master praised the manager for his shrewdness.

Nonetheless, we must allow for the view that the debtors assumed the master had approved the transaction of reducing the amounts they owed. The debtors were told by the steward to lower the amounts, the one by 50 percent and the other by 20 percent. Changes like these were not at all unusual when partial crop failures struck due to weather or insects.[19] The debtors who supposed that the master had ordered these changes expressed their thanks to the manager. However, when the master learned what had transpired, he was unable to rectify the situation, namely, to demand full payment from the creditors and jail the manager. Thus, he resorted to publicly praising the ex-manager not for his dishonesty but for his sagacity.

Another objection is that first-century Jews who were actively engaged in international commerce were unable to abide by the Old Testament rule not to charge interest on loans. If we think of the large quantities of olive oil (868 gallons or 3,946 liters) and wheat (1,000 bushels), we see the master dealing with either wide-ranging traders or leaseholders of extensive fields. They no longer adhered to the rule of charging no interest.[20] Further, in those days the interest rate for wheat was 50 percent; even lower rates were known.[21] However, it is difficult to determine the exact lending practices of first-century Israel and to what extent Jewish moneylenders observed concomitant legal aspects.[22]

Explanations of this scenario can be multiplied, but because the details given in the parable are limited an interpreter is forced to resort to speculation. These points can be stated with certainty. First, the manager handled money that did not belong to him. Next, the time of his dismissal had come and he was facing poverty. Third, by acting shrewdly he befriended his master's creditors and looked to them for financial help in the near future. And last, although the master had his own reservations about his manager, he gave him credit for his astute business transactions.[23]

APPLICATION

What precisely does the parable mean? The story of the dishonest manager, clarified in the light of the original Jewish setting, still conveys a message that is relevant today. What, then, is that message?[24] Jesus summed it up in a rather comprehensive statement by saying, "For the people of this world are more shrewd in dealing with their own kind than are the people of the light. I tell you, use worldly wealth to gain friends for yourselves, so that when it is gone, you will be welcomed into eternal dwellings" (v. 9).[25] Is verse 8 or verse 9 the end of the parable? Most translations correctly show a paragraph break at verse 8, but the next verse is its conclusion. Jesus uses the phrase "I tell you," which occurs at the close of many parables (e.g., Luke 18:14). A related question is whether Jesus is condoning unethical business practices. The answer is no because the parable teaches a lesson.

The point of the parable is that the manager, who had gained a reputation of being dishonest and who realized that his future was at stake, sought approval by being charitable to his master's debtors. He did not cling to worldly wealth but generously gave it to those who were indebted to his master. Nevertheless, the money that he liberally gave to the debtors was not his, and in a sense not even his master's. Likewise the people of the light should not set their heart on worldly possessions. They can afford to be generous and give some of their assets away. They can afford to do so because these assets do not belong to them but to God. When they donate money to the poor they are redistributing the wealth God has entrusted to them.[26] Jesus put the same truth in these words, "Do not store up for yourselves treasures on earth . . . but store up for yourselves treasures in heaven" (Matt. 6:19, 20). And what Jesus taught finds its roots in many forms and ways in the teaching of the Old Testament. David in the presence of God's people prayed, "But who am I, and who are my people, that we should be able to give as generously as this? Everything comes from you, and we have given you only what comes from your hand" (1 Chron. 29:14). By means of the parable of the shrewd manager, Jesus counsels his followers to give their money away and be generous, so that they may gain God's favor and be welcomed to live in his house eternally.[27] Note the parallel of verse 4, "I know what I'll do so that, when I lose my job here, people will welcome me into their houses."

A point of contrast, although not expressed, is implied here. Indirectly Jesus says: the dishonest manager, by reducing the amounts his master's debtors owed, looked to the future; how much more should God's people share their possessions and look toward their eternal home. God's people must use their earthly possessions for spiritual investments just as worldly people use their money to obtain material gains. The time comes when money is a thing of the past. When death comes, man's spirit returns to God who gave it (Eccles. 12:7). God welcomes all his people who have not set their hearts on earthly treasures but have gathered treasures in heaven.[28]

The people of the world know how to use worldly possessions and apply materialistic ways. At times they show remarkable shrewdness in handling financial assets. On the other hand, Christians who have learned the standard of God's Law are often inclined to relax and modify Christian principles. They want the best of two worlds: they want to have the Christian faith couched in the comfort of an affluent society; they want to be loved by God and at the same time be praised by man. Jesus said, "The people of this world are more shrewd in dealing with their own kind than are the people of the light." If the people who do not profess to serve God live by the standards of the world, should not those who profess to be his people uphold the Law of God and live by divine standards? Should they not practice what they preach, and show by word and deed that money will ultimately fail but heavenly riches will last forever? In his pastoral letter, James admonishes Christians who opt for a double life. "You adulterous people, don't you know that friendship with the world is hatred toward God? Anyone who chooses to be a friend of the world becomes an enemy of God" (James 4:4).

35 Rich Man and Lazarus

> **Luke 16:19–31**
>
> [19]"There was a rich man who was dressed in purple and fine linen and lived in luxury every day. [20]At his gate was laid a beggar named Lazarus, covered with sores [21]and longing to eat what fell from the rich man's table. Even the dogs came and licked his sores.
>
> [22]"The time came when the beggar died and the angels carried him to Abraham's side. The rich man also died and was buried. [23]In hell, where he was in torment, he looked up and saw Abraham far away, with Lazarus by his side. [24]So he called to him, 'Father Abraham, have pity on me and send Lazarus to dip the tip of his finger in water and cool my tongue, because I am in agony in this fire.'
>
> [25]"But Abraham replied, 'Son, remember that in your lifetime you received your good things, while Lazarus received bad things, but now he is comforted here and you are in agony. [26]And besides all this, between us and you a great chasm has been fixed, so that those who want to go from here to you cannot, nor can anyone cross over from there to us.'
>
> [27]"He answered, 'Then I beg you, father, send Lazarus to my father's house, [28]for I have five brothers. Let him warn them, so that they will not also come to this place of torment.'
>
> [29]"Abraham replied, 'They have Moses and the Prophets; let them listen to them.'
>
> [30]"'No, father Abraham,' he said, 'but if someone from the dead goes to them, they will repent.'
>
> [31]"He said to him, 'If they do not listen to Moses and the Prophets, they will not be convinced even if someone rises from the dead.'"

The parable of the shrewd manager and that of the rich man and Lazarus have a few things in common. First, a most obvious point: the introductory clause of the two parables is identical: "There was a rich man . . ." Second, the teaching of the parable of the shrewd manager is the admonition not to store up treasures on earth but in heaven. This is also one of the themes in the parable of the rich man and Lazarus. And third, the two parables present the call to repent before it is too late. They challenge the listener to turn to the teaching of God's Law in regard to the use of wealth, the exercise of honesty and respect, and the application of mercy and love.

The parable of the rich man and Lazarus may be viewed as a drama in two acts followed by a conclusion. The first scene is a presentation of life and death on earth, and the second portrays heaven and hell. The conclusion is given in the form of implicit application.

The Here and Now

Jesus told a vivid story of a rich man and a poor man.[1] The rich man was dressed in the purple garments worn by kings;[2] his underwear was made of fine Egyptian linen. Day after day he spent his time at banquets, for he did not have to work. He spent his life feasting. Yet in spite of all his wealth, the man is not known by name.[3] All we know is that he had five brothers who, like himself, showed a habitual disregard for the revealed Word of God.

The second person introduced in the story lived on the other end of the economic spectrum, in abject poverty. Moreover, he could not even walk. His friends had to carry him about and prop him up near the gate of the rich man's mansion. Because of a lack of medical care and personal hygiene, he suffered from a skin disease and was covered with sores. His body had wasted away, hunger was his constant companion, and his longing eyes were focused on the scraps of food that had been swept from the dining room floor[4] and were distributed to dogs and beggars outside. This human wretch had no companions other than the dogs that came to lick his sores. Although he went through life as a nobody, he had a name. He was called Lazarus, the abbreviated form of Eleazar, which means "God helps."[5]

Both men were Jews, but the rich man ignored God's commands to care for his poverty-stricken fellow Jew. The rich man could not be totally ignorant of the Scriptures, for the teachers of the Law diligently instructed the people in the divine precepts. Besides, the rich man had become acquainted with Lazarus and even knew him by name. The poor man who never complained and never addressed the rich man, trusted in God, his helper.

Death came and put an end to Lazarus's suffering. His body, which was nothing but skin and bones, was quickly removed. Because there was no one to show or to receive sympathy, his funeral was not even worth mentioning. But Lazarus was not alone in death. God's angels came to take him to the place of honor in heaven. He was seated next to Abraham, where he might enjoy a messianic banquet.[6]

The rich man also died. His life of ease, luxury, comfort, pleasure, and pomp suddenly ended. Perhaps he suffered a heart attack. The funeral of the rich man was elaborate. His five brothers took care of all the arrangements. Flute players and mourners came, and all his friends were in attendance. The deceased had lived in luxury; he was buried in luxury. But all those who came to mourn the death of the rich man could not see beyond the grave. They continued to think of him as the rich man, although now departed.[7] While Lazarus was taken by angels to Abraham's side, the rich man without his earthly possessions entered hell.

The Then and There

Everything changed at the moment of death. Lazarus was given a place of highest honor next to the father of believers. Angels had brought him to Abraham's side, where he would enjoy the company of God's people. The rich man, who on earth was surrounded by friends, no longer bore the name *rich* in hell. Stripped of all his wealth, he was alone.

On the other side of the grave, Lazarus remained silent toward the rich man, although understandably he conversed with Abraham. It was Abraham who answered the rich man's requests. Not Lazarus but Abraham instructed the rich man in the realities of eternal destinies. The rich man was in torment, while Lazarus enjoyed the pleasure of Abraham's company. The torment of hell involved extreme thirst and the agony of fire.[8]

The rich man in hellish torment saw Abraham in the distance with Lazarus next to him.[9] He recognized Abraham, the father of believers, and as a Jew he acknowledged him as his father. He desired to have this kinship count, although he was much more a physical than a spiritual son of Abraham. Even in hell he did not seem to realize that his utter neglect of God's commands on earth had ended any claim to spiritual heritage.[10] In his lifetime he himself had severed the spiritual ties with Abraham by ignoring the needs of his fellowman. Instead of loving his neighbor as himself, he had lived neither for God nor his fellowman but for himself. He had pursued the goal of self-gratification. And now in hell he was left to himself.

The rich man did not find himself in hell because he had lived wickedly on earth.[11] His many relatives and friends could testify that he had been a prominent citizen and that in entertaining guests he had proved to be a most generous host. They could speak of him in glowing words of praise and commendation. However, the rich man did not deserve hellish torment for what he had done in his life on earth but for what he had failed to do. He had neglected to love God and the neighbor. He had disregarded God and his Word.

Even in hell, the rich man remained unrepentant. He did not appeal to God for mercy but to Abraham. He called Abraham his father and expected the patriarch to have pity on one of his descendants.[12] He instructed Abraham on how to show mercy and send relief: "Send Lazarus to dip the tip of his finger in water and cool my tongue." He had put aside conceit because he would readily avail himself of the services of a former beggar, if possible. Yet his tone of voice implied that he considered Lazarus to be a servant who could be sent at his call with the approval of Abraham. On earth the rich man never helped Lazarus; in hell, however, he expressed a need for human help. He recognized Lazarus, yet did not address him directly. He wanted Abraham to send Lazarus as a humble servant who would readily respond to the bidding of the rich man. In a sense, he acted as if he were still on earth.

While Lazarus enjoyed heavenly pleasures, presumably in the setting of a flowing stream, the rich man suffered the burning agony of hellish fire.[13] He cried out for water to cool his tongue, and saw that Lazarus had access to it. On earth Lazarus longed to still his hunger with the crumbs that fell from the rich man's table but had nothing. In hell the rich man longed for a drop of water to cool his tongue but received no comfort.[14]

Abraham addressed the rich man as "son," by which he acknowledged only the physical relationship. Even this relationship could not bring the man relief for two reasons: (1) the law of retribution, and (2) the irrevocability of God's verdict. First, the law of retribution stipulated that a man's earthly life in words and deeds stood in direct relation to his fate in the next life. The rich man had chosen a lifetime of good things on earth; in hell he suffered agony. Lazarus, by contrast, spent his lifetime in misery, but enjoyed the comforts of heaven afterward. Second, God's irrevocable judgment was confirmed by the unbridgeable chasm fixed between heaven and hell. No one could go from heaven to hell or vice versa.[15] God had pronounced judgment without the possibility of appeal. The die was cast at the moment of death.

Lazarus entered heaven and the rich man entered hell. And between the two places God had fixed a great chasm, making it impossible to pass from one state to the other.[16]

The rich man realized the permanency of his state. His own lot was fixed, but that of his five brothers on earth was not. They could still change their way of life and thus avoid spending eternity in hell. Once more he called Abraham "father," and once more he wanted to use Lazarus as his servant. He begged Abraham to send Lazarus to his father's house to warn his five brothers, so that they would not come to the place of torment to which he had come. He was fully aware of the great chasm between heaven and hell, but he thought that someone could readily go from heaven to earth. He was of the opinion that Abraham had authority to send Lazarus who could be an eyewitness and testify to them. Somehow he realized that he himself could not leave hell to return to earth. He had to stay where he was.[17]

During his life on earth, as well as during the discourse the rich man conducted with Abraham, Lazarus remained silent. Not a word came from his lips about the rich man's audacity in telling Abraham what to do. It was Abraham whom the rich man addressed, and it was Abraham who responded.

Abraham refused to grant the five brothers of the rich man a sign from heaven. He did not allow even a semblance of the occult. God's revelation had been given and that was sufficient for salvation. Abraham told the rich man that his father's household had access to the five books of Moses and all the prophetic books. That is, they had the Old Testament Scriptures. "Let them listen to them."

The rich man knew that his father and his brothers did not take the Scriptures seriously. His five unmarried brothers were still at home with their father (five is a round number) and lived a life similar to that of the rich man on earth. It was not the riches they enjoyed that caused the rich man concern[18] but their disregard for the Scriptures. A third time he called Abraham "father," assuring him that his father and brothers would repent if someone would rise from the dead and go to them. He no longer asked that Lazarus be sent. Anyone would do.

Abraham replied that someone risen from the dead would not be able to tell them God's revelation any more plainly than they had been told in the Scriptures. If a man rejects the written Word of God, he will not be brought to repentance by someone risen from the dead. King Saul saw Samuel brought up by the witch of Endor, yet he did not repent (1 Sam. 28:7–25). And the Pharisees saw Lazarus, the brother of Mary and Martha, come forth from the grave. They did not repent but instead tried to kill him (John 12:10).[19] Use of the name *Lazarus* in the parable and in the raising of Lazarus at Bethany is striking. The question is asked whether this use can be regarded as coincidental.[20] However, because the precise historical setting in which the parable was told is lacking, an attempt to link it to the resurrection account of Lazarus in Bethany, although well meant, is hardly convincing. On the other hand, the resurrection of Lazarus and the resurrection of Jesus indicate unmistakably that those who refuse the testimony of God's revelation "will not be convinced even if someone rises from the dead."

APPLICATION

The parable of the rich man and Lazarus is devoid of an introduction and lacks a specific conclusion. The parable as such could have been told anytime during Jesus' earthly ministry. But because Luke has recorded the parable as a sequel to the parable of the shrewd manager, and because he reveals the reaction of the Pharisees to Jesus' teaching, "You cannot serve both God and Money" (Luke 16:13), we may assume that the Pharisees were present when Jesus sketched the story of the rich man and Lazarus.[21] The Pharisees were the most likely to have heard the parable. The immediate context shows that because they loved money they sneered at Jesus (Luke 16:14). Also because they justified themselves in the eyes of men, as Jesus said, they were self-righteous (Luke 16:15). God, however, knew their hearts. Jesus saw the inconsistency in their lives and taught a story of a man who loved money, lived in luxury, and thought that being a descendant of Abraham guaranteed salvation. The content of the parable relates to comments addressed to the Pharisees on such vices as love of money and self-righteousness.[22]

In the broader context of the series of parables recorded by Luke, these questions ought to be posed: Whom do the rich man and Lazarus represent? Why did Jesus not tell a story of a rich tax collector and a poor teacher of the Law? The Pharisees regarded the tax collectors as "sinners" who had run the risk of forfeiting the claim to being sons of Abraham and belonging to God's covenant people. The characters Jesus portrays in the parable, however, are two men, the one rich and the other poor. The rich man lived a respectable life, called Abraham his father, and spent eternity in hell. The poor man never opened his mouth on earth or in heaven, yet he occupied the seat of honor next to father Abraham.

The Pharisees were able to recognize themselves in the rich man. They had reacted adversely and vehemently to Jesus' remark that they could not serve both God and money. By sneering at Jesus, they ostensibly revealed that they were the ones who loved money. Also, they were the ones who readily called Abraham their father and thought that their relationship to the patriarch secured their future. The rich man called Abraham his father three times. But Abraham, although admitting the physical descent by calling him "son" the first time, made clear in subsequent answers that a physical relationship was insufficient.[23] Therefore, the Pharisees were unable to count on mere physical descent from Abraham to guarantee them a place in heaven.

Furthermore, the Pharisees were the ones who taught the law of retribution in regard to the future life. This doctrine simply does not fit the teaching of Jesus.[24] It is foreign to him. But Jesus put the doctrine of the Pharisees in the mouth of Abraham. "Son, remember that in your lifetime you received your good things, while Lazarus received bad things, but now he is comforted here and you are in agony." Jesus applied the law of retribution to the Pharisees, who heard their own theology from the lips of Abraham. They were the ones who had created a great chasm between themselves and the social and moral outcasts of society. These outcasts lived in utter religious and economic poverty. No one in the Jewish community would provide them spiritual food; they were consigned to starvation. Should anyone ever question the Pharisees' attitude toward these outcasts, he would be told that they had Moses and the Prophets, let them listen to the Law and repent. The Pharisees heard their own remarks, distinct and direct, from Abraham. They were the ones depicted by the rich man in hell, while Lazarus represented the outcasts.

Encountering Jesus, the Pharisees on more than one occasion had asked him to give them a sign from heaven.[25] They had asked him this for the purpose of testing him; they probably would not have believed him even if he gave them a supernatural sign. Now these Pharisees heard the rich man in the parable ask Abraham for a sign from heaven. But Abraham refused his request. He said, "If they do not listen to Moses and the Prophets, they will not be convinced even if someone rises from the dead." In the rich man's request the Pharisees heard the echo of their own words. The parable was addressed to them.[26]

CONCLUSION

The lesson Jesus taught is timeless: it is the abiding rule of listening to God's Word obediently and thankfully. Scripture teaches us to love the Lord our God with all our heart, soul, and mind, and to love our neighbor as ourselves. This love ought to be materially expressed in cheerfully giving our gifts to the Lord and to our needy neighbors (Ps. 112:9; 2 Cor. 9:7). Also, it should be shown spiritually, first, by growing "in the grace and knowledge of our Lord and Savior Jesus Christ" (2 Peter 3:18) and, second, by teaching our neighbor to "know the Lord" (Jer. 31:34; Heb. 8:11).

The rich are truly rich if they share their material and spiritual blessings with the needy. Indeed they are poverty-stricken if they keep these blessings to themselves. Anyone who gathers material wealth selfishly suffers spiritual bankruptcy. Likewise, any church that fails to evangelize dies a spiritual death.

Christians in affluent societies cannot close their eyes and ears to the needs of the poor in Africa, Asia, and Latin America. By means of the news media, they find the needy lying at their door. These are the needy who have both a physical and a spiritual hunger, who long for the food that falls from the rich man's table.

Scripture nowhere teaches that being rich is sinful. Repeatedly, however, it warns God's people that riches may be a trap and temptation "that plunge men into ruin and destruction" (1 Tim. 6:9). When man relegates God and man's needy neighbors to a secondary place, and Scripture to willful neglect, his responsible answer to the call to repent may never come.[27]

The parable, therefore, sounds a note of urgency for man to listen to God's Word wisely and obediently. It directs him away from dabbling in the occult; it calls him to repentance and faith; it tells him that he is living in a period of grace; it instructs him to put aside self-righteousness; and it reminds him that man's destiny is irrevocably sealed at the time of death. Concisely, the parable reiterates the words of the psalmist, "Today, if you hear his voice, do not harden your hearts" (Ps. 95:7, 8).

36 Farmer and Servant

Luke 17:7–10

⁷"Suppose one of you had a servant plowing or looking after the sheep. Would he say to the servant when he comes in from the field, 'Come along now and sit down to eat'? ⁸Would he not rather say, 'Prepare my supper, get yourself ready and wait on me while I eat and drink; after that you may eat and drink'? ⁹Would he thank the servant because he did what he was told to do? ¹⁰So you also, when you have done everything you were told to do, should say, 'We are unworthy servants; we have only done our duty.'"

In the workaday world of Western society, the parable of the farmer and his servant seems somewhat out of place. Labor disputes of one kind or another are the order of the day. Higher wages and fewer hours on the job are some of the demands made by the labor force. Also, an employee working in one sector of the job market cannot readily cross over into another sector. Each worker must do the job for which he has been hired.

The parable Jesus tells reveals an aspect of the employer-employee relationship of his day. Although the actual setting belongs to another age, the application of the parable is timeless. The message conveyed in this little vignette of first-century agricultural life has abiding validity and is relevant today.

"Suppose," Jesus says, "one of you has a servant whom you had put to work plowing a field or tending sheep. Would you welcome him to the table at the end of the day and invite him to sit down and eat the food you had to prepare? Would you not rather put the servant to work in the kitchen and tell him to prepare supper for you, to wait on you while you eat and drink, and to have his own supper after you are finished? And when the servant has done what you told him, do you thank him? Of course not!" "Likewise," Jesus continues, "when you have done everything God has told you to do, you will have to agree that you are nothing but servants who have only done your duty."[1]

The context of the parable is the cold, impersonal relationship of the ancient world in which a slave was expected to obey whatever his master told him to do. If the owner instructed the servant to plow the field during the day and to prepare supper upon returning home, he merely obeyed because he knew that this was his task. It was as simple as that. And for doing his task the slave did not receive a "thank-you," for it was not customary to thank slaves.

What is Jesus saying in this parable? He wants his followers to know what it means to be a servant. His own disciples, who lived in a religious climate of merits and demerits, argued more than once as to which of them would be the greatest in the kingdom of heaven.[2] Jesus had to teach them: "If anyone wishes to be first, he must be the very last, and the servant of all" (Mark 9:35). He himself set the example when he washed his disciples' feet (John 13:1–17) and, after the institution of the Lord's Supper, instructed them to be servants: "the greatest among you should be like the youngest, and the one who rules like the one who serves. For who is greater, the one who is at the table or the one who serves? Is it not the one who is at the table? But I am among you as one who serves" (Luke 22:26, 27).[3]

Constantly Jesus had to teach his disciples not to work in God's kingdom for the sake of rewards. God does not employ his servants in order to reward them for their services. No servant can ever say, "God is indebted to me." God does not buy services like an employer buying the time and skills of an employee. And because God does not enter into an employer-employee relationship, no one can ever put a claim on God for services rendered.[4]

To give his disciples a perspective on the meaning of servanthood, Jesus told the parable of the farmer and his slave. The farmer could make far-reaching claims on the time and skills of his servant. He could do this justifiably for his own benefit and pleasure. If this is true for the farmer and his servant, Jesus intimated, how much more is it true for God's servants[5] who have been called to love and serve God with heart, soul, mind, and strength? If God tells his servants to be holy for he is holy, then no one can come to him and expect a reward for labors performed. No one can claim a word of appreciation from him for doing his duty. If God grants favors and gives rewards, he does so out of grace and not because of merit.

37 Unjust Judge

Luke 18:1–8

¹Then Jesus told his disciples a parable to show them that they should always pray and not give up. ²He said: "In a certain town there was a judge who neither feared God nor cared about men. ³And there was a widow in that town who kept coming to him with the plea, 'Grant me justice against my adversary.'

⁴"For some time he refused. But finally he said to himself, 'Even though I don't fear God or care about men, ⁵yet because this widow keeps bothering me, I will see that she gets justice, so that she won't eventually wear me out with her coming!'"

⁶And the Lord said, "Listen to what the unjust judge says. ⁷And will not God bring about justice for his chosen ones, who cry out to him day and night? Will he keep putting them off? ⁸I tell you, he will see that they get justice, and quickly. However, when the Son of Man comes, will he find faith on the earth?"

This parable is also known as the parable of the persistent woman. It is a companion to the one on the friend at midnight (Luke 11:5–8). Luke presents the two as similar accounts: one about a man, the other about a woman. (This parable is found only in Luke.) Although it appears somewhat detached from the context, the conclusion, "However, when the Son of Man comes, will he find faith on the earth?"(18:8), connects it with the eschatological teaching of the preceding chapter (17:20–37). In addition, the subject of prayer surfaces in the parable of the Pharisee and the publican (Luke 18:9–14), which immediately follows.

WIDOW AND JUDGE

Only two people assume leading roles: the widow and the judge. The widow's adversary is only mentioned in passing. The companion parable of the friend at midnight likewise shows two leading characters, the host and the neighbor, while the traveler, again, is a person mentioned only in passing.

Widows in Israel seem to have experienced great difficulty; the numerous protective laws indicate that oppression and hardship were their lot. God himself defends the cause of the widow (Deut. 10:18) and places a curse upon the man who withholds justice from her (Deut. 27:19). The widow took the place of her deceased husband and in court was considered equal to a man: "Any vow or obligation taken by a widow or divorced woman will be binding on her" (Num. 30:9). Anyone wishing to deprive the widow of her rights would have to face God, the defender of widows (Ps. 68:5).

Nevertheless, widows were mistreated. The prophet Isaiah complains that the rulers of the land are rebels and thieves. "They do not defend the cause of the fatherless; the widow's case does not come before them" (Isa. 1:23). And Malachi states that God will be quick to testify against those who oppress the widow and the fatherless (Mal. 3:5).

Jesus tells his disciples about a widow in a certain town who has no one to support her against an adversary except an unjust judge.[1] Her adversary does not even have to appear in court, which may indicate that the issue was a money matter. She cannot afford the services of a lawyer. Instead she goes directly to the judge and wants him to be both her lawyer and her judge.[2]

Instead of going to a community court, she goes to a worldly judge of ill repute.[3] This judge is devoid of religious principles and immune to public opinion. He lacks any shame in the sight of the community and is devoid of morals and scruples.[4] He simply could not care less what God or man says. To such a judge the widow goes. Details are lacking, for we are not told how old the woman is,[5] whether she is rich or poor, and why she goes to a judge who "neither feared God nor cared about men."

As a widow she is a picture of vulnerability. Her only recourse is to take her case to the judge with the plea, "Grant me justice against my adversary." The phrase "grant me justice" is legal language and really means "take up my case," or "help me to justice."[6]

The widow asks the judge to help her in spite of the judge's reputation of disregard toward such requests. True to form, the judge refuses to act. He probably dismisses the widow by sending her home with the customary remark, "Next case, please."

The only weapon the woman has is to go to the judge day after day with the same request, "Grant me justice against my adversary." The widow is getting on the judge's nerves, so that he talks to himself and says, "Even though I don't fear God or care about men, yet because this widow keeps bothering me, I will see that she gets justice, so that she won't eventually wear me out with her coming!" He does not fear any physical action;[7] rather, her persistence is getting the best of him. Instead of quietly going away, which he had expected, she returns to him with the same plea. The judge cannot take any more of this persistent woman. He relents, investigates her case, and executes justice.

APPLICATION

In the parable of the unjust judge, Jesus is more specific than in the one of the friend at midnight. In fact, the interpretation and application of the message of the parable in Luke 11:5–8 must be gleaned from the general context, while the parable of the unjust judge contains both the message and the application.

Says Jesus, "Listen to what the unjust judge says."[8] He wants the disciples to pay close attention to the very words of the judge. They are important for a correct understanding of the parable. As in the parable of the friend at midnight, Jesus used the rule of contrasts. He contrasts the worst in man to the best in God: "This is what the unjust judge says and does. What do you think God does in regard to his chosen ones who cry to him day and night?" In other words, no one should picture God as an unmovable deity comparable to the earthly judge of the parable. The meaning is that if this surly judge, who by his own admission listened to neither God nor man, gave in to the widow's plea, how much more will God do justice for his own people who pray to him day and night? (Incidentally, this is the question that Islam puts to Christianity: Why did not God do justice to his great prophet Jesus by letting him die on a cross? The answer to that question is that God has manifested his justice by raising Jesus to life eternal as the forerunner of all God's people.)[9]

Moreover, no relationship exists between the widow and the judge, whether it be social, communal, or religious. The judge wants to be rid of her so that even the lawyer-client relationship will end. And yet this unscrupulous judge listens to this widow and does her justice. By contrast, God has chosen his own people. He has a special interest in them because they belong to him.[10] When his people cry to him day and night, God takes up their case and brings about justice. Thus, should the widow cry out to God, she would receive justice, because God hears and answers prayer.[11] The judge listened to the widow for the wrong reason: to get her off his back. God listens to his people because he loves them and vindicates their cause. The judge acts selfishly; God acts in behalf of his people.

Must God's people pray continually? The parable indicates that they should continually bring their cause before God in prayer. They should always pray and not become weary when an answer is not immediately given. Jesus teaches the power of prayer. By word and example he demonstrates that God's children must pray day and night and not lose heart. Likewise, Paul in his Epistles repeatedly refers to praying continually (night and day) and most earnestly, for example, with regard to his desire to be with the church at Thessalonica (1 Thess. 3:10).

If God's people cry to him day and night, why does he at times delay in answering?[12] Jesus continues, "Will he keep putting them off?" And the implied answer to this rhetorical question is: of course not. He may keep his people waiting, he may exercise their patience, he may strengthen their faith, but at the proper time God will answer the prayers of his people.[13]

God is not like the unjust judge who refused to listen to the widow's plea. God may keep his people waiting, but justice will be meted out and that right quickly: "I tell you, he will see that they get justice, and quickly." On the surface, it appears that Jesus utters a contradiction of sorts. But this is not at all the case if we pose two simple questions and supply the answers. First, will God bring about justice for his people? The answer is: of course he will. God's people can rely on God's faithfulness. He is not like the unjust judge whose character could not be trusted. And second, must God's people wait long before their prayers are answered? In contrast to the judge, God is not annoyed when his people cry out to him day and night. The hearing of prayers is not to be understood as God's relenting from a set determination not to answer. Rather, God answers prayer in his time and in accordance with his plan.[14] And when that time is near, prayer is answered speedily. God does not delay at all, for his ear is attuned to the voice of his children. The time of waiting in periods of distress may seem long, but afterward when God's people see their prayers answered and see the design of God's plan, they admit that God exercised justice in their behalf without delay.[15]

Jesus concludes the application of the parable by calling attention to his return: "However, when the Son of Man comes, will he find faith on the earth?" The statement at first seems unrelated to the preceding. But in the last part of the previous chapter Luke has recorded the teaching of Jesus on the coming of the Son of Man in the last day.[16]

By referring to his second coming, Jesus links the concept of justice to the day of judgment in which he is the judge of the living and the dead (Acts 10:42). Jesus reminds his followers of the day of his return. Will he at that time find simple, childlike faith?

The return of the Son of Man cannot be called into question; that event will be fulfilled in God's appointed time. Of Jesus' promise to return, the believer can be sure. The other side of the coin is whether the believer will be faithful in his prayers. Will the follower of Jesus continually pray for the coming of God's kingdom (Matt. 6:10; Luke 11:2) and the return of Christ (1 Cor. 16:22; Rev. 22:17, 20)? Jesus fulfills and eventually completes his redemptive work through the body of believers of which he is the head. Jesus does the work entrusted to him. But will a believer be faithful to Jesus by constantly communicating with him in prayer? And will there be faith that perseveres when he returns?

In a way, the persistent widow is a picture of the church in prayer.[17] The world oppresses the followers of Jesus, who have nowhere to turn but to God. They wait in prayerful expectation upon God's intervention in the knowledge that he will honor their request. The similarity between the persistent host who called his neighbor out of bed and the widow who kept coming back to the judge is clear. Both had nowhere else to go. Both knew that if they kept asking, they would see their requests granted.

By means of these parables Jesus exhorts his followers to remain faithful even though his return may involve patient waiting. The souls of the ones slain because of the Word of God may cry out, "How long, Sovereign Lord, holy and true, until you judge the inhabitants of the earth and avenge our blood?" (Rev. 6:10). The answer they receive is to wait a little longer until the number of their fellow servants and brothers is complete.

38 Pharisee and Tax Collector

Luke 18:9–14

⁹To some who were confident of their own righteousness and looked down on everybody else, Jesus told this parable: ¹⁰"Two men went up to the temple to pray, one a Pharisee and the other a tax collector. ¹¹The Pharisee stood up and prayed about himself; 'God, I thank you that I am not like all other men—robbers, evil-doers, adulterers—or even like this tax collector. ¹²I fast twice a week and give a tenth of all I get.'

¹³"But the tax collector stood at a distance. He would not even look up to heaven, but beat his breast and said, 'God, have mercy on me, a sinner.'

¹⁴"I tell you that this man, rather than the other, went home justified before God. For everyone who exalts himself will be humbled, and he who humbles himself will be exalted."

The introductory verse to this parable is purposely wide in scope and does not pinpoint a specific group. There is a real temptation, however, to single out the Pharisees. Admittedly, many of the Pharisees displayed a self-righteous attitude and looked down upon their fellowman. It would be a deplorable mistake to ascribe this attitude to all Pharisees, for Nicodemus and Joseph of Arimathea do not fit this category.[1] For this reason, Luke has given the introductory verse in general terms.

The Pharisee

In this parable, Jesus depicts the attitude of a particular Pharisee who in his own view surpassed the rest of his countrymen in observing the details of the Mosaic Law.[2] Filled with a spirit of self-righteousness and casting disdainful looks at others around him, the Pharisee makes his way to the temple in order to pray. In his words and general conduct, the Pharisee shows that he does not need God because his trust is in himself.[3] His self-confidence is so great that he believes he is able to live up to the standard he has set. Consequently, he disdains the person who is unwilling or unable to meet this standard.

He goes to the temple in Jerusalem to pray. The hour may have been the mid-morning hour of 9 A.M. or the mid-afternoon hour of 3 P.M., the set times for prayer. He goes to the outer court to be seen and heard by men, because the inner court was accessible only to the priests. Here he stands, and looking up to heaven he prays about himself.[4] His prayer is self-centered, and is meant to be heard by those surrounding him. The prayer is short. It has an introduction, a negative element, and a positive element.

> God, I thank you
> that I am not like all other men—
> robbers, evildoers, adulterers—
> or even like this tax collector.
> I fast twice a week
> and give a tenth of all I get.

In this relatively short prayer, the emphasis is on the first-person singular. The pronoun *I* occurs at least four times. The Pharisee utters a prayer of thanksgiving. No petition is offered, for he trusts in himself and his own sufficiency. There is not need for confession, for he has kept the commandments. And references to his fellowman are listed in negative terms. Moreover, God should be pleased to have a law-abiding Pharisee address him in prayer. He is not aware that God's grace has kept him from falling into hideous sins such as robbery, fraud, and adultery. He does not realize what it means to live with a guilty conscience, as does the tax collector.

In his self-glorification he enumerates two extras he has done. First, over and above the requirements of the Law, he fasts twice a week. The Law prescribed a public day of fasting once a year on Yom Kippur (the Day of Atonement),[5] but gave permission for voluntary fasting at any time. The Pharisees instituted Monday and Thursday as days of fasting during which prayer was offered for the nation.[6]

Second, although the produce he buys has already been tithed by the grower, the Pharisee makes sure that everything that becomes his is tithed.[7] He himself wants to uphold the Law of God even though its requirements have already been met by others.

The prayer of the Pharisee is not at all unusual. A similar prayer, recorded in the Talmud and originally uttered by Rabbi Nedhunya ben Ha Kana in about A.D. 70, reads as follows:

> I give thanks to Thee, O Lord my God, that Thou hast set my portion with those who sit in the Beth ha-Midrash [house of learning] and Thou has not set my portion with those who sit in [street] corners, for I rise early and they rise early, but I rise early for words of Torah and they rise early for frivolous talk; I labour and they labour, but I labour and receive a reward; and they labour and do not receive a reward; I run and they run, but I run to the life of the future world and they run to the pit of destruction.[8]

The Pharisee, looking around him in the temple court, notices a tax collector. He thanks God that he is different from other men, and certainly from the tax collector. He is free from sins committed by this traitor. How does this scoundrel dare to come into the temple area? Does not David ask, "Who may ascend the hill of the LORD? Who may stand in his holy place? He who has clean hands and a pure heart, who does not lift up his soul to an idol or swear by what is false" (Ps. 24:3, 4). Do not the words of David condemn this tax collector?

THE TAX COLLECTOR

Synagogues were found throughout the countryside and at numerous places in Jerusalem. The tax collector does not dare enter a synagogue. What he needs is a place where he is able to pray to God undisturbed. As a Jew he has access to the outer court of the temple and may go there at the hour of prayer in the morning or afternoon. All he needs is a place where he can be away from others who come to the temple for prayer.

The tax collector has heard the Word of God that has convicted him of his sin. His conscience is bothering him; he needs spiritual help. He wants to go to God, but he is overburdened by his own unworthiness in the sight of God and man. He does not even dare look up to heaven, let alone lift up his hands in prayer (1 Tim. 2:8). He is ashamed of the sin he has committed against God and against his fellowman. Employed by the Romans, he is the object of scorn and derision among his own people. He knows that he has defrauded them, so that they look upon him as a robber and a traitor. It is not surprising that the Pharisees see him as a sinner who has transgressed God's Law.

The financial debt the tax collector owes the people he has cheated is staggering. He cannot possibly pay it all back, and besides, he does not remember how many people have been duped.[9] The Law clearly speaks to the sin of stealing by deception when it says, "If anyone sins and is unfaithful to the LORD by deceiving his neighbor . . . he must return what he has stolen or taken by extortion, or what was entrusted to him, or the lost property he found, or whatever it was he swore falsely about. He must make restitution in full, add a fifth of the value to it and give it all to the owner on the day he presents his guilt offering" (Lev. 6:2–5). The tax collector does not dare come near the altar to approach the priest about the guilt offering. He stands at a distance from the altar. He has nowhere to go but to God in prayer.

Because of his occupation he has neglected the worship of God in synagogue and temple. Now the time has come to confess his sin before God, even though he cannot think in terms of a guilt offering. His debts to the people are too great and varied. He is too much of a sinner for such an offering. All he can do is pray to God. But because he has neglected his spiritual life for quite some time, he does not even know how to pray. Words of praise, adoration, and thanksgiving fail him. The burden of sin presses him down. He must give expression to his guilt, and he does so by means of a cry for mercy. He cries out, "God, have mercy on me, a sinner." And as he is saying this he keeps on beating his breast, marking, so to speak, the source of sin—his heart.

The sinner, as the tax collector calls himself, comes to God with empty hands. He has no merits and no claims. Excuses and explanations do not enter his mind. Comparisons with others are out of the question. He knows that he is *the* sinner pleading for mercy. His cry, "God, have mercy on me," is a plea to God to forgive his sin and to turn divine wrath from him.[10] He asks for mercy, and that is all he dares to ask.[11] He prays and waits for God to answer.

ANSWERS

Jesus reveals how God answers the prayers of the Pharisee and the tax collector in a concluding statement: "I tell you that this man [the tax collector], rather than the other [the Pharisee], went home justified before God." God hears and answers the anguished cry of a sinner in a spiritual agony.

The people surrounding the Pharisee consider him a worthy saint who strives most diligently to keep the Law of God. They believe that God will certainly hear the Pharisee's prayer because it is an expression of his gratitude. The prayer of the tax collector, on the other hand, is unaccompanied by the prescribed guilt offering and cannot meet approval. Should anyone, therefore, be asked to judge the two prayers, he or she could commend the Pharisee and condemn the tax collector.[12]

God hears the prayers and looks at the hearts of the two men. The heart of the Pharisee is self-sufficient, whereas that of the tax collector has been completely emptied of self-reliance. The Pharisee is justified in his own eyes and therefore does not need God's mercy. He has kept the Law and is not aware of any sins of commission or omission. The tax collector, however, addresses God by using the first line of Psalm 51, the penitential psalm of David. He prays the very language of Scripture, "Have mercy on me, O God . . ." (Ps. 51:1).[13] The tax collector adds the words "the sinner" to his petition, but even these words echo the sentiment of David's psalm. It is this scriptural prayer that God answers.

The tax collector went home justified before God, Jesus said. The man who called himself "the sinner" relied completely on God's mercy.[14] His attitude toward God was right, and this admitted him to the kingdom of heaven as a child of God. In simple trust he relied upon his God, who did not put his faith to shame. Before God, the tax collector was acquitted. The Pharisee was not. The one went home a saint, the other a sinner.

Jesus concluded the parable of the Pharisee and the tax collector with the same words he used for the parable of the places of honor at the table: "For everyone who exalts himself will be humbled, and he who humbles himself will be exalted" (Luke 14:11).

The application of the parable is not limited to time or culture. "Pharisees" and "tax collectors" are present in the church today. If we look in the mirror of God's Word, we can catch glimpses of them in our own lives. Jesus teaches that true humility leads to exaltation. He tells us to look only to him for our salvation. When we are fully aware of our own unworthiness in the sight of God and ask for mercy, God forgives our sins and saves us through his Son. In the words of Paul, "Christ Jesus came into the world to save sinners—of whom I am the worst" (1 Tim. 1:15).

39 Pounds

Luke 19:11–27

¹¹While they were listening to this, he went on to tell them a parable, because he was near Jerusalem and the people thought that the kingdom of God was going to appear at once. ¹²He said: "A man of noble birth went to a distant country to have himself appointed king and then to return. ¹³So he called ten of his servants and gave them ten minas. 'Put this money to work,' he said, 'until I come back.'

¹⁴"But his subjects hated him and sent a delegation after him to say, 'We don't want this man to be our king.'

¹⁵"He was made king, however, and returned home. Then he sent for the servants to whom he had given the money, in order to find out what they had gained with it.

¹⁶"The first one came and said, 'Sir, your mina has earned ten more.'

¹⁷"'Well done, my good servant!' his master replied. 'Because you have been trustworthy in a very small matter, take charge of ten cities.'

¹⁸"The second came and said, 'Sir, your mina has earned five more.'

¹⁹"His master answered, 'You take charge of five cities.'

²⁰"Then another servant came and said, 'Sir, here is your mina; I have kept it laid away in a piece of cloth. ²¹I was afraid of you, because you are a hard man. You take out what you did not put in and reap what you did not sow.'

²²"His master replied, 'I will judge you by your own words, you wicked servant! You knew, did you, that I am a hard man, taking out what I did not put in, and reaping what I did not sow? ²³Why then didn't you put my money on deposit, so that when I came back, I could have collected it with interest?'

²⁴"Then he said to those standing by, 'Take his mina away from him and give it to the one who has ten minas.'

²⁵"'Sir,' they said, 'he already has ten!'

²⁶"He replied, 'I tell you that to everyone who has, more will be given, but as for the one who has nothing, even what he has will be taken away. ²⁷But those enemies of mine who did not want me to be king over them—bring them here and kill them in front of me.'"

When Jesus was coming to the city of Jerusalem, the people believed that the kingdom of God was about to appear. During his healing and teaching ministry Jesus had healed the blind, cleansed the lepers, and raised the dead, besides preaching the good news.[1] Accompanying Jesus to Jerusalem, the people expected the kingdom of God to become a reality.

Jesus knew that the crowd failed to understand the coming of the kingdom in spiritual terms. They failed to see that he would not and could not be an earthly king in God's kingdom. However, in order to help them understand the implication of the kingdom, Jesus told the parable of the pounds. He did this by indirectly referring to events that had taken place more than thirty years earlier and that were engraved in their memories.

HISTORY

The people of Israel vividly remembered the sudden calamities inflicted on the Jews during the Passover feast of 4 B.C. in the temple area of Jerusalem. Herod the Great had died not long before that Passover feast, and in his will he had stipulated that Archelaus was to be king.[2] However, Archelaus's kingship was not to become effective until Caesar had approved it. Before the new appointee could travel to Rome to be officially crowned king—even though officers and soldiers acclaimed him as their king—a minor disturbance in the temple area degenerated into a bloodbath in which three thousand Jews were killed by Archelaus's soldiers. Thereupon Archelaus ordered the rest of the Jews to return home; they abandoned the celebrations of the Passover feast and departed.

While Archelaus went to Rome, his officers were in charge. In view of the turmoil and turbulence in the land, Archelaus was hard-pressed before Caesar to defend himself. Fifty Jewish deputies appeared before the Roman emperor to plead for the autonomy of Israel and to accuse Archelaus of murdering three thousand of their countrymen in the temple area of Jerusalem. These fifty deputies were supported by more than eight thousand Jews in Rome.[3] They asked Caesar to entrust their country to governors instead of Archelaus.

After a few days of deliberation, Caesar appointed Archelaus as ethnarch of Idumaea, Judea, and Samaria, and promised to make him king if he proved himself capable. In the mind of the people, Archelaus as well as his brother Antipas (ruling Galilee and Perea as tetrarch) were regarded as kings.[4]

Archelaus must have spent considerable time in Rome because he was involved in at least two lawsuits before Caesar: one against his immediate relatives, who wished to take the claim to the throne from him, and the other against the fifty Jewish deputies who were pleading for autonomy. Also, the Jews in Jerusalem revolted during Archelaus's absence. At the feast of Pentecost in 4 B.C. they sought to obtain national independence.

When Archelaus eventually returned to take possession of his ethnarchy, he handed out swift punishment. Thus, the high priest Joazar was removed from office because he had supported the Jewish rebels. Archelaus treated not only the Jews but even the Samaritans with great brutality.[5] By his actions he made himself a most hated ruler who, because of complaints against him, was removed from office and banished in A.D. 6. After his reign, governors ruled Idumea, Judea, and Samaria. But the people retained vivid recollections of the rule of Archelaus.

PARABLE

Approaching the city of Jerusalem together with numerous pilgrims to the Passover feast, Jesus had only to say, "A man of noble birth went to a distant country to have himself appointed king and then to return," and all the people knew that he referred to Archelaus. They recalled the massacre of the three thousand Jews during the Passover celebrations of three decades earlier. Jesus continued to call attention to this incident. He said, "But his subjects hated him and sent a delegation after him to say, 'We don't want this man to be our king.' He was made king, however, and returned home."

Jesus used the reference to contemporary history to set the stage for his teaching about the kingdom of God. "A man of noble birth," Jesus said, "called ten of his servants together before he left and gave each one a mina." The amount was the equivalent of about three months' wages.[6] It was not an excessive amount that each servant received, but it was sufficient to prove his faithfulness to the king. The instruction each one had to follow was: "Put this money to work." The king expected his servants to be trustworthy in managing a relatively small amount of money and to show an increase at the time of his return. Also, the instruction should be seen and understood against an oriental background in which daily trading and bargaining are part of life.

The absence of any terms of contract may indicate a circumventing of the divine law against usury. Repeatedly God had told his people not to charge their countrymen usurious rates.[7] But numerous ways of bypassing the injunction were found. Thus huge profits were made in some instances, mostly when money was invested in high-risk business ventures. The first servant put his money to work and upon his master's return was able to show a 1,000 percent return. The second servant showed a 500 percent return.[8] Although the parable does not mention the increases the other servants gained, the context justifies the implication that they enjoyed varying degrees of success. From an oriental point of view, therefore, it was unusual for a person to keep his money in a piece of cloth and not to put it to work. It was part of that culture to trade.

When the king returned and summoned his servants, he was pleased with the faithfulness of the servant who had gained another ten minas. He praised him for his diligence and wisdom; he called him "good," and he rewarded him by putting him in charge of ten cities.[9] The second servant, upon showing his additional five minas, received the same proportionate reward. He was placed in charge of five cities. The third servant, by returning only the one mina he had received, was condemned.

The three servants in the parable portray three classes. The first represents those who gained immense profits; the second stands for those whose profit was considerable; and the third for the one who had gained no profit at all. The third servant, therefore, is of an entirely different kind.[10] He is the unprofitable one.

When the third servant appeared before the king and returned the one mina, he made it known that the mina did not belong to him but to the king and that he had kept the money safely in a cloth. He had not squandered it, and thieves had not robbed him. Fear had kept him from putting the money to work. He knew the demanding nature of the king and could describe his characteristics rather accurately. He said, "You are a hard man. You take out what you did not put in and reap what you did not sow." He knew his master as an aggressive person who did not shrink from taking that which really was not his at all. The servant realized his own timidity. He had a genuine fear for the harshness of the king. He only hoped that by returning the total amount of money intact the king would let him go in peace.

The king, however, was not at all pleased with the servant's insolence. He could not understand the servant's fear and had no patience with his inept excuse. He did see himself accurately reflected in the character sketch the servant provided. But if the servant had believed what he said about the king, he should have done the very least and put the money on deposit.[11]

The praise and commendation given the other servants became scorn and condemnation for the third. The king, acting now as a judge, told the servant that on the basis of his own words he would be judged. If the servant knew his master to be a hard man, he should have had enough faith in the king's ability to claim the money with appropriate interest from the bankers. The bankers most certainly would have known firsthand that the king took out what he did not put in and reaped where he did not sow. Although the servant knew the king's bent for driving a hard bargain, he did not even avail himself of that possibility by depositing his money with the bankers. Aptly, the king called him wicked, implying that the servant was incompetent, unfit, and useless.[12]

The parable is told in vivid colors. Even the bystanders are addressed by the king, "Take this mina away from him and give it to the one who has ten minas." The bystanders express their surprise to the king: "Sir, he already has ten minas!"[13] The objection to the king's order is that the first servant already has the greatest amount of all. Why should he receive an extra mina? Does this command support the saying that the rich are getting richer and the poor poorer? And furthermore, if the servant already has been given authority over ten cities, would he feel rewarded by receiving the comparatively small amount of one mina? Should not all the money that the servants had received from the king and what they had gained by trading be put in the king's treasury? It is relatively easy to multiply the questions, but most of them are resolved if we understand the implied symbolism in the parable.

The money entrusted to the servants was given to them as a test. The king wanted to test their loyalty to him and wished to reward them accordingly. This he did by putting the one servant in charge of ten cities and the other in charge of five. As a reward for his loyalty to the king, the first servant was given money from the third. By means of this action the king made it known that he permanently ended the relationship he had had with the third servant.[14] And he showed that he placed his full confidence in the first servant by entrusting him with the responsibility taken from the other one. The amount of money must be seen, therefore, in terms of responsibility.

The king did not answer the bystanders directly.[15] By using a somewhat proverbial remark,[16] he implicitly told them why he gave the mina to the servant who had ten minas. "To everyone who has, more will be given, but as for the one who has nothing, even what he has will be taken away." The remark points to common practice in the business world. That is, people readily lend money to a person whose capital returns show a substantial profit. They have confidence in a successful business for they know that their invested money will bear dividends. But when investors realize that a person who has borrowed money shows no profit on his capital, they are quick to withdraw the amount they have invested and thus reduce the borrower's capital.[17] Money is given to a man who courts success and taken from him who faces bankruptcy.

Jesus ended the parable by calling attention to the delegates who had protested the appointment of the king. There was no love lost between these two parties. As the text indicates, "his subjects hated him and sent a delegation after him to say, 'We don't want this man to be our king'" (v. 14). The wording reveals the personal animosity these people fostered to their own detriment.[18]

When the king returned to his kingdom, he at once called to his court those citizens who did not want him to rule them. When they appeared in his presence, the king had them slain in front of him. There is no record that Archelaus upon his return from Rome executed the fifty Jews who had brought suit against him in Caesar's court. Yet it is known that he removed the high priest from office for having aided the rebels. He also treated the people most cruelly after he returned from his visit to Rome.

INTERPRETATION

In a sense, the parable of the pounds is a kingdom parable, even though it is not introduced by the familiar phrase, "The kingdom of heaven is like . . ." The parable, based on actual history, was taught at a time when the people thought that the kingdom of God was about to appear. From their own recent history Jesus taught his contemporaries a lesson concerning the coming of his kingdom.

The parable is intended to teach the people that an interim is to occur between his first and second comings. As Archelaus departed for Rome but would eventually return, so the Son of Man will leave and, in God's appointed time, come back. The king gave his servants a certain amount of money with the explicit order to put it to work. When he eventually assumed the responsibility of governing his ethnarchy (ruling a nation), he summoned his servants to the palace to have them give an account of their activities. Likewise Jesus, upon his departure from earth to heaven, endows his followers with gifts and expects them to work with these gifts most faithfully and fruitfully in his absence. When the time for his return has come, he will summon his servants to appear before him to receive words of praise and rewards or condemnation and severe punishment.[19]

The kingdom of God exists in the present, but is also in a state of expectant fulfillment. It is therefore *now*, but at the same time *not yet*. Jesus, although King eternally, fully brings his kingdom to realization only upon his return. Then he awards the faithful servants with greater opportunities to serve him, and he metes out punishment for the slothful and wicked servants. During Jesus' absence, he allows ample time for service as well as for rebellion.[20]

Those people who accompanied Jesus on his way to Jerusalem should not have thought that the kingdom would immediately bring joy and happiness to all. Rather, they should have thought in terms of an interim during which they would be tested. Then, after the period of probation, those who had rebelled would be punished.

No one in Jesus' audience would identify Jesus with the cruel Archelaus of earlier days.[21] But his listeners were able to understand that the interim of Archelaus's absence in some way would parallel Jesus' departure and subsequent return. The slaughter that Archelaus upon his return inflicted on his adversaries (v. 27) parallels the destruction of Jerusalem when in A.D. 70 God vented his wrath on the unbelieving inhabitants of that city (v. 44).[22]

The parable simply cannot be interpreted in all its detail because this would lead to absolute absurdity. The point of the parable is this: every follower of Jesus is given gifts and opportunities of service. No one can say that since he or she does not have the ability of a trained theologian or the eloquence of a gifted preacher, thus he or she cannot serve the Lord. Such reasoning does not stand the light of day. The parable teaches that all the servants received one mina each, and each servant was held accountable for the entrusted money. Likewise, everyone who follows Jesus has been endowed with gifts and is given opportunities to put these gifts to work. Each one is expected to make the most of these avenues of service. Soon the time, which God in his providence has allotted, will be over, and then comes the judgment.

> Behold, I am coming soon!
> My reward is with me,
> and I will give to everyone
> according to what he has done.
>
> Revelation 22:12

Conclusion

Jesus' parables are unique in the context of Scripture. Although few parables have been recorded in the Old Testament, the great number of parables and parabolic sayings in the Gospels is striking. Of course, a few graphic examples from the Old Testament indicate that storytelling was not unknown. For example, the prophet Nathan told David the story of the poor man whose little ewe lamb was forcefully taken from him by a rich man. The application "you are the man" was most direct.[1] In rabbinic literature also, teaching in the form of a parable was not unknown. However, to attribute more than two parables to any one person is difficult indeed.[2] It is estimated that about one-third of Jesus' instruction has been given in parabolic form. Counting parables and short figurative sayings, some scholars come to a total of sixty parables.[3] All of these are called parables of Jesus.

As John writes at the conclusion of his Gospel that not everything Jesus did has been written down (John 21:25), we may assume that not every parable Jesus taught has been recorded. Perhaps some of the sayings of Jesus that are found in sources other than the New Testament may be authentic.[4] Also, by teaching orally as the teachers of his day were accustomed to do, Jesus taught his sayings repeatedly. As a teacher he had complete freedom to teach a certain parable twice, with different settings in each case. When he traveled from Jericho to Jerusalem to celebrate the Passover for the last time, he taught the parable of the pounds by placing it in the historical setting of Archelaus going to a distant country to have himself appointed king. A few days later Jesus taught his disciples the parable of the talents. The two parables undoubtedly have much in common, yet in scope and purpose they differ.

Jesus not only told the parables; he told them well. Most of them are marked by brevity, and in their brevity they sparkle. Jesus drew his material from a variety of sources. At times he turned to the Old Testa-

221

ment—as he did for the parable of the vineyard and the tenants when he took his theme from the "Song of the Vineyard" recorded in Isaiah 5. On other occasions he took his examples directly from the times, culture, and environment in which he lived. Parables such as the sower, the barren fig tree, and the unjust judge are cases in point. Jesus could also rely on events that were well known to his audience: the nobleman who went to a distant country to be appointed king, and the hapless man who fell among robbers along the Jericho road. Jesus is the Great Teacher of all these parables. Even though the evangelists have transmitted them, in the parables we are confronted with the teaching of Jesus. The parables are his. That is, they did not originate in the mind of an evangelist,[5] and they were not composed by the early Christian community that needed a particular story for the purpose of teaching doctrine.[6] Jesus is the originator of the parables.

Of course, the evangelists recorded the parables of Jesus, and in their work of writing the Gospels they show their own individuality. Differences in wording in the parallel accounts of the same parables clearly reveal the hand of the individual evangelists. Besides, the fact that Jesus taught his parables in Aramaic, whereas the Gospels present them in Greek, is sufficient to prove that the recovery of the very words of Jesus remains problematic.[7] The question of origin, not authority, in regard to specific wording in a given parable is not always easy to answer. If a parable has been recorded by only one evangelist, the authenticity of Jesus' words need not be debated. But when a parable occurs in parallel Gospel accounts and shows variations in wording, the question of editorial work of the individual evangelist is real. Matthew, Mark, and Luke display their own characteristics and inclinations as they record the parables of Jesus.

GENERAL CHARACTERISTICS

Because the Gospel of Mark has only six parables, we cannot say much about Mark's characteristics. Of these six parables only one is peculiar to Mark; that is, the one of the seed growing secretly. The other parables are paralleled in Matthew and Luke. They are the parables of the sower, the mustard seed, the vineyard and the tenants, the fig tree, and the doorkeeper. The parable of the doorkeeper, which is not recorded in Matthew's Gospel, is the only one of the six in Mark that is not a nature parable. Of all the parables of Jesus, Mark selected five that describe growth in nature. The evidence seems to indicate that Mark was a person acquainted with rural life.

The world of Matthew is broad, ranging from kings to servants. He records parables depicting ministers of finance, housebuilders, a farmer who employs temporary farm laborers, tenant farmers, fishermen, a jeweler, a woman baking bread, a shepherd, a father and his two sons, a burglar, children at play, bridesmaids, and guests invited to a wedding banquet. In these parables the focus is on people.[8] And Matthew reveals himself as a man who has an interest in them.

This interest is even more pronounced in the Gospel of Luke.[9] In the parables that are peculiar to Luke, individual persons take a central place: the friend who arrives at midnight, the prodigal son and his brother with the father, the woman who lost her coin and the shepherd who found his sheep, the rich man and Lazarus, the widow and the judge, the Pharisee and the tax collector, and the Samaritan caring for the robbers' victim. By means of these parables, Luke demonstrates an interest in individual people, even to the point of recording names (Lazarus and Abraham), nationality (Samaritan), and occupation (tax collector).

Luke seems to move among the common people, particularly those of moderate means. The two debtors owe the moneylender an amount of three months' wages and six weeks' wages each, and each of the ten servants receives the equivalent sum of three months' wages from the nobleman. The farmer has only one servant, who plows his field and cooks his supper. Likewise, the man who prepares a banquet has only one servant who invites the guests and who brings in the poor and the lame. The rich in the parables presented by Luke belong to the upper-middle class.[10] They are the farmer who had a bumper crop and had to build bigger barns to store the harvest; the man who dressed in purple and fine linen and lived in luxury every day; the rich man whose manager shrewdly diminished the debts of his master's debtors; and the father who apportioned the inheritance at the request of his younger son. In Luke's parables, the common folk are portrayed: a Samaritan with his donkey, the beggar visited by dogs, the shepherd and his sheep, the woman and her coin, the widow uttering her complaint, and the tax collector beating his breast.

By contrast, some of Matthew's parables portray grandeur, splendor, and extravagance. The minister of finance owes the king an amount that runs into the millions; a man entrusts a total of eight talents to three of his servants; a king arranges a wedding banquet by sending out servants to invite the guests and then deploys soldiers to punish them when they refuse to come; and the owner of a vineyard dispatches his servants in groups to collect the tenants' revenue. Matthew moves among kings and millionaires. Many of his people are the upper crust of society. Others, like the pearl merchant and the master who entrusted his servant with authority, are among the moderately rich.

In the selection of parables that are peculiar to each Gospel writer, some characteristics come to light. It is Matthew who dwells on stories with financial interests; Luke is a man for the poor and the citizen of average income; while Mark, although his parables are few in number, displays an interest in nature. Moreover, each writer arranges parables more or less in groups. In one grouping (Matthew 13), Matthew includes seven, which are not put together haphazardly. These seven reveal a definite pattern.[11] After the introductory parable of the sower, the ones on the wheat and weeds and the fishnet form a pair. In between these two, there are two sets of twins: first the set of mustard seed and the yeast, then the set of the hidden treasure and the pearl. And the parables Matthew records in chapters 24 and 25 of his Gospel have an eschatological perspective. The parables of the fig tree, the burglar, the servant entrusted with authority, the ten virgins, the talents, and the last judgment point in this direction. Luke also has arranged his material in such a way that, with the exception of the parables of the two debtors and the pounds, the parables peculiar to him are found in the so-called travel narrative or great insertion from Luke 9:51–19:27. And the parable of the pounds, which is the last of Luke's parables, has been strategically placed to serve as a bridge passage between the section on Jesus' journey to Jerusalem and that on Jesus' ministry in Jerusalem.[12]

Some parables that have been recorded by more than one Gospel writer reflect the life situation in which they were written.[13] For example, on the interpretation of the parable of the sower, specifically the seed sown on rocky ground, Matthew and Mark write, "When trouble or persecution comes because of the word, they (he) quickly fall(s) away" (Matt. 13:21; Mark 4:17). But Luke has: "but in the time of testing they fall away" (Luke 8:13). Each in his own way expresses the same truth: in hard times people will abandon the faith. Similarly, the parable of the two builders is related by Matthew in a version understandable to a Jew living in Judea or Galilee and by Luke in a version that is meaningful to a Hellenist living abroad.

Literary Characteristics

The style of the evangelists differs noticeably in respect to the parables they record. While Mark's style is rather simplistic, Matthew's, especially in the longer parables, is marked by the use of contrast. In fact, the longer parables in Matthew's Gospel are presented in black-and-white caricatures.[14] The builders put their house on either rock or sand;

the farmer sows wheat, and his enemy sows weeds in the same field; the fishnet yields both good and bad fish; the king shows a forgiving spirit but his minister of finance does not; the vineyard workers who are hired first grumble and those who are hired last rejoice; of the two sons only one obeys his father; the servant entrusted with authority can be either faithful or lazy; five virgins are wise and five are foolish; two servants put their talents to work and one buries his talent in the ground; at the wedding banquet all the guests are appropriately dressed except one who is not. Even in one of the shorter parables the contrast is evident: the children in the marketplace are either glad or sad. In Matthew's parables people are either wise or foolish, good or bad, faithful or lazy.

Whereas Matthew takes his pictures on black-and-white film, Luke uses color. His people are colorful, picturesque, and well developed. The Samaritan is a figure of compassion; the friend who knocks at the door of his neighbor in the middle of the night, and the widow who makes her periodic visits to the judge, portray the art of persistence. That is not to say that Luke avoids contrast. On the contrary, he puts the priest and the Levite over against the Samaritan; the rich man is the opposite of Lazarus; and the Pharisee is contrasted with the tax collector. But Luke presents his figures with more color and detail than the other evangelists. In Matthew's Gospel, the good and the bad are invited to the wedding banquet. In Luke's presentation of the parable of the great supper, the poor, the crippled, the blind, and the lame are welcomed. In the parable of the talents, the one servant buries his in the ground. In his description of the parable of the pounds, Luke depicts the one servant wrapping his coin in a piece of cloth. The people Luke portrays are real; they think, they talk, they act. Matthew's pearl merchant is nondescript and in a sense fails to come to life. Luke's rich man who is cashing in on a bumper crop is a lifelike figure. He is talking to himself, he is making plans, and he is ready to act. Matthew generally omits detail; he presents a bare outline. It is Luke who, by means of his facile pen, adds depth and dimension to the parables.

THEOLOGICAL CHARACTERISTICS

In parables peculiar to the Gospel of Luke, the theme of repentance and salvation is rather prominent. Luke shows much clearer than Matthew that Jesus calls to salvation the outcasts, the poor, the lost, and the despised.[15]

The theme spelled out in Luke 19:10, "For the Son of Man came to seek and to save what was lost," is exemplified in several of Luke's parables. They are the two debtors, the lost sheep, the lost coin, the prodigal son, and the Pharisee and the tax collector. The parable of the two debtors was told after the Sabbath incident when a sinful woman entered the home of Simon the Pharisee. Although she was despised in the eyes of the righteous Pharisee, she found remission of sin and peace of heart. The wayward son came to his senses in a filthy pigpen, returned home, and was restored. The tax collector, considered a social outcast by the Pharisee, beat his breast, prayed to God, and was justified. There is joy in heaven when a sinner repents, a feast in the father's house when the son returns, and peace in the heart of an outcast when God justifies.

It is Luke who unfolds the theme of Jesus' love toward the poor and the downtrodden. When the invited guests refuse to come to the great banquet, the poor, the crippled, the blind, and the lame are brought in. When there is still room left in the house, the servant is told to make them come in. The poor man who is carried daily to the rich man's gate is carried by angels to Abraham's side in heaven.

Luke shows that Jesus loves the poor, but warns the rich to come to repentance and faith. The parable of the rich man and Lazarus is intended to picture the afterlife misery of a man who on earth had lived in luxury without regard for God and fellowman. The parable of the rich man who wished to store his material wealth in bigger barns uncovers the naked poverty of a man who puts his trust in riches and not in God. And the parable of the shrewd manager teaches us not to depend on worldly wealth but to distribute it to gain friends and to be welcomed into eternal dwellings.

Love to one's neighbor is a theme much more sharply defined in Luke's Gospel than in the others. By means of Jesus' parable of the good Samaritan, Luke indicates that the concept is limitless and its application universal. The command to love one's neighbor, therefore, transcends barriers of race, culture, age, nationality, and language.

In at least three parables peculiar to his Gospel, Luke develops the theme of faithfulness. The cost of being a disciple of Jesus is unwavering loyalty in doing one's duty. That a follower of Jesus serves him with wholehearted devotion is shown most vividly in the parable of the farmer whose servant plows the field during the day, prepares supper for him upon returning home, and does not even receive thanks, because it is all in a day's work. The parable of the man who wished to build a tower and the king who was going to war against another king illustrates the cost of discipleship. Following Jesus means a willingness to give up everything; nothing may take precedence over being a disciple.

This loyalty comes to expression in the parable of the pounds. Nine servants put their money to work and each is able to gain additional pounds. But one servant keeps his coin in a handkerchief and is publicly condemned for his uselessness. The other servants are praised and given the reward of greater responsibilities. The theme of faithfulness is also spelled out in the parables of the other evangelists. That is, Matthew elucidates it in the parables of the two sons, the burglar, the servant entrusted with authority, the virgins, and the talents. Mark depicts it in the parable of the doorkeeper.

Last but not least, the theme of prayer is expounded in three of Luke's parables. The friend who knocks at his neighbor's door at midnight and the widow who makes her regular appearance before the judge are parallel accounts. Both parables teach the doctrine of persistence in prayer, which in the early Christian community was summed up in the apostolic precept: "Pray continually."[16] The parable of the Pharisee and the tax collector mentions prayer, yet is primarily concerned with righteousness.[17]

Except for the Synoptic parallels of the mustard seed and the yeast, Luke does not have any parable that he introduces as a kingdom parable. Mark provides this introduction for the parables of the seed growing secretly and the mustard seed. It is Matthew who lists kingdom parables. A total of ten parables have the kingdom introduction: wheat and weeds, mustard seed, yeast, hidden treasure, pearl, fishnet, unforgiving servant, workers in the vineyard, wedding banquet, and ten virgins. By implication, the parable of the talents may also be considered a kingdom parable because of its link with the parable of the ten virgins. Also the parable of the sower is in the context of "the knowledge of the secrets of the kingdom of heaven," for in this parable Jesus conveys a basic understanding of the coming of the kingdom.[18]

Many of the kingdom parables in Matthew's Gospel have an eschatological perspective. The wheat and weeds and the fishnet parables are similar in their conclusions: both speak of separation at the end. Likewise, the wedding banquet scene ends in the casting out of the man who did not wear wedding clothes. The parables of the ten virgins and the talents picture five foolish girls shut out and a lazy servant thrown out into the darkness. Matthew concludes his parables with the one on the last judgment in which the separation of the people is compared to a shepherd separating his sheep on the right from his goats on the left.

In his methodical way, Matthew has grouped together a total of seven parables in chapter 13. Four of these can be taken as two pairs: the mustard seed and the yeast are similar, and the treasure and the pearl have the same message. In the first set, the victorious power of the message of salvation is expressed externally in the growing of the mustard plant and internally in the rising of the batch of dough. And in the second set, both the farmer who sold everything to buy the field that contained the hidden treasure, and the merchant who liquidated his assets in order to buy the costly pearl, exemplify the total surrender to Christ and the infinite value of his kingdom.

Because of the paucity of parables in Mark's Gospel, it is difficult to ascertain whether Mark selected his parables for any theological purpose. Two of his parables have an eschatological motif. They are the fig tree and the doorkeeper. In the other parables he demonstrates the action of God at work either in nature or in human relations. They are the parables of the sower, the seed growing secretly, the mustard seed, and the tenants. In general, it may be said that in all of Mark's parables the power and rule of God are evident.

RECIPIENTS AND RESPONSE

Who were the people who heard the parables when Jesus taught them in public or in private? They fall into three categories: the disciples, the crowds, and the opponents of Jesus. Most of the parables were addressed either to the crowds or to the disciples.[19] According to Matthew, the crowds listened to the parables of the two builders, the children in the marketplace, the sower, the wheat and weeds, and the mustard seed and the yeast. The disciples heard those of the treasure and the pearl, the lost sheep, the unforgiving servant, and the workers in the vineyard. In addition, the eschatological parables of the virgins, talents, and last judgment were given to the disciples in private. The chief priests and elders of the people were Jesus' opponents. They heard the parables of the two sons, the tenants, and the wedding banquet applied to them.

It is Luke who indicates that Jesus frequently countered his opponents by teaching them parables even in their own homes. On at least five different occasions Jesus instructed Pharisees, an expert in the Law, or teachers of the Law. Invited for dinner to the home of Simon the Pharisee, he taught the parable of the two debtors. Second, during a similar dinner engagement, a prominent Pharisee and his guests heard Jesus' parables of the chief place at the table and the great banquet. Third, an expert in the Law asked Jesus to explain the meaning of the word *neighbor* and heard the explanation in the form of the good Samaritan parable. Fourth, when the Pharisees and teachers of the Law muttered that Jesus entered the homes of moral and social outcasts and ate with them, they were asked to look into the mirrors of the lost sheep, lost coin, and lost son parables and see in true perspective the spiritual relationships of the outcasts to themselves. And fifth, when Jesus told the Pharisees, "You cannot serve both God and Money," they sneered at Jesus because they loved money. In this setting Jesus taught the parable of the rich man and Lazarus.

The crowds, Luke writes, were delighted with all the wonderful things Jesus was doing, although all his opponents were humiliated (Luke

13:17). They heard the parables of the two builders, the sower, the rich fool, the mustard seed and the yeast, the tower builder and the king going to war, and the pounds. The disciples were instructed privately in such parables as the friend at midnight, the unjust judge, the doorkeeper, the burglar, the servant entrusted with authority, the shrewd manager, and the farmer and his servant.

The crowd heard three of Mark's parables: the sower, the seed growing secretly, and the mustard seed. Two were told in private for the benefit of the disciples: the fig tree and the doorkeeper. And last, the parable of the tenants was addressed to the chief priests, the teachers of the Law, and the elders.

Those parables that have parallels generally have the same audiences, although the one evangelist may be more specific than the other. Thus, Matthew relates that the parables of the mustard seed and the yeast were presented to the crowd (Matt. 13:34); Luke indicates that the crowd was a synagogue audience that included many of Jesus' opponents (Luke 13:10, 17). The parable of the lost sheep is addressed to Jesus' opponents (Luke 15:1) according to Luke, and to his disciples (Matt. 18:1) according to Matthew. It is not at all impossible that Jesus taught this parable twice to two different audiences.[20] In fact, this is the case when Jesus taught the crowd the parable of the pounds upon approaching the city of Jerusalem for his last Passover feast. A few days later, he used the same motif to teach his disciples the parable of the talents.

Most of Matthew's parables have an indirect appeal. Usually they are introduced by the clause, "The kingdom of heaven is like . . ." The kingdom is compared to a sower, a seed, a treasure, a merchant, a net, a king, or a landowner. Other parables are much more direct in calling for a personal response. For example, Jesus applies the parable of the two builders to "everyone who hears these words of mine and puts them into practice." The message is—*listen* and, in response, *act*. In Matthew's parable of the unmerciful servant, a personal appeal is given: "This is how my heavenly Father will treat each of you unless you forgive your brother from your heart" (Matt. 18:35). The same direct appeal comes to expression in the parables of the two sons, the fig tree, the burglar, the servant entrusted with authority, and the ten virgins. In these parables, the response elicited is in the form of a call to constant readiness, and an exhortation to watch and repent. The parable of the tenants evokes immediate negative response from the chief priests and Pharisees; they seek to arrest Jesus.

Luke's parables, much more so than those of Matthew, invite response. Simon the Pharisee is asked to respond to the parable of the two debtors; the expert in the Law, after hearing the good Samaritan parable, is told, "Go and do likewise." A number of parables are told in the setting of a situation that calls for an answer. They are the parable of the rich fool, which Jesus teaches when he is asked to divide an inheritance; the parable of the barren fig tree, which results from a discussion of the sinfulness of Galileans whom Pilate had killed and whose blood he had mixed with their sacrifices; the parables of the places of honor at the table and the great supper, which come in response to a dinner invitation Jesus had received; the parables of the lost sheep, coin, and son, which are an answer to the Pharisees and teachers of the Law disapproving Jesus' table-fellowship with outcasts; and the parable of the pounds, which is directed to the crowd thinking that the kingdom of God was about to appear.

Jesus appeals to his disciples not to cling to earthly possessions in the teaching of the shrewd manager, and to see the end result of money worship in the parable of the rich man and Lazarus. The appeal in the parable of the unjust judge is to faithfulness in prayer and, in that of the Pharisee and tax collector, to humility before God. In many of Luke's parables the basic message is: repent from sin. This is true of the parables on the barren fig tree, the great supper, and the triad of the lost sheep, coin, and son.

At times, Luke's parables involve the audience by means of the "one of you" type of introduction. Thus, the audience is directly part of the parable and each one is compelled to respond. The friend at midnight parable begins with the clause, "Suppose one of you has a friend." The parables of the tower builder and the king going to war, the lost sheep and the lost coin, and the farmer and his servant have similar introductions. Whether the audience consists of friend or foe, the parable that begins with an inclusive introductory clause elicits response. Matthew has the engaging question, "What do you think?" as an approach to the parables of the lost sheep and the two sons.

REPRESENTATION

In his Gospel, Matthew presents Jesus to his readers as the Christ, the Son of God. It is therefore not at all surprising that in his selection of parables Matthew has taken many in which the representation of Jesus is apparent. Thus, in the application of the parable of the children playing in the marketplace, it is the Son of Man who comes eating and drinking and is called a glutton, drunkard, and a friend of tax collectors and "sinners." When Jesus explains the parable of the wheat and weeds, he identifies himself with the landowner. "The one who sowed the good seed is the Son of Man" (Matt. 13:37). In the parable of the tenants, the landowner's son is sent to the tenants and is killed by them. The wedding banquet is held because the king's son is getting married. And the parable of the sheep and the goats is introduced by a description of the Son of Man coming in his glory, accompanied by his angels, judging the nations, and separating the people.

In the so-called eschatological parables, references to Jesus are implicit as well as explicit. The doorkeeper has to watch because the owner of the house may return anytime during the night. The parable of the burglar is more direct in its application: "So you also must be ready, because the Son of Man will come at an hour when you do not expect him" (Matt. 24:44). The parables of the ten virgins, the talents, and the pounds refer to Jesus' imminent return.

God is presented as Father in a number of Matthew's parables. The king in the parable of the unmerciful servant is a personification of God the Father. "This is how my heavenly Father will treat each of you unless you forgive your brother from your heart," Jesus says in the application (Matt. 18:35). In the parable of the two sons, one son obeys and the other disobeys his father. The implication is that tax collectors and prostitutes obey the will of God the Father and thus enter his kingdom. Both the parables of the tenants and the wedding banquet portray the father sending out his son and the father preparing a banquet for his son.

Although Luke presents the father figure only in the parable of the lost son, the third evangelist does submit some parables in which God is mentioned directly. Thus, God demands the life of the rich fool. The name of God is mentioned a few times in the parable of the unjust judge. And the Pharisee and the tax collector address God in prayer.

It is characteristic of Matthew's Gospel to represent Jesus in many of the parables—a feature that is lacking in the parables of Luke's Gospel. Likewise, it is Matthew who brings out the role of God the Father in a number of his parables. Luke, by contrast, stresses interpersonal relationships, as exemplified in the good Samaritan, the friend at midnight, the prodigal son, and the rich man and Lazarus.

Each writer introduces the parables of Jesus, but each one employs his own skills, insights, and abilities in presenting them. Nevertheless, the parables originated with Jesus. He created them, he now speaks through them, and in them he makes himself known to his people. The parables, then, coming to us in forms presented by individual evangelists, give us the assurance that we are indeed listening to the voice of Jesus.

Abbreviations

AB	Anchor Bible
ATR	Anglican Theological Review
AV	Authorized Version
BA	Biblical Archaeologist
BECNT	Baker Exegetical Commentary on the New Testament
Bib	Biblica
BibLeb	Bibel und Leben
BibSac	Bibliotheca Sacra
BJRL	Bulletin of the Jon Rylands University Library of Manchester
BTB	Biblical Theological Bulletin
CBQ	Catholic Biblical Quarterly
É et T	Église et Théologie
EQ	Evangelical Quarterly
EvQ	Evangelical Quarterly
ExpT	Expository Times
HeyJ	The Heythrop Journal
HTR	Harvard Theological Review
ICC	International Critical Commentary
Interp	Interpretation
JBL	Journal of Biblical Literature
JETS	Journal of the Evangelical Theological Society
JTS	Journal of Theological Studies
KoinJ	Koinonia Journal. Princeton Theological Seminary
Miss	Missiology: An International Review
NAB	New American Bible
NASB	New American Standard Bible
NEB	New English Bible
NIDNTT	New International Dictionary of New Testament Theology

NIV	New International Version
NovT	*Novum Testamentum*
NovTSupp	*Novum Testamentum Supplement*
NRSV	New Revised Standard Version
NTS	*New Testament Studies*
QR	*Quarterly Review*
RB	*Revue biblique*
REB	Revised English Bible
RefR	*Reformed Review*
RevExp	*Review and Expositor*
SB	H. L. Strack and P. Billerbeck, *Kommentar*
Scot JT	*Scottish Journal of Theology*
StTh	*Studia Theologia*
SWJT	*Southwestern Journal of Theology*
TB	*Tyndale Bulletin*
TDNT	*Theological Dictionary of the New Testament*
TrinJ	*Trinity Journal*
TS	*Theological Studies*
Tyn Bul	*Tyndale Bulletin*
TZ	*Theologische Zeitschrift*
VC	*Vigiliae Christianae*
WTJ	*Westminster Theological Journal*
W&W	*Word & World*
ZNW	*Zeitschrift für die Neuentestamentliche Wissenschaft*
ZPEB	*Zondervan Pictorial Encyclopedia of the Bible*
ZTK	*Zeitschrift für Theologie und Kirche*

Notes

Introduction

1. R. Schippers, "The Mashal-character of the Parable of the Pearl," in *Studia Evangelica*, ed. F. L. Cross (Berlin: Akademie-Verlag, 1964), 2:237.

2. F. Hauck, *TDNT*, V:752.

3. Consult C. L. Blomberg, *Interpreting the Parables* (Downers Grove, Ill.: InterVarsity, 1990), pp. 171–253.

4. A. M. Hunter, *The Parables Then and Now* (London: Westminster, 1971), p. 12.

5. I. Epstein, ed., "Seder Zeraim Berakoth 13a," in *The Babylonian Talmud* (London: Soncino, 1948), p. 73; see also H. K. McArthur and R. M. Johnston, *They Also Taught in Parables: Rabbinic Parables from the First Centuries of the Christian Era* (Grand Rapids: Zondervan, Academie Books, 1990), p. 40.

6. Hauck, *TDNT*, V:758. J. Jeremias, in the 8th edition of his *Die Gleichnisse Jesu* (Göttingen: Vandenhoeck & Ruprecht, 1970), p. 8, remarks that Jesus' parables may have contributed to the development of the literary genre of rabbinic parables.

7. J. Jeremias, *The Parables of Jesus* (New York: Scribner, 1963), pp. 13–18, contends that these words of Jesus have been misplaced and belong to another tradition; they must be interpreted without reference to the context of Mark 4. According to Jeremias, the writer inserted the passage from the other tradition because of the catchword *parable*, which Jeremias asserts originally meant *riddle*. He thus ascribes two meanings to the word *parable* in Mark 4. One has the meaning of the true parable, the other the riddle. The rules of exegesis, however, do not support Jeremias's interpretation, for unless the evangelist shows a difference in the understanding of a word, one should keep the same meaning throughout the passage.

8. W. Lane, *The Gospel according to Mark* (Grand Rapids: Eerdmans, 1974), p. 158; W. Hendriksen, *The Gospel of Mark* (Grand Rapids: Baker, 1975), p. 145; H. N. Ridderbos, *The Coming of the Kingdom* (Philadelphia: Presbyterian & Reformed, 1962), p. 124.

9. C. E. B. Cranfield, "St. Mark 4:1–34," *Scot JT* 4 (1951): 407.

10. Lane, *Mark*, p. 160.

11. C. E. van Koetsveld, *De Gelijkenissen van den Zaligmaker* (Schoonhoven, 1869), vols. 1, 2.

12. A. Jülicher, *Die Gleichnisreden Jesu* (Tübingen: Buchgesellschaft, 1963), vols. 1, 2. See also R. H. Stein, *An Introduction to the Parables of Jesus* (Philadelphia: Westminster, 1981), pp. 53–56; and his article "The Parables of Jesus in Recent Study," *W&W* 5 (1985): 249–50.

13. Blomberg, *Interpreting the Parables*, p. 17; G. Bray, *Biblical Interpretation: Past and Present* (Downers Grove, Ill., and Leicester: InterVarsity, 1996), p. 501.

14. Stein, *Parables of Jesus*, p. 156 n. 7.

15. Compare J. W. Sider, "Proportional Analogy in the Gospel Parables," *NTS* 31 (1985): 1–23; M. L. Bailey, "Guidelines for Interpreting Jesus' Parables," *BibSac* 155 (1998): 29–38.

16. R. H. Stein, "Interpreting the Parables of Luke," *SWJT* 40 (1997): 6–16.

17. Consult the interesting studies of M. Black, "The Parables as Allegory," *BJRL* 42 (1960): 273–87; R. E. Brown, "Parable and Allegory Reconsidered," *NTS* 5 (1962): 36–45.

18. C. H. Dodd, *The Parables of the Kingdom* (London: Nesbit, 1935), p. 26.

19. Jeremias, *Parables*, pp. 113, 114.

20. A. M. Brouwer, *De Gelijkenissen* (Leiden: Brill, 1946), p. 247; G. V. Jones, *The Art and Truth of the Parables* (London: SPCK, 1964), p. 38.

21. M. A. Tolbert, *Perspectives on the Parables* (Philadelphia: Fortress, 1979), p. 20.

22. D. O. Via Jr., "A Response to Crossan, Funk, and Peterson," *Semeia* 1 (1974): 222, asserts, "I have no interest at all in even the Persona of the historical Jesus."

23. J. D. Crossan, "The Good Samaritan: Towards a Generic Definition of Parable," *Semeia* 2 (1974): 101, seems to indicate that it is more important for a proposition to be interesting than to be true.

24. Among others, refer to J. D. Crossan, *In Parables: The Challenge of the Historical Jesus* (New York: Harper & Row, 1973), p. 5.

25. L. Berkhof, *Principles of Biblical Interpretation* (Grand Rapids: Baker, 1952), p. 100.

26. A. B. Mickelsen, *Interpreting the Bible* (Grand Rapids: Eerdmans, 1963), p. 229.

27. K. Aland, *Synopsis of the Four Gospels* (Stuttgart: Württembergische Bibelanstalt, 1976).

28. Some commentators list Luke 12:57–59 as a parable; see, e.g., I. H. Marshall, *The Gospel of Luke* (Grand Rapids: Eerdmans, 1978), pp. 550–51; others do not, e.g., J. A Fitzmyer, *The Gospel according to Luke X–XXIV*, AB 28A (Garden City, N.J.: Doubleday, 1985), p. 1002, who calls these verses pragmatic advice.

Chapter 1: Salt

1. Deut. 29:22, 23; Judg. 9:45; Job 39:6; Ps. 107:34; Jer. 17:6; Zeph. 2:9.

2. Jeremias, *Parables*, p. 169; Marshall, *The Gospel of Luke*, p. 596; Hauck, *TDNT*, I:229.

3. E. P. Deatrick, "Salt, Soil, Saviour," *BA* 25 (1962): 47, mentions that in modern Israel "savorless salt" is spread on flat rooftops that are covered with soil. Because of the salt, the soil hardens. Rooftops are used as gathering places and playgrounds.

4. The verb in Matt. 5:13 and Luke 14:34 for "to lose its saltiness" is *mōrainein*, which has the primary meaning of "to make foolish" in the active voice and "to become foolish" in the passive; W. Bauer, W. F. Arndt, F. W. Gingrich, and F. Danker, *A Greek-English Lexicon of the New Testament* (Chicago: University of Chicago Press, 1978), p. 531.

5. W. Nauck, "Salt as a Metaphor," *StTh* 6 (1953): 176.

Chapter 2: Two Builders

1. E. F. F. Bishop, *Jesus of Palestine* (London: Lutterworth, 1955), p. 86, refers to mud houses between Gaza and Ashkelon, built far enough removed from a sudden change in direction of a watercourse. But during one winter in the Negev Desert, a dry creek suddenly filled, changed course, and washed away an entire Bedouin encampment with loss of human life and cattle.

2. Jeremias, *Parables*, p. 27. Hellenistic houses were often built with cellars (basements), an unusual feature in Palestine.

Chapter 3: Children in the Marketplace

1. Jeremias, *Parables*, p. 161, follows the suggestion made by Bishop, *Jesus of Palestine*, p. 104. Jeremias writes: "That some children were sitting perhaps implies that they

were content with 'piping' or 'wailing,' leaving the more strenuous exercises for the others." However, there is a real danger of reading too much into the text at this point.

2. Marshall, *Luke*, p. 300.

3. F. Mussner, "Der nicht erkannte Kairos (Mt 11, 16–19 = Lk 7, 31–35)," *Bib* 40 (1959): 600, pictures all the children sitting down and calling out.

4. A. Plummer, *The Gospel of Luke (ICC)* (New York: C. Scribner & Sons, 1902), p. 163.

5. Matt. 9:11; Luke 5:30; 15:1–2; 19:7.

6. Piska 26, in W. G. Braude, *Pesikta Rabbati*, 2 vols. (New Haven: Yale University Press, 1968–1969), 1:526–27. Also see *SB*, II:161.

7. Jeremias, *Parables*, p. 162 n. 44.

Chapter 4: Sower

1. W. Neil, "Expounding the Parables," *ExpT* 78 (1965): 74.

2. J. Jeremias, "Palästinakundliches zum Gleichnis vom Säemann," *NTS* 13 (1967): 48–53. Also see his *Parables*, p. 12; R. A. Foster and W. D. Shiell, "The Parable of the Sower and the Seed in Luke 18:1–10: Jesus' Parable of Parables," *RevExp* 94 (1997): 259–67.

3. N. Levison, *The Parables: Their Background and Local Setting* (Edinburgh: Clark, 1926), p. 15.

4. Jeremias, "Palästinakundliches," p. 53; and see K. D. White, "The Parable of the Sower," *JTS* 15 (1964): 300–307; P. B. Payne, "The Order of Sowing and Ploughing," *NTS* 25 (1978): 123–39. That the earth is to bring forth fruit in abundance in the messianic age seems to be the teaching of the Old Testament (Amos 9:13; Jer. 31:27; Ezek. 36:29, 30) and of the pseudepigrapha and rabbinic writings. N. A. Dahl, "The Parables of Growth," *StTh* 5 (1951): 153; *SB*, IV:880–90; R. K. McIver, "One Hundred-Fold Yield—Miraculous or Mundane? Matthew 13.8, 23; Mark 4:8, 20; Luke 8.8," *NTS* 40 (1994): 606–8.

5. H. N. Ridderbos, *Studies in Scripture and Its Authority* (St. Catharines: Paideia, 1978), p. 50.

6. I. H. Marshall, "Tradition and Theology in Luke," *Tyn Bul* 20 (1969): 63.

7. F. F. Bruce, *Second Thoughts on the Dead Sea Scrolls* (London: Paternoster, 1956), p. 101.

8. B. Van Elderen, "The Purpose of the Parables according to Matthew 13:10–17," in *New Dimensions in Evangelical New Testament Studies*, ed. R. N. Longenecker and M. C. Tenney (Grand Rapids: Zondervan, 1974), p. 185.

9. W. Hendriksen, *The Gospel of Matthew* (Grand Rapids: Baker, 1973), p. 553. J. R. Kirkland rejects this explanation and holds that wise and discerning people see the truth hidden in parables, but the dull and unperceptive do not. See his "The Earliest Understanding of Jesus' Use of Parables: Mark IV 10–12 in Context," *NovT* 19 (1977): 13. Kirkland's contention flies in the face of Jesus' prayer: "I praise you, Father, Lord of heaven and earth because you have hidden these things from the wise and learned and revealed them to little children" (Matt. 11:25).

10. J. D. Kingsbury, *The Parables of Jesus in Matthew 13* (Richmond: John Knox, 1969), p. 13.

11. Kirkland, "Earliest Understanding," pp. 16–20.

12. Hendriksen, *Mark*, p. 154.

13. Marshall, *Luke*, p. 323.

14. B. Gerhardsson, "The Parable of the Sower and Its Interpretation," *NTS* 14 (1967–1968): 192, concludes that the parable and its interpretation go together like hand in glove. "If the parable—in the form we know it—is from Jesus, then so is the interpretation." See C. F. D. Moule, "Mark 4:1–20. Yet Once More," *Neotestamentica et Semitica* (1969): 95–113.

15. *Revised English Bible, With the Apocrypha* (Oxford and Cambridge: Oxford and Cambridge University Presses, 1989).

16. Gerhardsson, "Parable of the Sower," p. 187.

17. Dodd, *Parables* 182.

18. Gerhardsson, "Parable of the Sower," p. 175.

19. Jülicher, *Gleichnisreden*, 2:528.

20. *The Gospel of Thomas*, trans. B. M. Metzger, Saying 9, reads as follows: "Jesus said: 'Behold, the sower went out, he filled his hand, he sowed [the seed]. Some [seeds] fell on the road. The birds came [and] gathered them up. Others fell on the rock and did not send a root down to the earth, and did not send an ear up to heaven. And others fell among thorns. They choked the seed and the worm ate it [*lit.* them]. And others fell upon the good earth; and it brought forth good fruit up to heaven. It bore sixty-fold and one hundred and twenty-fold.'"

It is obvious that the writer of the Gospel of Thomas has cast the parable of the sower in a Gnostic mold. The reason why the writer concludes the parable with "One hundred and twenty-fold" may very well be that he understood the number 12 to be the number of perfection. See H. Montefiore and H. E. W. Turner, *Thomas and the Evangelists* (London: SCM, 1962), p. 48.

21. Kingsbury, *Parables of Jesus*, p. 62.

Chapter 5: Seed Growing Secretly

1. See, for example, Mark 4:2, 10, 13, 33, where the plural form *parables* is consistently used.

2. Lane, *Mark*, p. 149. Ridderbos, *Coming of the Kingdom*, p. 142, is of the opinion that Mark chose these three parables to teach the "positive meaning of the delay of judgment."

3. When Mark writes that the soil "all by itself" produces grain, he does not imply that the soil produces a crop without God's provision, but that the farmer's help is not needed in the growing process of the wheat. W. Michaelis, *Die Gleichnisse Jesu* (Hamburg: Furche-Verlag, 1956), p. 38. Furthermore, the emphasis in producing grain should not be put on the soil as much as on the seed itself. R. Stuhlmann, "Beobachtungen zu Markus IV.26–29," *NTS* 19 (1972–1973): 156.

4. Jülicher, *Gleichnisreden*, 2:540.

5. Parallels in apostolic literature include 1 Clement 23:4, "O senseless ones! Compare yourselves to a tree. Take a vine, for instance: first it sheds its leaves, then comes a bud, then a leaf, then a flower, and only after this, first a green grape and then a ripe one," *Apostolic Fathers*, vol. 2, ed. R. M. Grant and H. H. Graham (Camden, N.J.: Thomas Nelson & Sons, 1965), p. 48. Also see 2 Clement 11:3, and the Gospel of Thomas, Saying 21.

6. H. B. Swete, *The Gospel according to St Mark* (London: Macmillan, 1909), p. 85.

7. For a comprehensive classification of these interpretations, see C. E. B. Cranfield, "Message of Hope, Mark 4:21–32," *Interp* 9 (1955): 158–62; P. R. Jones, "The Seed Parables of Mark," *RevExp* 75 (1978): 519–38.

8. J. Calvin, *Harmony of the Evangelists* (Grand Rapids: Eerdmans, 1949), 2:128. Although Calvin directs attention to the period of growth, he places equal emphasis on the one who sows the seed. Cranfield's criticism has some validity: Calvin considered the parable to be addressed to Jesus' disciples. However, the application in Calvin's commentary seems much broader than the mere circle of the twelve disciples. See Cranfield, "Message of Hope," p. 159.

9. Jeremias, *Parables*, p. 152.

10. Farmers in America's Midwest have a saying that corn should be "knee-high by the fourth of July."

11. Hendriksen, *Mark*, p. 170. See J. P. Heil, "Reader-Response and the Narrative Context of the Parables about Growing Seed in Mark 4:1–34," *CBQ* 54 (1992): 271–86.

Heil points out that the "teaching or 'sowing' of the seed/word will steadily and inevitably . . . grow into a delightful 'harvest' of seed/people to populate God's kingdom" (p. 284). And see G. Thiessen, "Der Bauer und die von selbst Frucht bringende Erde: Naiver Synergismus in Mk 4,26–29?" *ZNW* 85 (1994): 167–82.

Chapter 6: Wheat and Weeds

1. Bauer et al., *Lexicon*, p. 339.

2. I. Löw, *Die Flora der Juden* (Hildersheim, 1967), 1:725; *SB*, I:667.

3. My father-in-law bought a farm in western Canada in the late 1930s. He soon found the fields covered with a weed called "daisy." From the previous owner he learned the cause: some years before, a neighbor who bore a grudge had ridden one day on horseback through the fields scattering daisy seed. The result is still evident today.

4. Jülicher, *Gleichnisreden*, 2:548, asserts that weeds mature before the wheat.

5. Compare Matt. 15:15, where the same question of parable explanation is asked. Consult M. de Goedt, "L'Explication de la Parable de L'Ivraie (Mt XIII, 36–43)," *RB* 66 (1959): 35. And see J. Jeremias, "Das Gleichnis vom Unkraut unter dem Weizen," in *Neotestamentica et Patristica* (Leiden: Brill, 1962), p. 59.

6. R. Schippers, *Gelijkenissen van Jezus* (Kampen: J. H. Kok, 1962), p. 71.

7. Jeremias, *Parables*, pp. 84–85, confidently asserts that "it is impossible to avoid the conclusion that the interpretation of the tares is the work of Matthew himself." According to Kingsbury, *Parables of Jesus*, p. 109, it is Jesus the exalted Lord who exhorts the Christians in Matthew's church to be obedient to the will of God. However, as R. H. Gundry observes, "The answer to the question of origin is the teaching of Jesus." *The Use of the Old Testament in St. Matthew's Gospel* (Leiden: Brill, 1967), p. 213. In short we do not have to go to the imaginative mind of Matthew. Rather, the origin of this teaching lies in Jesus himself.

8. Ridderbos, *Coming of the Kingdom*, p. 139.

9. Schippers, *Gelijkenissen*, p. 71.

10. W. G. Doty, "An Interpretation of the Weeds and Wheat," *Interp* 25 (1971): 189.

11. With thanks to Hunter, *Parables*, p. 48, who seems to have a boundless store of rhymes, poems, and sayings.

12. Calvin, *Harmony of the Evangelists*, 2:120.

13. Numerous examples may be found in the series, *Works of the Fathers*, collected by Thomas Aquinas. See *Commentary on the Four Gospels*, I, *St. Matthew* (Oxford: n.p., 1842).

14. Stein, *Parables of Jesus*, pp. 48–49.

Chapter 7: Mustard Seed

1. A. B. Bruce, *The Parabolic Teaching of Christ* (New York: A. C. Armstrong, 1908), p. 91.

2. Michaelis, *Gleichnisse*, p. 55. In the Gospel of Thomas the parables of the mustard seed and of the yeast are separated. They do have the same wording (with slight variations) as the canonical accounts: see Sayings 20 and 96.

3. A number of leading manuscripts have the reading "great tree" in Luke 13:19. B. M. Metzger, *A Textual Commentary on the Greek New Testament*, 2d ed. (Stuttgart: Deutsche Bibelgesellschaft, 1994), p. 137, writes, "Although copyists may have deleted *mega* to harmonize Luke with the prevailing text of Matthew (13:32), it is much more probable that, in the interest of heightening the contrast between a mustard seed and a tree, *mega* was added—as it was added also in a few witnesses in the Matthean parallel."

4. The mustard seed *(Sinapis nigra)* is black and grows predominantly in the southern and eastern areas of Mediterranean countries, Mesopotamia and Afghanistan. It is the smallest seed of the three or four varieties of mustard plants. P. R. Jones, "The Seed Parables in Mark," *RevExp* 75 (1978): 519–38; Löw, *Die Flora der Juden,* 1:521; O. Michel, *TDNT,* III:810–12. Near the Lake of Galilee, even today this mustard grows to a height of 10 feet (3 meters).

5. For rabbinic examples, see *SB,* I:669.

6. It is possible that the two evangelists have added this explanation as a help to the reader.

7. J. W. Wevers, *Ezekiel* (Greenwood, S.C.: Attic, 1969), p. 139. C. L. Feinberg, *The Prophecy of Ezekiel* (Chicago: Moody, 1969), p. 97, says that the concluding verses of Ezekiel 17 "without question introduce a Messianic prophecy." Also see D. M. G. Stalker, *Ezekiel* (London: SCM, 1968), p. 154; J. B. Taylor, *Ezekiel* (Downers Grove, Ill.: InterVarsity, 1969), p. 146; and J. Mánek, *Und Brachte Frucht* (Stuttgart: Calwer, 1977), p. 28.

8. Scholars hesitate to refer to the mustard plant as a tree. See R. W. Funk, "The Looking-Glass Tree is for the Birds," *Interp* 27 (1973): 5. Nevertheless, it reaches a height of 10 to 12 feet. Popular speech in that day described the growing phenomenon of the mustard plant as "a tree."

9. Rabbis used to call Gentiles "the birds of the air." See Hunter, *Parables,* p. 45, and Kingsbury, *Parables of Jesus,* p. 82. Also, H. K. McArthur, "The Parable of the Mustard Seed," *CBQ* 33 (1971): 208; O. Kuss, "Zum Sinngehalt des Doppelgleichnisses vom Senfkorn und Sauerteig," *Bib* 40 (1959): 653.

Chapter 8: Yeast

1. Jeremias, *Parables,* p. 147, summarily states, "No housewife would bake so vast a quantity of meal."

2. For a lengthy description, see C. L. Mitton, "Leaven," *ExpT* 84 (1973): 339–43.

3. R. C. H. Lenski, *Interpretation of St. Matthew's Gospel* (Columbus: Lutheran Book Concern, 1943), pp. 530–32.

4. F. Godet, *Commentary on St. Luke's Gospel* (Grand Rapids: Kregel, reprint of 1870 ed.), 2:122. R. W. Funk, "Beyond Criticism in Quest of Literary: The Parable of the Leaven," *Interp* 25 (1971), understands the number 3 eschatologically and writes, "Three measures of meal points to the sacramental power of the Kingdom, to the festive occasion of an epiphany," p. 163. The emphasis, however, should fall on the inherent power of the yeast and not on the significance of the flour or the number 3.

5. Hendriksen, *Matthew,* p. 568.

6. For a comprehensive study, see Ridderbos, *Coming of the Kingdom,* especially pp. 342–56.

Chapter 9: Hidden Treasure and Pearl

1. For example, scholars point to the Gospel of Thomas, where the two parables are separated (Hidden Treasures, Saying 109; and Pearl, Saying 76). This is also true for the parables of the mustard seed and the yeast. Nevertheless, the available evidence is inconclusive. The issue is discussed by O. Glombitza, "Der Perlenkaufmann," *NTS* 7 (1960–1961): 153–61. Also see J. C. Fenton, "Expounding the Parables: IV. The Parables of the Treasure and the Pearl (Mt. 13:44–46)," *ExpT* 77 (1966): 178–80; J. Dupont, "Les Paraboles du Trésor et de la Perle," *NTS* 14 (1967–1968): 408–18.

2. E. A. Armstrong, *The Gospel Parables* (New York: Sheed and Ward, 1967), p. 154.

3. Because we lack the necessary details of ownership laws in Jesus' day, we need not call the man's morality into question. The parable does not stress the ethical conduct of

the man who found the treasure. For an extensive discussion, see J. D. M. Derrett, *Law in the New Testament* (London: Longman and Todd, 1970), pp. 1–16.

4. B. T. D. Smith, *The Parables of the Synoptic Gospels* (Cambridge, England: SPCK, 1937), p. 145.

5. Smith, *Parables*, p. 146. And see Schippers, *Gelijkenissen*, p. 103; Jeremias, *Parables*, p. 199; Hauck, *TDNT*, IV:472.

6. E. Linnemann, *Parables of Jesus: Introduction and Exposition* (London: SPCK, 1966), p. 100.

7. Hunter, *Parables*, p. 80. Also Michaelis, *Gleichnisse*, p. 66.

Chapter 10: Fishnet

1. In the Gospel of Thomas, Saying 8, a similar parable is found, but the emphasis differs radically: "And he said: Man is like a fisherman who cast his net into the sea; he drew it out of the sea when it was full of little fishes. Among them the wise fisherman found a large good fish. The wise fisherman cast all the little fishes down into the sea (and) chose the large fish without difficulty. He who has ears to hear, let him hear."

2. Mánek, *Frucht*, p. 50. See also Jeremias, *Parables*, p. 226.

3. Michaelis, *Gleichnisse*, pp. 68–69. Also consult B. Gerhardsson, "The Seven Parables in Matthew XIII," *NTS* 19 (1972–1973): 18–19.

4. G. Cansdale, *Animals of Bible Lands* (Grand Rapids: Zondervan, 1970), p. 216. Consult also Dalman, *Arbeit und Sitte*, 4:351, who refers to twenty-four species.

5. An interesting description is provided by W. O. E. Oesterley, *The Gospel Parables in the Light of Their Jewish Background* (New York: Macmillan, 1936), pp. 85–86.

6. Dodd, *Parables*, p. 188.

7. For example, Lenski, *Matthew's Gospel*, p. 547, says that the "net is the Gospel."

8. In an interesting short study, J. Mánek, "Fishers of Men," *NovT* 2 (1958): 138–41, shows that the sea is at enmity with God (Rev. 21:1). "Because the sea is the place of revolt against God, it cannot participate in the new world of the future. It will cease with other demonic powers as it is shown in the vision of a new heaven and a new earth in Rev. XXI 1," p. 139. Fishers of men, therefore, rescue them from a sphere hostile to God.

9. See W. F. Albright and C. S. Mann, *Matthew* (New York: Doubleday, 1971), p. cxliv.

Chapter 11: Unforgiving Servant

1. The phrase may also be translated "seventy times seven." See Gen. 4:24.

2. When an oriental monarch summoned his secretaries of the treasury, he bypassed all the minor officials. He met the highest placed public servants. See K. H. Rengstorf, *TDNT*, II:266, who points out that the word *servant* "is the usual linguistic form for the relation of the subject to the king in the despotic monarchies of the ancient Orient."

3. H. G. Liddell and R. Scott, *A Greek-English Lexicon* (Oxford: Clarendon, 1968), p. 1154. The sum of ten thousand talents amounts to numerous millions of dollars.

4. Josephus, *Antiquities*, 17.11.4 [318–20]. See also *Antiquities*, 12.4.4. [176], where he writes that a certain Joseph son of Tobias offered the Egyptian king Ptolemy to collect eight thousand talents in taxes from Coelosyria, Phoenicia, Judea, and Samaria and even to double the amount.

5. The minister of finance confessed inability to pay and asked for deferment. In another year he promised to pay the total sum. Thus he became indebted to the king and owed him the money from which the king a year later would receive interest as well. Thus when the king forgave the minister his debt *(daneion)*, it was actually a loan. Derrett, *Law in the New Testament*, pp. 39–40. Bernard Brandon Scott interprets the story not as reality but as fiction. See his *Hear Then the Parable: A Commentary on the Parables of Jesus* (Minneapolis: Fortress, 1989), p. 271; and his "The King's Accounting: Matthew 18:23–24," *JBL*

104 (1985): 433; and Martinus C. De Boer, "Ten Thousand Talents? Matthew's Interpretation and Redaction of the Parable of the Unforgiving Servant [Matt 18:23–35]," *CBQ* 50 (1988): 214–32.

6. For a study on symmetry in the parable, see F. H. Breukelman, "Eine Erklärung des Gleichnisses vom Schalksknecht," in *Parrhesia*, Festschrift honoring Karl Barth (Zürich, 1966), pp. 261–87.

7. The reason the fellow servant could not pay was that he was on the way to the king to pay his annual revenue. The minister of finance by jailing his follow-minister offended the king by depriving him of the revenue due that day. Consult Derrett, *Law in the New Testament*, pp. 41–42.

8. "Torture was regularly employed in the East against a disloyal governor, or one who was tardy in his delivery of the taxes, in order to discover where they had hidden the money, or to extort the amount from their relations or friends." Jeremias, *Parables*, p. 212.

9. Ps. 103:6, 8; Micah 6:8. Consult F. Notscher, "Righteousness (justice)," in *Encyclopedia of Biblical Theology* (London, 1970), 2:782.

10. *SB*, I:800–801.

11. The Old Testament system of the Year of Jubilee did not work very well. This was not because of God's law but because of man's selfishness and greed. The Old Testament prophets constantly preached justice on the basis of law. See A. H. Leitch, "Righteousness," in *ZPEB*, 5:108.

12. Linnemann, *Parables*, pp. 111–13; Hunter, *Parables*, p. 69.

13. "Jewish law only permitted the sale of an Israelite in case of theft, if the thief could not restore what he had stolen; the sale of a wife was absolutely forbidden under Jewish jurisdiction; hence the king and his 'servants' are represented as Gentiles." Jeremias, *Parables*, p. 211. Also see *SB*, I:798. But the parable does not refer to Jewish people and therefore Jewish law does not apply. See Derrett, *Law in the New Testament*, p. 38.

14. R. S. Wallace, *Many Things in Parables* (New York: Harper and Brothers, 1955), p. 171.

15. Ibid., p. 174; Linnemann, *Parables*, p. 111.

16. D. O. Via Jr., *The Parables* (Philadelphia: Fortress, 1967), p. 142.

17. Also see Mark 11:25 and Col. 3:13.

Chapter 12: Workers in the Vineyard

1. Jeremias, *Parables*, p. 136, places the emphasis on the employer rather than on the workers and consequently speaks of the parable of the Good Employer. Also see Hunter, *Parables*, p. 70. Mánek, *Frucht*, p. 55, calls the parable "Equal Pay."

2. A. C. Schultz, "Vine, Vineyard," in *ZPEB*, 5:882, states that although the grapes begin to ripen in July, the harvest takes place in September. Consult Dalman, *Arbeit und Sitte*, IV:336; Derrett, "Workers in the Vineyard: A Parable of Jesus," *Journal of Jewish Studies* 25 (1974): 72, also published in *Studies in the New Testament* (Leiden: Brill, 1977), 1:56.

3. F. Gryglewicz, "The Gospel of the Overworked Workers," *CBQ* 19 (1957): 192. And see *SB*, I:830.

4. A wage of a denarius for a day's work was just and sufficient for the daily support of a workman and his family. See Mánek, *Frucht*, p. 56.

5. The difference between working conditions in ancient times and modern times is striking. See Oesterley, *Parables*, p. 107.

6. Clocks were not in use; the day was divided into hours beginning at sunrise, even though the Jewish day began at sunset. See Jeremias, *Parables*, p. 136 n. 21. Derrett, "Workers in the Vineyard," p. 56.

7. The introductory sentence, however, is only a starting point. Ridderbos, *Coming of the Kingdom*, p. 141. Yet the owner of the vineyard is the central figure in the parable and his word and deed illustrate the meaning of the kingdom.

8. The rabbinical rule was that a man employed by the hour for any kind of work might collect his wages all during the day. See Baba Mezia IIIa and Nezikin I, in *The Babylonian Talmud* (Boston: Bennet, n.d.), p. 633. Also see *SB*, I:832. By first paying the workers hired last, and by giving them an equal wage, the landowner avoided possible haggling, which could take considerable time. See Derrett, "Workers in the Vineyard," p. 63.

9. During the reign of King Agrippa II, about A.D. 60, the eastern cloisters of the temple at Jerusalem were built with the help of some eighteen thousand workers. The temple treasurer and his associates decided to pay every laborer a full day's wages even if he had worked only one hour of the day. See Josephus, *Antiquities*, 20:219–20; Derrett, "Workers in the Vineyard," p. 63.

10. The word *hetaire* occurs three times in the New Testament: (1) in the parable of the workers in the vineyard (Matt. 20:13); (2) in the parable of the wedding banquet, when the king addresses the guest who did not wear the wedding clothes (Matt. 22:12); (3) in the account of Jesus' arrest in Gethsemane, when Jesus says "Friend, do what you came for" (Matt. 26:50).

According to K. H. Rengstorf, *TDNT*, II:701, the term "always denotes a mutually binding relation between the speaker and the hearer which the latter has disregarded and scorned."

11. C. L. Mitton, "Expounding the Parables, VII. The Workers in the Vineyard (Matthew 20:1–16)," *ExpT* 77 (1966): 308.

12. Citizens in the kingdom of heaven must be fully cognizant of the principles operative in the kingdom. See Wallace, *Parables*, p. 125.

13. Oesterley, *Parables*, p. 104.

14. T. W. Manson, *The Sayings of Jesus* (London: SCM, 1950), p. 220.

15. The parallels of Matthew's and Mark's Gospels are identical except that in Matthew's the parable of the workers in the vineyard is added as an illustration of the saying "So the last will be first, and the first will be last" (Matt. 19:30; 20:16; Mark 10:31). In Luke 13:30 the saying also occurs, although in an entirely different context.

16. A. H. McNeile, *The Gospel according to St. Matthew* (London: Macmillan, 1915), p. 285.

17. Bible translations ascribe Matt. 20:16 to Jesus. The text is not part of the landowner's remarks, but is the conclusion Jesus repeats as a follow-up from Matt. 19:30. The REB, however, does not put the verse in quotation marks, implying that it is Matthew's conclusion to the parable. Jeremias, *Parables*, p. 36, goes so far as to suggest that "we disregard verse 16." On the other hand, Morison (*St. Matthew*, p. 356) and Derrett ("Workers in the Vineyard," p. 51) maintain that the words of Matt. 20:16 are Jesus' own application of the parable. The argument that Jesus did not utter the words of verse 16 lacks clarity and fails to convince.

18. The early church fathers indulged in fanciful interpretations. Irenaeus, for example, interpreted the five periods of work during which the workers were hired as five periods of history: from six to nine was the time of Adam to Noah. Next, the period from nine to twelve o'clock noon was that of Noah to Abraham. Third, from twelve to three included the period from Abraham to Moses. Fourth, the time from three to five denoted the time between Moses and Christ. And last, the one hour from five to six pointed to the period between the ascension and the return of the Lord. *Against Heresies* 4, 36, 7. For an extensive survey of interpretations given by authors from the second to the sixth centuries, see J. M. Tevel, "The Labourers in the Vineyard: The Exegesis of Matthew 20, 1–7 in the Early Church," *VC* 46 (1992): 365–80.

19. Mitton, "Expounding the Parables," p. 310.

20. Hunter, *Parables*, p. 72.

Chapter 13: Two Sons

1. J. D. M. Derrett, "The Parable of the Two Sons," *Studia Theologica* 25 (1971): 109–16, also published in *Studies in the New Testament*, I:76–84, follows Jülicher, *Gleichnisreden*, 2:367. Derrett points out that the first son was the elder and would be the father's successor. "An elder son might well take more interest in form than substance" (*Studies*, p. 81).

2. The textual evidence in regard to the reading of the text varies. Technically, three variations exist. (1) According to Codex Sinaiticus and other manuscripts, the first son says no but repents; the second son says yes but does not go. This is the reading in such translations as the AV, NRSV, and NIV. (2) According to Codex Vaticanus and other manuscripts, the first son says yes but does not go; the second son says no but repents. Who does the will of the father? The answer varies: "the latter," "the last one," "the second." Translations including NASB, NAB, and REB follow Codex Vaticanus. (3) The so-called Western text follows the order of Codex Sinaiticus except that the answer to the question, "Which of the two did what his father wanted?" is: "the last one." This would mean that the son who said yes but did nothing fulfilled his father's request. That is absurd. The choice is therefore either (1) or (2). See J. R. Michaels, "The Parable of the Regretful Son," *HTR* 61 (1968): 15–26. The order does not affect the meaning of the parable at all. Consult Metzger, *Textual Commentary*, pp. 44–46.

3. Metzger, *Textual Commentary*, pp. 45–46, indicates that the committee of the United Bible Societies' Greek New Testament opted for the order given by Codex Sinaiticus. To substantiate this choice, Metzger writes, "It could be argued that if the first son obeyed, there was no reason to summon the second."

Chapter 14: Tenants

1. Gospel of Thomas, Saying 65, "He said: 'A good man had a vineyard. He gave it to tenants that they might cultivate it and he might receive its fruit from them. He sent his servant so that the tenants might give him the fruit of the vineyard. They seized his servant [and] beat him; a little more and they would have killed him. The servant came [and] told it to his master. His master said, Perhaps he did not know them. He sent another servant; the tenants beat him as well. Then the owner sent his son. Since those servants knew that he was the heir of the vineyard, they seized him [and] killed him. He who has ears, let him hear.'" Interestingly, the Gospel of Thomas, Saying 66, continues, "Jesus said: Show me the stone which the builders rejected. It is the cornerstone." See W. G. Morrice, "The Parable of the Tenants and the Gospel of Thomas," *ExpT* 98 (1987): 104–7.

2. Derrett, *Law in the New Testament*, p. 290.

3. Whereas Mark and Luke, as well as the Gospel of Thomas, speak of one servant, Matthew uses the plural. According to Matthew, numerous servants are sent, and they are beaten, stoned, and killed. This may be a deliberate attempt on the part of Matthew to link the parable taught by Jesus to Israel's ecclesiastical history. A degree of allegorization is present, although not in relation to the person of the son: J. A. T. Robinson, "The Parable of the Wicked Husbandman: A Test of Synoptic Relationships," *NTS* 21 (1975): 451. That prophets were killed and stoned to death is evident from 1 Kings 18:13; 2 Chron. 24:21; Matt. 23:37; Luke 13:34; Acts 7:52; 1 Thess. 2:15; and Heb. 11:37.

4. Because the text states explicitly that the servant came to receive "some of the fruit of the vineyard" (Mark 12:2; Luke 20:10), we assume that the owner sent his servant when the vines yielded a harvest.

5. Some scholars see a parallel between the foreign domination of large parts of Galilee before and during the time of Jesus' ministry and the landowner portrayed in the parable. Dodd, *Parables*, p. 125; Jeremias, *Parables*, p. 74; M. Hengel, "Das Gleichnis von den Weingartner Mc 12:1–12 ins Lichte der Zenonpapyri und der rabbinische Gleichnisse," *ZNW* 59 (1968): 11–25; J. E. and R. R. Newell, "The Parable of the Wicked Tenants," *NovT* 14 (1972): 226–37. However, the parable does not at all indicate that the tenants were oppressed by a foreign landowner. On the contrary, the tenants and not the landowner are called wicked *(kakous)*, Matt. 20:41. Consult *SB*, I:871.

6. Derrett, *Law in the New Testament*, pp. 298–99, supposes that the second servant came to the tenants at the end of the second harvest, and the third at the end of the following harvest. Thus for three successive years the tenants kept the income of the vineyard. Although this may be correct, admittedly it remains an assumption.

7. Only Mark relates that after sending three servants in succession the owner sends many others. Matthew says that two groups of servants at two different occasions are sent. Luke speaks of three individual servants who successively come to the tenants.

8. Dodd, *Parables*, p. 125.

9. Derrett, *Law in the New Testament*, pp. 300–304. The tenants could even claim that Deut. 20:6 supported them, "Has anyone planted a vineyard and not begun to enjoy it? Let him go home, or he may die in battle and someone else enjoy it."

10. Both Matthew and Luke state that the tenants threw the son out of the vineyard and then killed him; Mark reverses the order by saying that they first killed him and then threw him out of the vineyard.

11. E. Werner, *The Sacred Bridge* (New York: Columbia University Press, 1959), p. 140.

12. Dodd, *Parables*, p. 131; Hengel, "Gleichnis," p. 37. Jeremias, *Parables*, pp. 72–73, observes that, although Jesus spoke prophetically of himself, "for the mass of his hearers the Messianic significance of the son could not be taken for granted." J. D. Kingsbury ("The Parable of the Wicked Husbandmen and the Secret of Jesus' Divine Sonship in Matthew: Some Literary-Critical Observations," *JBL* 105 [1986]: 643–55) points out that the Jewish leaders understood the metaphors Jesus used to portray his identity. However, this is doubted by J. Wehnert, "Die Teilhabe der Christen an der Herrschaft mit Christus—eine eschatologische Erwartung des frühen Christentums," *ZNW* 88 (1997): 81–96; A. Milavec, "The Identity of 'the Son' and 'the Others': Mark's Parable of the Wicked Husbandmen Reconsidered," *BTB* 20 (1990): 30–37.

13. Lane, *Mark*, p. 419.

14. It is not clear from the text who the other tenants may be. Jeremias (*Parables*, p. 76) on the basis of the Beatitude, "Blessed are the meek, for they will inherit the earth" (Matt. 5:5), asserts that the "others" are the poor. The logic of this assertion is not too convincing. Perhaps one can make the case of taking the word *people (ethnos)* in Matt. 21:43 to refer to the Gentiles.

15. A. Weiser, *The Psalms* (Philadelphia: Westminster, 1962), p. 724.

16. Although the quotation (Ps. 118:22) is also cited in Acts 4:11 and 1 Peter 2:7, there is no reason to maintain that the early Christian church added these words to the parable of the tenants.

17. Jeremias, *TDNT*, I:792. The rejected stone referred to Abraham, David, or the Messiah, according to the rabbis. The builders were depicted as the teachers of the Law. *SB*, I:875–76.

18. M. Black, "The Christological Use of the Old Testament in the New Testament," *NTS* 18 (1971–1972): 13, calls attention to the messianic interpretation of the stone and consequently speaks of the rejected stone and rejected Son. In Aramaic the words *ben* (son) and *eben* (stone) show a verbal relationship. See A. W. Martens, "Produce Fruit Wor-

thy of Repentance," in *The Challenge of Jesus' Parables*, R. N. Longenecker, ed. (Grand Rapids: Eerdmans, 2000), p. 160.

19. Gen. 22:2; Matt. 3:17; Mark 1:11; Luke 3:22; 2 Peter 1:17.

20. The textual evidence seems stronger for the inclusion than for the exclusion of Matt. 21:44. It is possible, of course, to regard the verse as an interpolation from Luke 20:18. Nevertheless, "the antiquity of the reading and its importance in the textual tradition" must be seen as decisive factors for its retention. Metzger (*Textual Commentary*, p. 47) nevertheless suggests that the verse may be an accretion to the text.

21. Some further references to the stone are Isa. 28:16; Dan. 2:34, 44, 45; Acts 4:11; Rom. 9:33; Eph. 2:20; and 1 Peter 2:6.

22. *The Belgic Confession*, Article 27.

Chapter 15: Wedding Banquet

1. An Old Testament parallel is Wisdom's invitation recorded in Prov. 9:2–5.

2. E. Schweizer (*The Good News according to Matthew* [London: SPCK, 1976], pp. 401–2) notes that the three successive parables in Matthew's Gospel are reminiscent of a court case against the Jewish clergy: the parable of the two sons pronounces the verdict, the parable of the tenants imposes the sentence, and the wedding banquet parable executes the verdict.

3. Mánek, *Frucht*, p. 61.

4. Derrett, *Law in the New Testament*, p. 139.

5. Ibid. Derrett calls attention to Sir Thomas More's refusal to attend the coronation of Queen Anne Boleyn in 1534.

6. A number of writers consider this detail, as well as others, to go beyond the limits of oriental exaggeration. See, for example, Armstrong, *Parables*, p. 103; Oesterley, *Parables*, p. 123; Linnemann, *Parables*, p. 94; and Jeremias, *Parables*, p. 68. However, K. H. Rengstorf, "Die Stadt der Mörder (Matt. 22:7)," in *Judentum, Urchristentum, Kirche*, Festschrift honoring J. Jeremias (Berlin: Töpelmann, 1960), pp. 106–29, has accumulated a comprehensive collection of incidents in which messengers dispatched by kings were scorned or killed.

7. 2 Chron. 30:1–10. Josephus, *Antiquities*, 9:264–265, writes that Hezekiah's messengers were scorned, seized, and killed. For comparison, see Judith 1:11.

8. The expression "his army," although in the plural in Greek, is a Semitism. Jeremias, *Parables*, p. 68 n. 75.

9. Rengstorf, "Stadt der Mörder," pp. 106–24. See especially his conclusions on pp. 125–29.

10. D. O. Via Jr., "The Relationship of Form to Content in the Parables: The Wedding Feast," *Interp* 25 (1971): 181, is of the opinion that the king is "unquestioned and unchanging." However, the king shows love, mercy, and patience on the one hand, and displeasure, anger, and vengeance on the other.

11. For a detailed discussion on the king providing the garments for his guests, see Hendriksen, *Matthew*, pp. 797–98. Consult scriptural references in 2 Kings 10:22; Isa. 61:10; Rev. 19:7, 8. D. C. Sim ("The Man without the Wedding Garment [Matthew 22:11–13]," *HeyJ* 31 [1990]: 172) suggests the possibility that the person without the wedding garment was an intruder. But the parable is not about a single intruder but about invited guests who either refuse to come or gladly accept the invitation.

12. Derrett, *Law in the New Testament*, p. 142, contrasts clean, white clothes to dirty clothes that signify mourning. Also see Jeremias, *Parables*, p. 187; *SB*, I:878–79.

13. Jeremias, *Parables*, p. 187.

14. Rev. 3:4, 5, 18 and 19:8. In this last verse, the writer adds the explanation that fine linen represents the righteous acts of the saints.

15. Jeremias, *Parables*, pp. 130, 189.

16. Calvin, *Harmony of the Evangelists*, 2:175.

17. G. Schrenk, *TDNT*, IV:187.

18. J. Morison, *A Practical Commentary on the Gospel according to St. Matthew* (Boston: Bartlett, 1884), p. 407.

Chapter 16: Fig Tree

1. Löw, *Die Flora der Juden*, I:240, points out that the word *summer* (Greek *theros*) in the Hebrew may have occasioned a play on words: *qayis* (summer; summer-fruit) and *qes* (end of life; time of final punishment). Also see J. Dupont, "La parable du figuier qui bourgeonne (Mc XIII, 28–29 et par.)," *RB* 75 (1968): 542, who refers to the prophecy of Amos 8:1, 2, in which the basket of summer fruit has eschatological significance.

2. Dupont, "Parable du figuier," p. 532. The words "even so" leave the impression that Jesus' disciples are compared with another group of people. The "you" of the preceding verse (Matt. 24:32; Mark 13:28; Luke 21:30) should be understood in the formal sense of "one knows that summer is near."

3. Another example of generalization may be seen in Luke 11:42, "you give God a tenth of your mint, rue and all other kinds of garden herbs." The parallel is given in Matt. 23:23, "You give a tenth of your spices—mint, dill and cummin."

4. The words of Matthew and Mark, "right at the door," point to the imminent arrival of the Lord who is coming as Judge and Redeemer. "You too, be patient and stand firm, because the Lord's coming is near. . . . The Judge is standing at the door!" (James 5:8, 9). Note the words of Revelation: "Here I am! I stand at the door and knock" (3:20). Mánek, *Frucht*, p. 34.

5. Lane, *Mark*, p. 448; C. B. Cousar, "Eschatology and Mark's *Theologia Crucis*, A Critical Analysis of Mark 13," *Interp* 24 (1970): 325; G. R. Beasley-Murray, *A Commentary on Mark Thirteen* (London and New York: Macmillan, 1957), p. 97.

6. Interpretations vary as to the meaning of the expression "this generation": (1) the Jewish people of Jesus' day (Beasley-Murray, *Commentary*, p. 100); (2) the Jewish people as a race (Hendriksen, *Matthew*, p. 868); (3) mankind in general (Jerome); (4) the faithful in the church (A. L. Moore, *The Parousia in the New Testament* [Leiden: Brill, 1966], pp. 131–32).

7. E. E. Ellis, *The Gospel of Luke* (The Century Bible) (London: Nelson, 1966), pp. 246–47. The expression is used in 1QpHab. 2:7; 7:2.

8. Mánek, *Frucht*, p. 34.

9. Marshall, *Luke*, pp. 777, 779.

10. Ridderbos, *Coming of the Kingdom*, p. 502.

Chapter 17: Watchful Servant

1. The present imperative, second-person plural, in the active voice is used here and in the parallel verse of Matt. 24:42.

2. The term *going away (apodēmos)* does not necessarily mean going to a distant country. It may imply going outside the province, for example, from Galilee to Decapolis.

3. *SB*, I:688. In Acts 12:4, Luke faithfully reports the Roman watches: "four squads of four soldiers each" guarded Peter during the night. Also see Matt. 14:25 and Mark 6:48, where Jesus is said to walk on the Lake of Galilee during the fourth watch of the night.

4. Dodd, *Parables*, p. 162.

5. The addition "and pray" may be derived from Mark 14:38. It is easier to account for its insertion than for its omission. Metzger, *Textual Commentary*, p. 95.

6. *SB*, II:47. According to the Mishna, when the courtyard consisted of more than one house, the owner could compel the residents to help pay the doorkeeper. Smith, *Parables*, p. 105.

7. J. Dupont, "La Parabole du Maître Qui Rentre dans la Nuit," in *Melanges Bibliques*, Festschrift honoring B. Rigaux (Gembloux: Duculot, 1970), p. 96. Jeremias, in *Parables*, p. 55, asserts that the parable was addressed to the scribes, who possessed the keys of the kingdom of heaven. It is difficult to see from text and context that this is actually the case. Consult Smith, *Parables*, p. 106.

8. Michaelis, *Gleichnisse*, p. 84.

9. The Gospel of Matthew does not have a parable similar to the one of the doorkeeper. Yet parallel verses are Matt. 24:42, "Therefore keep watch, because you do not know on what day your Lord will come"; and Matt. 24:13, "Therefore keep watch, because you do not know the day or the hour." Mark and Luke lack the parable of the ten virgins (Matt. 24:1–13). Because of his incorporation of this passage, Matthew may have deleted the parable of the doorkeeper.

10. Armstrong, *Parables*, p. 124; Dodd, *Parables*, pp. 161, 162; Jeremias, *Parables*, p. 55; Mánek, *Frucht*, p. 35. It is Michaelis, *Gleichnisse*, p. 82, who considers the possibility of two parables that differ from each other, but because of their affinity to a common theme are basically the same. Consult Marshall, *Luke*, p. 537. D. L. Bock (*Luke*, BECNT 3B, vol. 2:9:51–24–53 [Grand Rapids: Baker, 1996], p. 1171 n. 2) writes, "Mark 13:32–37 is at best a conceptual parallel to this Lucan unit."

11. Dupont, "Parabole," p. 105.

12. In the Greek the perfect participle of the verb *perizōnnumi* is used together with the imperative of the verb *eimi*. This use of the perfect tense is that of resultant state. That is, the command is to be dressed always for service: all along be ready!

13. Dodd, Jeremias, and others place this parable in the category of "crisis parables." The category consists of such parables as the waiting servants, the thief at night, the faithful and unfaithful servants, and the ten virgins. According to these scholars, Jesus warns his disciples of the immediate crises they will face when he is crucified. Although this observation is correct, the so-called crisis parables cannot be limited to the death of Jesus. They also focus on the second coming. Morris, *Luke*, p. 216; I. H. Marshall, *Eschatology and the Parables* (London: Tyndale, 1973), pp. 34–35.

14. Jeremias, *Parables*, p. 54 n. 18, calls Luke 12:37b secondary yet pre-Lucan. He notes the word *amēn* (which Luke uses only six times) as well as the Semitic redundancy of *parelthōn*. With other scholars, he considers this verse an allegorizing detail, which indeed it may be. Nevertheless, there is no reason to question the historicity and authenticity of the saying.

15. John 13:1–17; also Luke 22:27.

Chapter 18: Burglar

1. The Gospel of Thomas records the burglar parable in two of its sayings but does not have a christological application. "Therefore I say: If the householder knows that the thief is coming, he will be watching before he comes [and] will not let him break into his house of his kingdom to carry away his goods. But you must keep watch against the world; gird up your loins with great power, so that no robber may find a way to come to you" (Saying 21b). "Jesus said: Blessed is the man who knows in which part [of the night] the robber will come, so that he will arise and collect his . . . and gird up his loins before they come in" (Saying 103).

2. Some scholars hold that the reference to the Son of Man cannot be original but was introduced by the early Christian church. Jeremias, *Parables*, pp. 50–51; Mánek, *Frucht*, p. 66; G. Schneider, *Parusiegleichnisse im Lukas-Evangelium* (Stuttgart, 1975), p. 22. How-

ever, "the prediction of the coming of the Son of Man is a firm part of the teaching of Jesus." Marshall, *Luke*, p. 534. See R. Maddox, "The Function of the Son of Man," *NTS* 15 (1968–1969): 51.

3. Jeremias, *Parables*, p. 50, thinks that the disciples did not need to be warned. The parable, then, is an application of the early church to warn the people against the coming judgment. Marshall, *Eschatology*, p. 35, seriously questions this opinion.

Chapter 19: Servant Entrusted with Authority

1. Jeremias, *Parables*, p. 99, regards Luke 12:41 as a "created situation" even though its "linguistic usage shows that it was already in Luke's source." However, because of the reference to the disciples (Luke 12:22) as Jesus' immediate audience, one cannot rule out the historicity of Peter's question (Luke 12:41).

2. The expression "this parable" does not have to be taken literally as referring only to the one about the burglar. Taken comprehensively, it includes the parable of the door-keeper. This inclusive use of the word *parable* is also found in Luke 15:3, which covers the stories of the lost sheep, the lost coin, and the lost son.

3. The Greek term *oikonomos* may mean (1) a trustworthy slave given authority over his master's household (Luke 12:42); (2) a public official collecting rent (Rom. 16:23); (3) a manager (Luke 16:1), *SB*, II:219.

4. The parable of the faithful and unfaithful servants rings an echo in the story of Ahikar. See R. H. Charles, *Apocrypha and Pseudepigrapha* (Oxford: Clarendon, 1977), 2:715.

5. Bauer et al., *Lexicon*, p. 200, allow for the meaning "to punish with utmost severity."

6. O. Betz, "The Dichotomized Servant and the End of Judas Iscariot," *RQ* 5 (1964): 46, refers to 1QS 2:16, 17: "God will 'single out' the hypocrite for evil so that he will be cut off from the midst of all the Sons of Light; . . . He will have his allotted portion in the midst of those accursed forever." The verb *dichotomein* and the phrase *tithenai meros tinos* are hapax legomena in the New Testament and therefore open to various interpretations. Consult Jeremias, *Parables*, p. 57 nn. 30, 31.

7. Ps. 37:9a, 22b, 34b, 38b.

8. Jesus' characteristic use of *amēn* in Matt. 24:47 is *alēthōs* in Luke 12:44.

9. The two evangelists may have had access to a common source when they wrote their Gospels. It may also be possible that Luke was able to consult the Gospel of Matthew when he composed his own. W. C. Allen, *The Gospel according to St. Matthew (ICC)* (Edinburgh: T. & T. Clark, 1922), p. 262.

10. Michel, *TDNT*, V:150.

11. It occurs thirteen times in Matthew's Gospel (6:2, 5, 16; 7:5; 15:7; 22:18; 23:13, 15, 23, 25, 27, 29; and 24:51), once in Mark (7:6), and three times in the Gospel of Luke (6:42; 12:56; and 13:15).

12. Plummer, *Luke*, p. 333.

13. Michaelis, *Gleichnisse*, p. 74, and Jeremias, *Parables*, p. 56, apply the parable of Luke, because of Peter's question (Luke 12:41), to the apostles. But this interpretation would mean that the parable has little or no significance for the Christian.

14. Fitzmyer, *Luke X–XXIV*, pp. 986–87.

15. The saying is recorded six times by Matthew (8:12; 13:42, 50; 22:13; 24:51; 25:30) and once by Luke (13:28).

Chapter 20: Ten Virgins

1. P. Trutza, "Marriage," in *ZPEB*, pp. 4, 96, indicates that "rabbis fixed the minimum age for marriage at twelve for the girls and thirteen for the boys."

2. "The bridesmaids stood about the bride, all dressed in white—there were usually ten of them." Daniel-Rops, *Daily Life in Palestine at the Time of Christ* (London, 1962),

p. 124. Likewise J. A. Findlay, *Jesus and His Parables* (London: Epworth, 1951), pp. 111–12, refers to ten maidens whom he saw in a Galilean town making their way to the bride to keep her company while she waited for the arrival of the bridegroom.

3. Jeremias, "Lampades," *ZNW* 55 (1964): 199.

4. The textual evidence for the inclusion of the words "and the bride" at the end of verse 1 comes from an impressive combination of Western and Caesarean witnesses. Metzger, *Textual Commentary*, p. 52.

5. Oesterley, *Parables*, p. 136.

6. Jeremias, *TDNT*, IV:1100.

7. Jeremias, "Lampades," p. 198. Also *SB*, I:969 refers to this practice in the land of Israel, where the bride is brought from her father's home to that of her husband during the night. She is preceded by ten torches made of poles to which copper vessels are attached. In these vessels are oil-soaked rags that are lit and used to illumine the way.

8. Gen. 34:12; Exod. 22:16; 1 Sam. 18:25.

9. Daniel-Rops, *Daily Life*, p. 122.

10. For a detailed discussion, consult H. Granqvist, *Marriage Conditions in Palestinian Village* (Helsingfors, 1931), pp. 132–55. "If the bride price has also been given, the wedding can take place at any time; it may happen that the conclusion of the contract is postponed until the wedding day, but in any case the bridegroom may not go into his bride before it has taken place," p. 155.

11. An interesting sideline appears in Pirqe R. Eliezer 41, *Babylonian Talmud*, "Moses went (on the day of lawgiving) into the camp of the Israelites, and awoke them out of their sleep. 'Arise out of your sleep; the Bridegroom (God) is already on his way and claims his bride (Israel).'" *SB*, I:970.

12. In the New Testament, the meaning "to put in order" for *kosmeō* occurs only in Matt. 25:7. H. Sasse, *TDNT*, III:867.

13. Oesterley, *Parables*, p. 135.

14. In rabbinic literature the saying, "I don't know you," could be used by a teacher to expel a student for a week. *SB*, I:469; IV:1, 293.

15. Marshall, *Eschatology and the Parables*, p. 39, points out that with respect to Matt. 7:21–23 and Matt. 25:11, 12 "it is difficult not to hear in them the tones of the Son of Man."

16. G. Bertram, *TDNT*, IX:234.

17. Rabbi Johanan ben Zakkai, a contemporary of the apostles, taught a parable of a king who summoned his servants to a banquet without setting a time. The wise servants got dressed for the occasion and waited at the door of the palace. The foolish servants kept on working and had to come to the banquet in soiled clothes. The king was happy with the wise but angry with the foolish servants. Shabbath 153a, Moed I, *The Babylonian Talmud* (London: Soncino, 1938), p. 781.

18. Thomas Aquinas has collected numerous examples from the works of the church fathers. *Commentary on the Four Gospels, I, St. Matthew* (Oxford: n.p., 1842), pp. 844–50.

19. Jeremias, *Parables*, p. 51, writes that "Matthew saw in the parable an allegory of the *Parousia* of Christ." However, as Michaelis (*Gleichnisse*, p. 94) observes correctly, the parable has always been a parable on the return of Christ. There is no reason to designate it an allegory.

20. Schippers, *Gelijkenissen*, p. 114.

21. R. A. Batey, *New Testament Nuptial Imagery* (Leiden: Brill, 1971), p. 47.

22. Lenski, *St. Matthew's Gospel*, p. 961.

Chapter 21: Talents

1. Plummer, *St. Matthew*, p. 347.

2. Many commentators think that Jesus in his teaching "made more than one use of the basic idea" expressed in the two parables. Morris, *Luke*, p. 273. See also Geldenhuys, *Luke*, pp. 476–77; Plummer, *St. Luke*, p. 437; Th. Zahn, *Das Evangelium des Lucas* (Leipzig: A. Deichert, 1913), p. 628 n. 23; Lenski, *Matthew's Gospel*, p. 971. Others, among whom is Manson, *Sayings*, p. 313, want to see two versions of one original parable. Jeremias, *Parables*, p. 58, states that the parable of the talents has come down in three versions: Matt. 25:14–30; Luke 19:12–27; and in fragment 18 of the Gospel of the Nazaraeans. However, it is questionable indeed to hold that three versions descended from one original parable, especially when the fragment of the Nazarene Gospel seems to rely on the Matthew account. Indeed, P. Vielhauer (*New Testament Apocrypha*, ed. E. Hennecke and W. Schneemelcher [Philadelphia: Westminster, 1963], 1:140) concludes "that the content of the [Gospel of the Nazaraeans] was roughly identical with that of Matthew and consequently that the [Gospel of the Nazaraeans] was merely a secondary form of Matthew."

3. J. Ellul, in "Du texte au sermon (18). Les talents. Matthieu 25/13–30," *Études Théologiques et Religieuses* 48 (1973): 125–38, questions whether it is possible to discover the oldest form of the parable. The message of the parable is too complex.

4. J. D. M. Derrett, "The Parable of the Talents and Two Logia," *ZNW* 56 (1965): 184–95, published in *Law in the New Testament*, pp. 17–31. See especially p. 18.

5. *SB*, I:970. From rabbinic sources it is evident that both capital and profit belonged to the master of the servant. However, if the servant happened to be a Hebrew, he might accumulate the profit for himself.

6. According to the rabbis, "Money can only be guarded [by placing it] in the earth," Baba Mezia 42a, Nezikin I, *The Babylonian Talmud*, 250–51.

7. Matt. 18:23.

8. In the light of Lev. 26:1–13 and Deut. 28:1–14, the Jew acknowledged that God grants rewards for faithful obedience. Through these blessings obedient Jews would be at the top economically and politically, never at the bottom.

9. The expression "enter the joy" of the master is equivalent to "enter the kingdom" and "enter life." J. Schneider, *TDNT*, II:677. Happiness or joy points to a feast, Jeremias, *Parables*, p. 60 n. 42; it can be used as a synonym for banquet, Smith, *Parables*, p. 166; G. Dalman, *The Words of Jesus* (Edinburgh: T. & T. Clark, 1902), p. 117.

10. Derrett, *Law in the New Testament*, p. 26.

11. Michaelis, *Gleichnisse*, p. 110.

12. Daniel-Rops, *Palestine*, p. 253, indicates that the rabbis tried to lay down rules for business procedure, but that these were not always observed. Although lending at interest was forbidden in the Mosaic Law, the rabbis circumvented this by making a distinction between lending at interest and practicing usury. Usury was condemned. See also J. B. Carpenter, "The Parable of the Talents in Missionary Perspective: A Call for an Economic Spirituality," *Miss* 25 (1997): 165–81.

13. Bauer et al., *Lexicon*, p. 443.

14. Derrett, *Law in the New Testament*, p. 28.

15. Matt. 25:29, except for minor variations, is identical to Matt. 13:12 (and parallels, Mark 4:25; Luke 8:18). Also, the conclusion to the parable of the servant entrusted with authority has similar wording, Luke 12:48. Also see Luke 19:26.

16. Matt. 8:12; 13:42, 50; 22:13; 24:51; 25:30; and Luke 13:28.

17. Rom. 3:2. In his pastoral Epistles to Timothy, Paul exhorts him to guard what had been entrusted to him. 1 Tim. 6:20; 2 Tim. 1:14.

18. Dodd, *Parables*, p. 151; Jeremias, *Parables*, p. 62; Smith, *Parables*, p. 168; E. Kamlah, "Kritik und Interpretation der Parabel von den anvertrauten Geldern: Matt. 25, 14ff.; Luke 19, 12ff.," *Kerygma und Dogma* 14 (1968): 28–38; J. Dupont, "La parabole des tal-

ents (Matt. 25:14–30) ou des mines (Luc 19:12–27)," *Revue de Théologie et de Philosophie* 19 (1969): 376–91.

19. Mánek, *Frucht*, p. 73

Chapter 22: Last Judgment

1. Surveying the theology of Matthew, G. Gray, "The Judgment of the Gentiles in Matthew's Theology," in *Scripture, Tradition and Interpretation*, Festschrift honoring E. F. Harrison (Grand Rapids: Eerdmans, 1978), 199–215, concludes that "the judgment of the Gentiles cannot assuredly be the final judgment of all men," p. 213. J. R. Michaels, "Apostolic Hardships and Righteous Gentiles: A Study of Matthew 25:31–46," *JBL* 84 (1965): 27–38; R. C. Oudersluys, "The Parable of the Sheep and Goats (Matthew 25:31–46): Eschatology and Mission, Then and Now," *RefR* 26 (1973): 151–61. The fact remains, however, that the parable as a whole concerns the last judgment, and that judgment includes all men and is final.

2. Cansdale, *Animals of Bible Lands*, p. 44.

3. Armstrong, *Parables*, p. 191; Jeremias, *Parables*, p. 206.

4. Dalman, *Arbeit und Sitte*, VI:217.

5. Jeremias, *Parables*, p. 206; Mánek, *Frucht*, p. 76.

6. Zech. 14:5; Matt. 16:27; 19:28; 2 Thess. 1:7; Jude 14, 15; Rev. 3:21; 20:11, 12. In the section called "Parables" in the Book of Enoch 62:5, the unrighteous "see that Son of Man sitting on the throne of his glory." He, that is, the Messiah, slays all the sinners by the word of his mouth. Charles, *Apocrypha and Pseudepigrapha*, 2:228.

7. The perfect passive tenses of "blessed" *(eulogēmenoi)* and "prepared" *(hētoimasmenēn)* denote the perfect of resultant state in which an act performed in the past has lasting significance for the present and future.

8. Hendriksen, *Matthew*, p. 888.

9. Plummer, *St. Matthew*, p. 350; Mánek, *Frucht*, p. 75; Manson, *Sayings*, p. 249.

10. In the *Testaments of the Twelve Patriarchs*, Joseph 1:5, 6, a faint echo is heard, although admittedly the thought differs markedly from the Matthean passage:
"I was sold into slavery, and the Lord of all made me free:
I was taken into captivity, and His strong hand succored me.
I was beset with hunger, and the Lord Himself nourished me.
I was alone, and God comforted me:
I was sick, and the Lord visited me:
I was in prison, and my God showed favour unto me." Charles, *Apocrypha*, 2:346.

11. For a comprehensive survey, see G. E. Ladd, "The Parable of the Sheep and the Goats in Recent Interpretation," in *New Dimensions in New Testament Study*, ed. R. N. Longenecker and M. C. Tenney (Grand Rapids: Zondervan, 1974), pp. 191–99.

12. Matt. 10:40, 42; Mark 13:13; John 15:5, 18, 20; 17:10, 23, 26; Acts 9:4; 22:7; 26:14; 1 Cor. 12:27; Gal. 2:20; 6:17; Heb. 2:17.

13. J.-C. Ingelaire, "La 'parabole' du jugement dernier (Matthieu 25/31–46)," *Revue d'Histoire et de Philosophie Religieuses* 50 (1970): 52.

14. H. E. W. Turner, "The Parable of the Sheep and the Goats (Matthew 25:31–46)," *ExpT* 77 (1966): 245, interprets Acts 9:4 by saying, "Certainly here is mysticism, but it is a mysticism of self-identification rather than of unification." Also see C. L. Mitton, "Present Justification and Final Judgment—A Discussion of the Parable of the Sheep and the Goats," *ExpT* 68 (1956): 46–50.

15. J. A. T. Robinson, "The 'Parable' of the Sheep and the Goats," *NTS* 2 (1956): 225–37, also published in *Twelve New Testament Studies* (Naperville, Ill.: A. R. Allenson, 1962), pp. 76–93, calls attention to this passage but does so for linguistic reasons.

16. Plummer, *St. Matthew*, p. 350. D. A. De Silva ("Renewing the Ethic of the Eschatological Community: The Vision of Judgment in Matthew 25," *KoinJ* 3 [1991]: 175) speaks of "those who bear the name but not the fruits of a disciple."

17. Manson, *Sayings*, p. 251. J. M. Court ("Right and Left: The Implications for Matthew 25.31–46," *NTS* 31 [1985]: 223–33) refers to non-Christians who are judged for rejecting Christian missionaries in Matthew's day. Although this rings true, his interpretation is too restrictive.

18. "There is, therefore, an exact correspondence between the character of their sin as 'without the law' and the final destruction visited upon them as also 'without the law,'" J. Murray, *The Epistle to the Romans* (Grand Rapids: Eerdmans, 1959), 1:70.

19. The perfect passive tense in the participles cursed *(katēramenoi)* and prepared *(hētoimasmenon)*, like the ones in Matt. 25:41, are perfects of resultant state, in which an act that took place in the past has validity in present and future.

20. For example, Isa. 33:14; 66:24; Matt. 5:22; 13:42, 50; 18:8, 9; Luke 16:19–31; Jude 7; Rev. 19:20; 20:10, 14, 15; 21:8.

21. L. Cope, "Matthew XXV:31–46. 'The Sheep and the Goats' Reinterpreted," *NovT* 11 (1969): 43.

22. J. Mánek, "Mit wem identifiziert sich Jesus? Eine exegetische Rekonstruktion ad Matt. 25:31–46," in *Christ and Spirit in the New Testament*, ed. B. Lindars and S. S. Smalley (Cambridge: Cambridge University Press, 1973), p. 19.

23. A number of commentators see the hidden Christ confronting us in the needy and unfortunate people of the world. For example, Hunter, *Parables*, p. 118; Armstrong, *Parables*, p. 193.

24. Mánek, "Exegetische Rekonstruktion," p. 22; Mánek, *Frucht*, p. 79.

25. Matt. 5:47; 12:48; 18:15; 23:8; 28:10.

26. Manson, *Sayings*, p. 217.

27. For example, Dan. 7:9, 10; Rev. 20:11–15.

Chapter 23: Two Debtors

1. Jeremias, *Parables*, p. 126.

2. The custom of anointing someone with oil goes back to antiquity. Pss. 23:5; 45:7; 104:15; Ezek. 23:41; Amos 6:6. Daniel-Rops, *Palestine*, p. 208.

3. A servant would take the sandals of the guests and keep them until the end of the meal. A. C. Bouquet, *Everyday Life in New Testament Times* (New York: Scribner, 1954), p. 71.

4. Daniel-Rops, *Palestine*, p. 207.

5. Derrett, *Law in the New Testament*, p. 268.

6. Some manuscripts have the definite article before "prophet." The expression *"the prophet"* would then refer to the great prophet whom God would raise up (Deut. 18:15).

7. Marshall, *Luke*, p. 309; Calvin, *Institutes of the Christian Religion*, III.4.33 (Grand Rapids: Eerdmans, 1944), p. 722.

8. Jeremias, *Parables*, p. 127, points out that the Hebrew, Aramaic, and Syriac languages have no word for "thank" and "thankfulness." The concept is expressed by means of such words as love or bless.

9. H. Drexler, "Die grosze Sünderin Lucas 7, 36–50," *ZNW* 59 (1968): 166.

10. Some Roman Catholics understand the text (Luke 7:47) to say that love merits forgiveness. The NAB translates the text as follows, "I tell you, that is why her many sins are forgiven—because of her great love." See also the NJB. The NRSV reads, "Therefore, I tell you, her sins, which are many, have been forgiven; hence she has shown great love." Blomberg (*Interpreting the Parables*, p. 185 n. 39) refers to "a long list of Roman Catholic

scholars, both ancient and modern, who agree with the interpretation" that the woman believed in Christ prior to coming to Simon's house and that Jesus made that fact public.

11. With thanks to Hunter, *Parables*, p. 55.

12. Morris, *Luke*, p. 149.

Chapter 24: Good Samaritan

1. Matt. 19:16. For rabbinic sources, consult *SB*, I:808.

2. Deut. 6:5 and Lev. 19:18.

3. B. Gerhardsson, *The Good Samaritan—The Good Shepherd?* (Lund, Copenhagen: Gleerup, 1958), p. 7. When a Jewish soldier loses his life in armed conflict, the nation mourns because a *brother* has died.

4. E. F. F. Bishop, "People on the Road to Jericho. The Good Samaritan—and the Others," *EvQ* 42 (1970): 2.

5. The phrase "ascent of blood" may be a corruption of the Hebrew "going up to Adummim." Consult Bishop, "People on the Road to Jericho," p. 3. Also see Josh. 15:7 and 18:17; Bishop, "Down from Jerusalem to Jericho" *EvQ* 35 (1963): 97–102.

6. Stories of highway robberies along the Jericho road have been recorded from ancient times to the present. For example, see Jerome's commentary on Jer. 3:2.

7. Jericho was one of the cities with a high concentration of priests who had taken up residence in the "city of palms." *SB*, II:66, 182.

8. Rev. 6:6: "do not damage the oil and the wine." Oil and wine made up a first aid kit in ancient times. *SB*, I:428. The oil soothed and the wine was antiseptic.

9. The two silver coins were two denarii, an amount sufficient for several days of room and board. In the parable of the workers in the vineyard (Matt. 20:1–16), the laborer's daily wage is one denarius.

10. C. Daniel, "Les Esséniens et l' arriére-fond historique de la parabole du Bon Samaritan," *NovT* 11 (1969): 71–104, portrays the victim as an Essene who was robbed by Zealots. The Zealots hated the Essenes. Likewise the priest and Levite bypassed the man because they belonged to a different religious order. However, does Jesus merely teach a lesson to condemn the hatred of rival religious sects? If so, he would have been more explicit. It is well to assume that the man was a Jew, because that is what the initial audience would have understood Jesus to mean. See also B. Reicke, "Der barmherzige Samariter," in *Verborum Veritas*, Festschrift honoring G. Stählin (Wuppertal: Brockhaus, 1970), p. 107.

11. Lev. 21:1; Num. 19:11.

12. Derrett, "Law in the New Testament: Fresh Light on the Parable of the Good Samaritan," *NTS* 11 (1964–1965): 22–37, published in *Law in the New Testament* (London: Longman and Todd, 1970), pp. 208–27. K. E. Bailey (*Through Peasant Eyes* [Grand Rapids: Eerdmans, 1980], p. 45) notes that a priest who contracted uncleanness would have to endure humiliation and would have to buy and reduce to ashes a red heifer for the purification ritual that "took a full week."

13. The motives for the attitude of priest and Levite have been discussed by many exegetes. But explanations by and large rest on assumptions, because Jesus does not specify the reason the clergy refused to help. By deliberately refraining from giving the reason, he keeps the parable from becoming an outright attack on the religious establishment of his day. Instead, he attacks the failure to show mercy. See Oesterley, *Parables*, p. 162; H. Zimmerman, "Das Gleichnis vom barmherzigen Samariter: Lukas 10, 25–37," in *Die Zeit Jesu*, Festschrift honoring H. Schlier (Freiburg, Basel, Vienna, 1970), p. 69; Jeremias, *Parables*, pp. 203–4; Michaelis, *Gleichnisse*, p. 208.

14. Josephus, *Antiquities*, 18:30.

15. *SB*, I:538. Matt. 10:5; Luke 9:52, 53; John 4:9. In the Jewish synagogue services, Samaritans were cursed. The Jews prayed that God would exclude them from the life here-

after. The Jews slandered Jesus by asking him, "Aren't we right in saying that you are a Samaritan and demon-possessed?" (John 8:48). See Stein, *Parables of Jesus*, p. 76.

16. Mánek, *Frucht*, p. 87.

17. Bailey, *Through Peasant Eyes*, p. 52.

18. F. Scott Spencer ("2 Chronicles 28:5–15 and the Parable of the Good Samaritan," *WTJ* 46 [1984]: 317–49) calls attention to the parallel of parables and the Chronicles passage. He constructs the following structural patterns (pp. 325–26):

Luke 10:30–35

1 Victim attacked by robbers (v 30)
2 Victim neglected by priest (v 31)
2' Victim neglected by Levite (v 32)
1' Victim ministered to by Samaritan (vv 33–35)

2 Chronicles 28:2–15

1 Victims attacked by northern armies (vv 5–8)
2 Prophet's response to victims (vv 9–11)
2' Leader's response to victims (vv 12–13)
1' Victims ministered to by Israelites (vv 14–15)

See also K. E. Bailey, *Poet and Peasant* (Grand Rapids: Eerdmans, 1976), pp. 72–74; B. Van Elderen, "Another Look at the Parable of the Good Samaritan," in *Saved by Hope*, ed. J. I. Cook (Grand Rapids: Eerdmans, 1978), pp. 109–19.

19. Mánek, *Frucht*, p. 88, considers the parable a Midrash, commentary, or sermon on the Word of God recorded in Hosea 6:6, "For I desire mercy, not sacrifice." Likewise, Derrett, *Law in the New Testament*, p. 227.

20. Derrett, *Law in the New Testament*, pp. 222–23, points out that Jesus "plays a role similar to that of Moses."

21. Jesus' word, "Do this and you will live" is reminiscent of Deut. 5:33; 6:24; Lev. 18:5.

22. Linnemann, *Parables*, p. 52.

23. Armstrong, *Parables*, p. 165.

24. Lev. 19:34. Also see Michaelis, *Gleichnisse*, p. 210.

25. Hunter, *Parables*, p. 111.

26. Augustine, *Quaestiones Evangeliorum*, II, 19. Dodd, *Parables*, pp. 11–12. Consult Mánek, *Frucht*, pp. 88–89, for a useful survey of modern interpretations. And see Gerhardsson, *Good Samaritan*, pp. 1–31, for an elaborate study of possible verbal derivatives; J. Daniélou, "Le Bon Samaritain," in *Mélanges Bibliques rédigés en l' honneur de A. Robert* (Paris, 1956), pp. 454–93; H. Binder, "Das Geheimnis vom barmherzigen Samariter," *TZ* 15 (1959): 176–94.

27. Morris, *Luke* (Grand Rapids: Eerdmans, 1974), p. 191. W. Monselewski, *Der barmherzige Samariter. Eine auslegungsgeschichtiliche Untersuchung zu Lukas 10, 25–37* (Tübingen: Mohr-Siebeck, 1967), p. 16. G. Bray, *Biblical Interpretation: Past and Present* (Downers Grove, Ill., and Leicester: InterVarsity, 1996), p. 505.

Chapter 25: Friend at Midnight

1. Translations of Luke 11:5 differ in regard to the word *friend*. The NIV translates, "Suppose one of you has a friend, and he goes to him at midnight. . . ." But the REB reads as follows, "Suppose one of you has a friend who comes to him in the middle of the night. . . ." Is the friend the neighbor who lends bread, or is he the hungry traveler? It is really a question of who was a friend to whom.

2. Traveling during the night was common in the time of Jesus: the wise men traveled at night, and so did Joseph, Mary, and the baby Jesus (see Matt. 2:9, 14).

3. Cooking was normally done outside, or under a lean-to. See Daniel-Rops, *Palestine*, p. 220.

4. Dalman, *Arbeit und Sitte*, VII:70–72, 178–79; Armstrong, *Parables*, p. 80; Jeremias, *Parables*, p. 157.

5. Bailey, *Poet and Peasant*, p. 123.

6. The Greek word *anaideia* occurs only here in the entire New Testament. It may be translated as "shamelessness" to describe the impudence of the man who awoke his neighbor. Jeremias (*Parables*, p. 158) and Marshall (*Luke*, p. 465) allow the possibility that shamelessness may extend to the neighbor, too, for refusing his friend's request. The word then conveys the meaning of "not losing one's face." The neighbor therefore granted the request because he did not wish to bring shame on his house by his refusal. See also Bailey (*Poet and Peasant*, p. 133), who ascribes "avoidance of shame" not to the host but to the neighbor.

7. This rule, called *Kal Wa-homer* (from less important to the more important), was one of the seven hermeneutical rules compiled by Rabbi Hillel (c. 60 B.C.–A.D. 20). H. L. Strack, *Introduction to the Talmud and Midrash* (New York: Meridian, 1969), pp. 93–94.

8. N. Levison (*The Parables: Their Background and Local Setting* [Edinburgh: Clark, 1926], p. 84) writes the point of the parable is "that God is sure to help us when we are helpless ourselves."

9. Blomberg, *Interpreting the Parables*, p. 275.

10. Heidelberg Catechism, Question 129.

Chapter 26: Rich Fool

1. Ps. 133:1. Josephus indicates that the Essenes gave up the right to private property by living together, as brothers do on a family estate. *Wars*, 2:122.

2. Jews would appeal to rabbis and refer to Scripture, Num. 27:1–7; 36:2–10; Deut. 21:15–17.

3. Exod. 2:14; Acts 7:27, 35. The Gospel of Thomas, Saying 72, only pictures Jesus as a divider: "A man said to him: Speak to my brothers that they may divide my father's possessions with me. He said to him: O man, who made me a divider? He turned to his disciples and said to them: I am not a divider, am I?"

4. Col. 3:5.

5. 1 Cor. 6:9, 10. J. D. M. Derrett, "The Rich Fool: A Parable of Jesus Concerning Inheritance," in *Studies in the New Testament* (Leiden: Brill, 1978), 2:103.

6. Compare the parable to the story of Nabal, who in word and deed showed himself a slave to his possessions. 1 Sam. 25:11.

7. Prov. 3:10; Deut. 28:8.

8. Derrett, "The Rich Fool," p. 112.

9. Compare Ecclesiasticus 11:19.

10. Pss. 14:1; 53:1.

11. The parable of the rich fool in the Gospel of Thomas, Saying 63, differs in emphasis and scope from the canonical account: "Jesus said: There was a rich man who had many possessions. He said, I will use my possessions that I may sow and reap and plant and fill my storehouses with fruit so that I may lack nothing. These were his thoughts in his heart. And in that night he died. He who has ears, let him hear."

12. Derrett, "The Rich Fool," p. 114.

13. Ps. 24:1.

14. The general context obviously points to the teaching of the Sermon on the Mount. Therefore, the parable may be seen as an elaboration of Jesus' instruction not to store up treasures on earth but in heaven (Matt. 6:19, 20).

Chapter 27: Barren Fig Tree

1. 1 Kings 4:25; Micah 4:4.

2. Jer. 8:13; Hosea 9:10; Hab. 3:17.

3. The parable is reminiscent of that recorded in Isa. 5:1–7. Choice vines were planted in a vineyard on a fertile hill. Yet after all the care lavished on the vines, they yielded wild grapes. Also see the story of Ahikar. A father says to his son: "My son, you are like a tree which yielded no fruit, although it stood by the water, and its owner was forced to cut it down. And it said to him, Transplant me, and if even I bear no fruit, cut me down. But its owner said to it, When you stood by the water you bore not fruit; how then will you bear fruit if you stand in another place?" Jeremias, *Parables*, p. 170; Charles, *Apocrypha and Pseudepigrapha*, 2:775.

4. Isa. 34:4; Jer. 5:17; 8:13; Hosea 2:12; Joel 1:17.

5. Mánek, *Frucht*, p. 93.

6. The parable may be seen symbolically fulfilled in the cursing of the fig tree (Matt. 21:18, 19; Mark 11:12–14). It is rather striking that only Luke has recorded the parable of the barren fig tree; and of the Synoptic evangelists he is the one who does not have the account of Jesus cursing the fig tree.

7. J. Murray, *The Epistle to the Romans* (Grand Rapids: Eerdmans, 1965), 2:47.

Chapter 28: Places of Honor at the Table

1. *SB*, II:202.

2. A. Edersheim, *The Life and Times of Jesus the Messiah* (Grand Rapids: Eerdmans, 1953), 2:207. See also Morris, *Luke*, p. 231. Plummer, *St. Luke*, p. 356; *SB*, IV:2, 618.

3. For example, Matt. 18:4; 23:12; Rom. 12:15; 1 Peter 5:6.

4. Teachers of the Law were notorious for taking places of honor at banquets. See Matt. 23:6 and parallels Mark 12:39; Luke 20:46.

5. *Midrash Rabbah Leviticus*, I, 5 (London, 1961), p. 9.

Chapter 29: Great Supper

1. The practice of sending a servant to invited guests was rather common in ancient times. Esther 6:14; *SB*, I:880.

2. Schippers, *Gelijkenissen*, p. 45.

3. The farmer who bought five yoke of oxen owned vast tracts of land, most likely in excess of 45 hectares (111 acres). Jeremias, *Parables*, p. 177.

4. H. Palmer, "Just Married, Cannot Come," *NovT* 18 (1976): 241–57. See especially p. 248. The Gospel of Thomas, Saying 64, has an expanded sequence of excuses. The first excuse is, "Some merchants owe me some money; they will come to me this evening; I will go and give them orders. I pray to be excused from the dinner." The second guest said, "I have bought a house, and they request me for a day; I will have no leisure." The third said, "My friend will celebrate a wedding and I am to direct the banquet. I pray to be excused from the banquet." The fourth guest excused himself by saying, "I have bought a village; I go to collect the rent; I will not be able to come. I pray to be excused."

5. Plummer, *St. Luke*, p. 360.

6. Hunter, *Parables*, p. 94; Linnemann, *Parables*, p. 91.

7. Perhaps the distinction between the destitute who live in the town and those who are out in the country applies to the erring Jew who is "not far from the kingdom" and the Gentile devoid of religious instruction.

8. Palmer, "Just Married," p. 256.

9. E. Schürer, *A History of the Jewish People in the Time of Jesus Christ*, Division II, vol. I (Edinburgh: T. & T. Clark, 1885), p. 324.

10. Palmer, "Just Married," p. 256.

11. Morris, *Luke*, p. 234. P. H. Ballard, "Reasons for Refusing the Great Supper," *JTS* 23 (1972): 345.

12. Jeremias, *Parables*, p. 179, asserts that "the host is to be understood as a tax-gatherer who has become wealthy, and has sent out invitations in the hope that he may in this way be fully accepted in the highest circles." He bases this on the conviction that Jesus made use of a story current in his day of a rich tax collector, Bar Ma'jan, recorded in the Palestinian Talmud (J. Sanh. 6.23c par. J. Hagh 2.77d). It is debatable, however, whether the parable indeed goes back to the story of the tax collector. Linnemann, *Parables*, pp. 160–62; F. Hahn, "Das Gleichnis von der Einladung zum Festmahl," *Verborum Veritas*, p. 67; Derrett, *Law in the New Testament*, p. 143.

13. Derrett, *Law in the New Testament*, p. 141, contends that a host would send portions of a meal to friends who could not attend the banquet. By giving the food to the poor, the host withheld "even a token of recognition and continuing reciprocity."

14. Michaelis, *Gleichnisse*, p. 158. Stein (*Parables of Jesus*, p. 88) thinks it must be seen as "an eschatological proclamation rather than as an apologetical defense."

15. O. Glombitza, "Das Grosse Abendmahl. Luk XIV 12–24," *NovT* 5 (1962): 15.

16. Palmer, "Just Married," p. 253.

17. Consult K. E. Bailey, *Through Peasant Eyes* (Grand Rapids: Eerdmans, 1980), pp. 91, 106–9; Manson, *Sayings*, p. 130; Fitzmyer, *Luke X–XXIV*, p. 1053.

18. Wallace, *Parables*, p. 69.

Chapter 30: Tower Builder and Warring King

1. The theme "cost of discipleship" is elucidated in the book with that title by Dietrich Bonhoeffer. In this work, Bonhoeffer speaks of self-surrender and self-sacrifice to which he personally gave testimony when he was executed on April 9, 1945, in a German prison.

2. Smith, *Parables*, p. 220, reasons that because of the reference to the cost of the foundation, "some more substantial erection than the watch-tower of a vineyard is contemplated, perhaps a farm-building."

3. The Gospel of Thomas, Saying 98, has an interesting parallel to the parable of the warring king: "Jesus said: The kingdom of the Father is like a man who wanted to kill a powerful man. He drew the sword within his house and ran it through the wall, so that he might know whether his hand would be strong enough. Then he killed the powerful man."

4. P. G. Jarvis, "Expounding the Parables. V. The Tower-Builder and the King Going to War (Luke 14:25–33)," *ExpT* 77 (1966): 197; J. D. M. Derrett, "Nisi Dominus Aedificaverit Domum: Towers and Wars (Lk XIV 28–32)," *NovT* 19 (1977): 249–58. Both Jarvis and Derrett make God the subject of these two parables instead of Jesus' followers. This exegesis misses the point of the parables, namely, the cost of following Jesus calls for wholehearted commitment.

Chapter 31: Lost Sheep

1. Marshall, *Luke*, p. 600; Plummer, *St. Luke*, p. 368. For a detailed study, consult J. Jeremias, "Tradition und Redaktion in Lukas 15," *ZNW* 62 (1971): 172–89.

2. E. F. F. Bishop, "The Parable of the Lost or Wandering Sheep," *ATR* 44 (1962): 50.

3. M. Black, *An Aramaic Approach to the Gospels and Acts*, 3d ed. (Oxford: Clarendon, 1967), p. 133, suggests that the word *mountain* may have been influenced by the Aramaic *tura*, "which in Palestinian Syriac has the twofold use of 'mountain' and 'country,' the 'open country' as contrasted with inhabited places."

4. Bailey, *Poet and Peasant*, p. 149. See also Smith, *Parables*, p. 188 n. 2. Levison (*Parables*, p. 152) notes that in the Middle East he has never seen "a flock attended by a single person."

5. Armstrong, *Parables*, p. 185.

6. Jeremias, *Parables*, p. 134; and Brouwer, *Gelijkenissen*, pp. 225–26, portray the shepherd with a sheep around his neck, grasping front and hind legs with each hand. Also see *SB*, II:209; Kenneth E. Bailey, *Finding the Lost: Cultural Keys to Luke 15* (St. Louis: Concordia, 1992), p. 74.

7. The Gospel of Thomas, Saying 107, shows a Gnostic trend in the parable by stressing the shepherd's love for the one sheep because of its size: "Jesus said: The kingdom is like a shepherd who had a hundred sheep. One of them went astray; it was the largest. He left the ninety-nine and sought for the one until he found it. After he had exerted himself, he said to the sheep, I love you more than the ninety-nine."

8. Morison, *St. Matthew*, p. 317.

9. Jeremias, *Parables*, p. 39, translates Matt. 18:14 as follows, "Thus it is not the will of God that even one of the very least should be lost." He applies the expression "very least" to apostates with whom the Christian community should deal pastorally (p. 40).

10. K. H. Rengstorf, *TDNT*, I:327–28, provides a twofold interpretation of the word *sinner* as it was understood by the Jewish hierarchy. (1) A sinner is "a man who lives in conscious or witting opposition to the divine will (Torah) as distinct from the righteous who makes submission to this will the content of his life." And (2) he is the man "who does not subject himself to the Pharisaic ordinances."

11. The religious rulers of that and the following century spoke more about God's joy over the destruction of the unrighteous than over their salvation. *SB*, II:209.

12. Wallace, *Parables*, p. 52.

Chapter 32: Lost Coin

1. Some scholars question the order in which the parables are presented: Armstrong, *Parables*, pp. 182–83; Linnemann, *Parables*, p. 68. Oesterley, *Parables*, pp. 176–77, opposes any reversing of the order of the parables by stating the difference between the Western mind, which cares for logical sequence, and the oriental modes of thought, which cannot be bothered with logical symmetry.

2. Bishop, *Jesus of Palestine* (London: n.p., 1955), p. 191. Jeremias, *Parables*, p. 134.

3. J. Wilkinson, *Jerusalem as Jesus Knew It* (London: Thomas and Hudson, 1978), p. 28, comments on excavations in Nazareth of homes Jesus may have visited. He says, "The floors are uneven, being made of large smooth pieces of basalt with sizeable cracks between them. Even in the bright sunshine we can imagine the woman in the parable of Luke XV: 8 searching for her lost coin, especially in a room with basalt walls and floors, and small windows. No wonder she had to use a lamp." See J. D. M. Derrett, "Fresh Light on the Lost Sheep and the Lost Coin," *NTS* 26 (1979): 36–60.

4. Dalman, *Arbeit und Sitte*, VII:111–12.

5. A. F. Walls, "In the Presence of the Angels (Luke XV:10)," *NovT* 3 (1959): 316; *SB*, II:212.

Chapter 33: Lost Son

1. Jeremias, *Parables*, p. 128, states that the parable is not an allegory "but a story drawn from life." Also see Linnemann, *Parables*, p. 74; and Mánek, *Frucht*, p. 103. Hunter, *Parables*, p. 59, disagrees because "The father and his two sons . . . plainly have a representational significance." B. B. Scott (*Hear Then the Parable*, p. 112) points out that in Scripture the younger of two brothers is met with favor, for example, Cain and Abel, Ishmael and Isaac, Esau and Jacob.

2. G. Quell, *TDNT*, V:972–74; G. Schrenk, *TDNT*, V:978.

3. A parable remotely similar to that of the prodigal son comes from Rabbi Meir: "This can be compared to the son of a king who took to evil ways. The king sent a tutor to him

who appealed to him saying, 'Repent my son.' The son, however, sent him back to his father with the message, 'How can I have the effrontery to return? I am ashamed to come before you.' Thereupon his father sent back word, 'My son, is a son ever ashamed to return to his father? And is it not to your father that you will be returning.'" *The Midrash, Deuteronomy* (London: n.p., 1961), p. 53. Also consult F. W. Danker, *Jesus and the New Age* (St. Louis: Clayton, 1972), p. 170, for the text of a papyrus letter that contains a plea from a wayward son asking his mother to forgive him.

4. Emigration from Israel to the Diaspora was very common. It has been estimated that about eight times as many Jews (four million) lived in dispersion as in Israel (half a million). Jeremias, *Parables*, p. 129.

5. *SB*, II:212; see also Bailey (*Poet and Peasant*, p. 164), who notes that a father willingly may pass on the inheritance to his sons before his death, but that there is no evidence that this was ever done under pressure from any son. See also his *Finding the Lost*, pp. 113–14.

6. For a detailed discussion, consult Derrett, *Law in the New Testament*, p. 107.

7. Refer to K. H. Rengstorf (*Die Re-Investitur des Verlorenen Sohnes in der Gleichniserzählung Jesu Luk. 15, 11–32* [Köln, Opladen: Westdeutscher Verlag, 1967], pp. 19 and 22), who mentions the custom of cutting off someone in society.

8. The father may have followed the custom of that day, reflected in Ecclesiasticus 33:22–23: "In all that you do, keep the upper hand and allow no stain on your reputation. Let your life run its full course and then, at the hour of death, distribute your property" (REB).

9. W. Foerster, *TDNT*, I:507.

10. The Jews are strictly forbidden to raise pigs. "It is not right to breed pigs in any place whatever"; and, "Cursed be the man who would breed swine." Baba Kamma 82b, Nezikin I, *The Babylonian Talmud*, pp. 469–70.

11. Jeremias, *Parables*, p. 129, comments that the young man was "practically forced to renounce the regular practice of his religion."

12. Pods and seeds of the locust (carob) tree constituted fodder for cattle and pigs and at times were eaten by the poor. It is not necessary to say, as some scholars do, that the young man stole the pods in order to still his hunger. The universal truth, "Do not muzzle an ox while it is treading out the grain" (Deut. 25:4), is certainly applicable. Bailey (*Poet and Peasant*, p. 173) distinguishes the pods of the locust tree from the bitter berries of the wild carob shrub; he suggests that the prodigal ate not the pods but the bitter berries that had no food value. However, a farmer would seek to fatten his animals not with worthless fodder but with protein-laden feed. The clause, "but no one gave him anything," means that no human being gave him other food. See Fitzmyer, *Luke X–XXIV*, p. 1088.

13. Derrett, *Law in the New Testament*, p. 111.

14. The word *heaven* is a Jewish circumlocution for "God." *SB*, II:217. Bailey (*Finding the Lost*, pp. 132–38) redefines repentance as "acceptance to be found," that is, "something done for the believer." He finds the key to the prodigal's intentions in the words "he was 'looking out for number one,' namely himself." D. Buttrick (*Speaking Parables* [Louisville: Westminster / John Knox, 2000], p. 202) calls the prodigal's repentance a "soup kitchen conversion—he's hungry." But the text indicates that the younger son takes full responsibility by confessing his sin to both God and his father. The terms *repent* and *repentance*, although not present in this parable, are definitely implied and signify heartfelt regret for sins committed.

15. On a Jewish farm, three types of servants were employed: first, the bond-servant who belonged to his or her master's family and enjoyed numerous privileges; then, the lower class of manservants and maidservants (see Luke 12:45); and third, the temporary

hired help. The third category had more freedom than slaves had but at the same time less security. Consult Oesterley, *Parables*, pp. 185–86.

16. Michaelis, *Gleichnisse*, p. 138, thinks that the father was proud that his son wanted to go to a foreign land.

17. Schippers, *Gelijkenissen*, p. 170; H. Thielicke, *The Waiting Father* (New York: Harper, 1959), p. 28; Mánek, *Frucht*, p. 101.

18. In the account of David welcoming Absalom to the royal palace, the fatherly kiss symbolized forgiveness, 2 Sam. 14:33. Jeremias, *Parables*, p. 130.

19. Metzger, *Textual Commentary*, p. 139.

20. Compare Gen. 41:42. Joseph received a signet ring, robes of fine linen, and a gold chain from Pharaoh. Also see 1 Macc. 6:15.

21. Rengstorf, *Re-Investitur*, p. 29. E. R. Wendland notes that the prodigal's public elevation "is strikingly reminiscent of Joseph's elevation in Egypt (Gen. 41:41–43)." See his article, "Finding Some Lost Aspects of Meaning in Christ's Parables of the Lost—and Found (Luke 15)," *TrinJ* 17NS (1996): 46.

22. Bailey, *Poet and Peasant*, p. 187.

23. Rengstorf, *Re-Investitur*, p. 22, refers to the legal custom called *qeṣaṣah*, which is a cutting-off of a member of a Jewish community because of a conflict of interests. Derrett, *Law in the New Testament*, p. 116, remarks that this legal custom does not apply to the circumstances of the prodigal son because he was not penalized or ostracized by his family.

24. Consult L. Schottroff, "*Das Gleichnis vom Verlorenen Sohn,*" *ZTK* 68 (1971): 39–41.

25. Among others, J. T. Sanders, in "Tradition and Redaction in Lk XV: 11–32," *NTS* 15 (1968–1969): 433–38, argues for two separate parables. Also see J. J. O'Rourke, "Some Notes on Luke XV. 11–32," *NTS* 18 (1971–1972): 431–33; and Jeremias, "Tradition und Redaktion in Lukas 15," *ZNW* 62 (1971): 172–89, who refutes this stance. So does Tolbert, *Perspectives on the Parables*, pp. 98–100.

26. Rengstorf, *Re-Investitur*, p. 54, raises questions concerning the phrase "in the field." Does the phrase indicate that the son could not get along with his father and thus stayed away from the house?

27. Thielicke, *The Waiting Father*, p. 32.

28. Morris, *Luke*, p. 244.

29. The Greek word *teknon* (child) is much more affectionate than the word *huios* (son). The REB captures the meaning of *teknon* in its translation, "my boy."

30. Schippers, *Gelijkenissen*, p. 178.

31. To celebrate the prodigal's return "was a duty which the elder son had failed to recognize." Plummer, *St. Luke*, p. 379. Jeremias, *Parables*, p. 131, detects a reproachful tone of voice in the father's word to his son: "You ought to be glad and make merry, since it is *your* brother who has come home."

32. Thielicke, *The Waiting Father*, p. 29.

33. For a discussion of these questions, see Jülicher, *Gleichnisreden*, 2:364–65.

34. Bailey (*Finding the Lost*, pp. 194–211) and Wendland ("Lost Aspects," pp. 53–54) have listed and commented on some interesting similarities between the Shepherd psalm (Ps. 23) and the three parables in Luke 15.

Chapter 34: Shrewd Manager

1. In alphabetical order, recent representative literature is as follows: J. D. M. Derrett, "Fresh Light on St. Luke XVI; I. The Parable of the Unjust Steward," *NTS* 7 (1960–1961): 198–219, published in *Law in the New Testament* (London: Longman and Todd, 1970), pp. 48–77; J. D. M. Derrett, "Take Thy Bond . . . and Write Fifty (Luke XVI.6) The Nature of the Bond," *JTS* 23 (1972): 438–40, published in *Studies in the New Testament* (Leiden:

Brill, 1977), 1:1–3; J. A. Fitzmyer, "The Story of the Dishonest Manager (Luke 16:1–13)," *TS* 25 (1964): 23–42, published in *Essays on the Semitic Background of the New Testament* (London: Society of Biblical Literature, 1971), pp. 161–84; D. R. Fletcher, "The Riddle of the Unjust Steward: Is Irony the Key?" *JBL* 82 (1963): 15–30; T. Hoeren, "Das Gleichnis vom ungerechten Verwalter (Lukas 16, 1–8a)—zugleich ein Beitrag zur Geschichte der Restschuldbefreiung," *NTS* 41 (1995): 620–29; E. Kamlah, "Die Parabel vom ungerechten Verwalter (Luke 16:1ff) in Rahmen der Knechtsgleichnisse," in *Abraham Unser Vater*, Festschrift honoring O. Michel (Leiden: Brill, 1963), pp. 276–94; F. J. Moore, "The Parable of the Unjust Steward," *ATR* 47 (1965): 103–5; J. S. Kloppenborg, "The Dishonoured Master (Luke 16, 1–8a)," *Biblica* 70 (1989): 474–94; R. G. Lunt, "Expounding the Parables. III. The Parable of the Unjust Steward (Luke 16:1–15)," *ExpT* 77 (1966): 132–36; D. M. Parrott, "The Dishonest Steward (Luke 16.1–8a) and Luke's Special Parable Collection," *NTS* 37 (1991): 499–515; L. J. Topel, "On the Injustice of the Unjust Steward: Luke 16:1–13," *CBQ* 37 (1975): 216–27; F. E. Williams, "Is Almsgiving the Point of the 'Unjust Steward'?" *JBL* 83 (1964): 293–97.

2. Oesterley, *Parables*, pp. 192–203; Derrett, *Law in the New Testament*, p. 51; Fitzmyer, *Luke (X–XXIV)*, pp. 1097–99; Bock, *Luke 2*: 9:51–24–53, pp. 1329–30. Numerous Jewish traits and expressions are evident in the parable. Whether a non-Jewish audience understood the parable in Luke's day remains a question. The oral tradition existing alongside the written Gospel may have provided a key to a proper understanding of the parable. See Marshall, *Luke*, p. 615.

3. Bailey, *Poet and Peasant*, pp. 94–110; D. J. Ireland, *Stewardship and the Kingdom of God: An Historical, Exegetical, and Contextual Study of the Parable of the Unjust Steward in Luke 16:1–13*, NovT Supp 70 (Leiden: Brill, 1992), pp. 79–82; Blomberg, *Interpreting the Parables*, pp. 244–45.

4. Derrett, *Law in the New Testament*, p. 65.

5. Fitzmyer, *Essays*, p. 176.

6. Josephus, *Antiquities*, 18:157.

7. Derrett, *Studies*, I:1–3.

8. Derrett, *Law*, p. 71.

9. Fitzmyer (*Essays*, p. 177; *Luke [XXIV]*, p. 1098) is of the opinion that a manager received commissions on transactions. Because of these transactions he had become known as the dishonest steward. He habitually overpriced the debtors and pocketed the surplus. But when he on his own accord reduced the debts to the proper amounts, he gave up his own profits. But Derrett (*Law*, p. 74) indicates that all the money involving loan transactions belonged to the master. Note the wording of the question "How much do you owe *my master?*" Because the manager lacked financial resources, he made provisions for the immediate future.

10. By contrast, the minister of finance in the parable of the unmerciful servant (Matt. 18:21–35) fell on his knees and begged his master to be patient.

11. Ecclesiasticus 40:28 admonishes, "My son, do not live the life of a beggar; better die than beg" (REB).

12. *SB*, II:218, gives this calculation on the basis of Josephus, *Antiquities*, 8:57. Jeremias, *Parables*, p. 181, rounds this off to 800 gallons, which the translators of the NIV have adopted.

13. Dalman, *Arbeit und Sitte*, IV:192.

14. Ibid., III:155, 159. Also see Jeremias, *Parables*, p. 181; *SB*, II:218.

15. I. H. Marshall, "Luke XVI.8—Who Commended the Unjust Steward?" *JTS* 19 (1968): 617–19.

16. Derrett, *Law*, p. 73.

17. H. Drexler, "Zu Lukas 16:1–7," *ZNW* 58 (1967): 286–88, holds that because the master had been unfair to the manager by demanding an accounting and by dismissing him, the manager took revenge and cheated his master by summoning the debtors. S. I. Wright ("Parables on Poverty and Riches," in *The Challenge of Jesus' Parables*, Longenecker, ed., p. 227) points our that the appellation of *unrighteousness* applied to the manager "denotes an ordinary 'man of the world,' not a person of special wickedness." See also Ellis, *Luke*, p. 199.

18. The descriptive definite article and noun in the Greek *(tēs adikias)*, translated adjectivally in many versions, is the same in Luke 16:8 as in Luke 18:6.

19. Bailey, *Poet and Peasant*, pp. 100–101; Ireland, *Stewardship*, p. 80; Stein, *Parables of Jesus*, p. 109.

20. Hoeren, "Gleichnis," pp. 626–27.

21. Compare Kloppenborg, "Dishonoured Master," p. 483.

22. Parrott, "Dishonest Steward," p. 503.

23. M. Ball, "The Parables of the Unjust Steward and the Rich Man and Lazarus," *ExpT* 106 (1995): 329–30.

24. H. Preisker, "Lukas 16.1–7," *TLZ* 74 (1949): 85–92, contrasts the parable of the dishonest manager to that of the prodigal son. The manager remained enslaved to the power of money, whereas the prodigal son spent his money and repented.

25. Older translations, by following the Greek text verbatim, somehow obscure the meaning of the passage. The REB translates Luke 16:9 much the same as the NIV, "So I say to you, use your worldly wealth to win friends for yourselves, so that when money is a thing of the past you may be received into an eternal home." J. D. Stinson ("Friends of Mammon," *QR* 6 [1986]: 86) notes, "A friend of mammon is a person who treats money as something to be used when it suits him or her but who never is a vassal to mammon's power."

26. Derrett, *Law*, p. 74.

27. *SB*, II:221. Also consult Williams, "Almsgiving," p. 294; Lunt, "Parable," p. 134.

28. On the basis of studying the Qumran texts, the phrase "worldly wealth," the mammon of unrighteousness, is to be contrasted to heavenly wealth. Marshall, *Luke*, p. 621.

Chapter 35: Rich Man and Lazarus

1. Before Jesus' day a popular Egyptian folktale circulated depicting a rich man dressed in fine linen and a poor man on a straw mat, whose roles were reversed after death. See F. L. Griffith, *Stories of the High Priests of Memphis* (Oxford: n.p., 1900); and H. Gressmann, *Vom reichen Mann und armen Lazarus* (Berlin: n.p., 1918). This folktale was brought to Israel by Alexandrian Jews, was altered, and became part of Jewish lore. In this altered story a rich tax collector by the name of Bar Ma'jan and a poor teacher of the law were buried. After death, the teacher of the law strolled along the broad streams of paradise while the tax collector standing next to the water was unable to reach it to quench his thirst. G. Dalman, *Aramaische Dialektproben* (Leipzig: Deichert, 1927), pp. 33–34. The motif of the parable may have derived from these folktales, but the composition belongs to Jesus. Fitzmyer, *Luke X–XXIV*, p. 1127.

2. The purple dye was extracted from the purple snail. *SB*, II:220.

3. The name *Dives* is the Latin adjective for the word *rich* in all Latin versions. The rich man has been given such names as Amonofis, Finees, Finaeus, Nineue, and Neves in various manuscripts. H. J. Cadbury, "A Proper Name for Dives," *JBL* 81 (1962): 399–402; H. J. Cadbury, "The Name of Dives," *JBL* 84 (1965): 73; K. Grobel, ". . . Whose Name Was Neves," *NTS* 10 (1963–1964): 373–82. Metzger (*Textual Commentary*, p. 140) suggests that *horror vacui* (the dread of something missing) may have prompted scribes "to provide a name for the anonymous Rich Man."

4. The guests at a rich man's table used pieces of bread to dry off the grease on their fingers. These pieces could not be dipped into a meat or gravy dish and were not to be eaten by the guests. It was customary to throw them under the table. Oesterley, *Parables*, p. 205; Jeremias, *Parables*, p. 184.

5. Some scholars have sought to explain the name *Lazarus*. Consult R. Dunkerley, "Lazarus" *NTS* 5 (1958–1959): 321–37; J. D. M. Derrett, "Fresh Light on St. Luke XVI:11. Dives and Lazarus and the Preceding Sayings," *NTS* 7 (1960–1961): 364–480, published in *Law in the New Testament* (London, 1970), pp. 78–99; C. H. Cave, "Lazarus and the Lukan Deuteronomy," *NTS* 15 (1968–1969): 319–25. Compare L. Kreitzer, "Luke 16:19–31 and 1 Enoch 22," *ExpT* 103 (1992): 139–42.

6. The term *holpos* ("bosom") may be understood as an oriental expression for reclining at a feast or supper (John 13:23). It may also describe intimate fellowship (John 1:18). See T. W. Manson, *The Sayings of Jesus* (London: SCM, 1950), p. 299; *SB*, II:225–27.

7. Michaelis, *Gleichnisse*, p. 217.

8. Thirst and pain are the lot of those condemned to die separated from God. See 2 Esdras 8:59; 2 Enoch 10:1, 2.

9. In order to portray individuals in heaven and hell, Jesus used the imagery of human bodies and their functions, even though both Lazarus's and the rich man's bodies were buried on earth.

10. Paul in his Epistle to the Romans touches on this point when he writes: "It is not as though God's word had failed. For not all who are descended from Israel are Israel. Nor because they are his descendants are they all Abraham's children" (Rom. 9:6, 7).

11. R. F. Hock ("Lazarus and Micyllus: Greco-Roman Backgrounds to Luke 16:19–31," *JBL* 106 [1987]: 447–63) attempts to prove that the rich man lived self-indulgently and immorally. But the text does not say that (v. 19). R. Bauckham ("The Rich Man and Lazarus: The Parable and the Parallels," *NTS* 37 [1991]: 225–46) stays with the wording of the parable, namely, the rich man lived in luxury and Lazarus in poverty.

12. The Jew took pride in the fact that he was Abraham's descendant—Matt. 3:8, 9 and John 8:33–39. A Jew who was excommunicated might not claim Abraham as his father, but any Jew with some good deeds to his name belonged to Israel's covenant people and could call on father Abraham. See Oesterley, *Parables*, p. 208.

13. That Jesus taught a doctrine of hell in undisguised terms is evident from the many references to hellfire in the Gospels. Admittedly, the word for hell in these texts is the word *Gehenna* and not *Hades*. Jesus described hell as a place of punishment, so did the apostles. See among other passages Matt. 5:22, 29, 30; 7:19; 8:12; 10:28; 18:8, 9; 22:33; 25:41; and parallel verses.

14. Compare W. Vogels, "Having or Longing: A Semiotic Analysis of Luke 16:19–31," *É et T* 20 (1989):43.

15. Oesterley, *Parables*, p. 209, regards the doctrine of eternal damnation as anti-Christian. He asks whether Luke 16:26 is an interpolation and states that the passage "reads more smoothly without verse 26." Because he provides no textual evidence, such questioning is inadmissible and demonstrates a refusal to deal with the written Word of God. It is C. F. Evans, "Uncomfortable Words-V. (Luke 16:31)," *ExpT* 81 (1969–1970): 230, who writes: "To the present day the parable is appealed to as an authoritative ground for the belief that the state and status of the individual are irrevocably fixed at death."

16. The perfect tense of the Greek word *stērizō* in verse 26 denotes resultant state. Moreover, the *hopōs* construction implies purpose and not the result of something that occurred. Morris, *Luke*, p. 254; A. T. Robertson, *A Grammar of the Greek New Testament* (New York: Hodder & Stoughton, George H. Doran, 1919), p. 896.

17. Michaelis, *Gleichnisse*, p. 264 n. 151, suggests that Lazarus might appear in a dream or a vision to the rich man's brothers. However, if this were the case, the rich man himself could do this much more effectively.

18. The implication is not that a believer ought to go through life poverty-stricken in order to enter heaven. Abraham, during his life on earth, was numbered among the rich. The point at issue is man's relationship to God and his neighbor. Mánek, *Frucht*, p. 108.

19. Plummer, *St. Luke*, p. 397.

20. See J. Bretherton, "Lazarus of Bethany: Resurrection or Resuscitation?" *ExpT* 104 (1993): 169–73; K. Pierce, "The Lucan Origins of the Raising of Lazarus," *ExpT* 96 (1985): 358–61; Dunkerley, "Lazarus," p. 322.

21. Manson, *Sayings*, pp. 296–301, and Hunter, *Parables*, p. 114, suggest that the parable was addressed to the Sadducees because they deny the resurrection. This would be a helpful suggestion indeed, if the immediate context directly or indirectly referred to them.

22. Derrett, *Law*, p. 85, refers to the story of Dives and Lazarus as the "parable in reverse." Also see Oesterley, *Parables*, p. 203.

23. F. H. Capron, "Son in the Parable of the Rich Man and Lazarus," *ExpT* 13 (1901): 523.

24. Schippers, *Gelijkenissen*, p. 160.

25. Matt. 12:38; 16:1; Mark 8:11; Luke 11:16; John 6:30.

26. Schippers, *Gelijkenissen*, p. 161.

27. O. Glombitza, "Der reiche Mann und der arme Lazarus. Luk. XVI 19–31. Zur Frage nach der Botschaft des Textes," *NovT* 12 (1970): 173–74.

Chapter 36: Farmer and Servant

1. The adjective *unworthy* in the sentence "we are unworthy servants" does not convey the meaning of useless or unprofitable. It is more an expression of modesty in the sense of undeserving. "We are servants and deserve no credit" (NEB).

2. Matt. 18:1; 20:21; Mark 9:34; 10:37; Luke 9:46; 22:24; and see Matt. 23:11.

3. In the parable of the waiting servants (Luke 12:35–38), the master when he returns prepares a meal for his servants and waits on them.

4. Compare among other texts Ps. 61:12; Matt. 16:27; 2 Cor. 5:10; Rev. 22:12.

5. Manson, *Sayings*, p. 302; Bailey, *Through Peasant Eyes*, pp. 122–24.

Chapter 37: Unjust Judge

1. G. Schrenk, *TDNT*, I:375.

2. Derrett, "Law in the New Testament: The Unjust Judge," *NTS* 18 (1971–1972): 188, published in *Studies in the New Testament* (Leiden: Brill, 1977) 1:42.

3. According to Pharisaical law, the Jews were forbidden to go to non-Jewish courts. Paul indicates that in the early church this same rule should be followed (1 Cor. 5:12–6:8). People often went to a Gentile judge "if thereby, appealing to some political or fiscal argument, they could have their opponent's rights frustrated or could force him to do what the customary law would have left alone." Derrett, "Law in the New Testament," p. 184. Also consult Smith, *Parables*, p. 149.

4. Bailey (*Through Peasant Eyes*, p. 132; and *Poet and Peasant*, p. 132) points out that the concept *shame* has great significance in Middle Eastern culture.

5. Because marriages were contracted when a girl was fourteen or fifteen years of age, a widow could be rather young. Consult *SB*, II:374; Jeremias, *Parables*, p. 153.

6. Derrett, "Law in the New Testament," p. 187; Schrenk, *TDNT*, II:443.

7. Translations of the Greek word *hypōpiazē* vary, and range from expressing insult to committing acts of violence—"to hit under the eye." Derrett, "Law in the New Testament," p. 191, interprets the word to mean "losing prestige." It is, therefore, comparable to the

word *anaideia* in Luke 11:8, which may have the meaning of "losing one's face." See D. R. Catchpole, "The Son of Man's Search for Faith (Luke XVIII 8b)," *NovT* 19 (1977): 89. 1 Cor. 9:27 is the other place in the New Testament where the word *hypōpiazō* is used.

8. The expression "unjust judge" sets the stage for the contrast between unrighteousness personified in the worldly judge and God who listens to his chosen ones. See G. Delling, "Das Gleichnis vom gottlosen Richter," *ZNW* 53 (1962): 14.

9. See Bailey, *Through Peasant Eyes*, p. 140.

10. Delling, "Gleichnis," p. 15.

11. The language of the parable is reminiscent of Ecclesiasticus 35:12–20, which speaks about the justice of God. "For the Lord is a judge," says Jesus Ben-Sirach. "He never ignores the appeal of the orphan or the widow" (REB).

12. Many exegetes have tried to give a satisfactory explanation to Luke 18:7b. The abrupt change from the subjunctive mood in verse 7a to the indicative in verse 7b may mean that the verse consists of two independent sentences. The wording of the last part of verse 7 is similar to Ecclesiasticus 25:19. For interpretations of this verse, see H. Riesenfeld, "Zu *makrothumein* (Lk 18:7)," in *Neutestamentliche Aufsätze*, Festschrift honoring J. Schmid (Regensburg: Pustet, 1963), pp. 214–17; H. Ljungvik, "Zur Erklärung einer Lukas-Stelle (Luk. XVIII7)," *NTS* 10 (1963–1964): 289–94; A. Wifstrand, "Lukas xvii.7," *NTS* 11 (1964–1965): 72–74; C. E. B. Cranfield, "The Parable of the Unjust Judge and the Eschatology of Luke-Acts," *ScotJT* 16 (1963): 297–301; and Jeremias, *Parables*, p. 154; E. D. Freed, "The Parable of the Judge and the Widow (Luke 18:1–8)," *NTS* 33 (1987): 38–60.

13. Plummer, *St. Luke*, p. 414, comments that although the exact meaning cannot be determined, the import is clear enough; "however long the answer to prayer may *seem* to be delayed, constant faithful prayer always is answered."

14. Marshall, *Luke*, p. 676; Morris, *Luke*, pp. 263–64.

15. See Delling, "Gleichnis," p. 20; C. Spicq, "La parabole de la veuve obstinée et du juge inerte aux decisions impromptues (Lc. xviii 1–8)," *RB* 68 (1961): 82–83.

16. Linnemann, *Parables*, p. 121, boldly writes that the parable did not originate with Jesus; instead it is a word from the ascended Lord "spoken in the name and spirit of Jesus to the community of believers." Catchpole, "Son of Man's Search," p. 104, refutes her argument by showing the interrelatedness of parable and context. He concludes that in the parable "we hear the voice of the historical Jesus."

17. Delling, "Gleichnis," p. 24.

Chapter 38: Pharisee and Tax Collector

1. D. A. Hagner, "Pharisees," in *ZPEB*, 4:745–52.

2. Josephus, *War*, 1:110; Manson, *Sayings*, p. 309; *SB*, II:239.

3. Jeremias, *Parables*, p. 139 n. 38; Manson, *Sayings*, p. 309. Paul describes his former life as a Pharisee in his letter to the Philippians: "If anyone else thinks he has reasons to put confidence in the flesh, I have more: circumcised on the eighth day, of the people of Israel, of the tribe of Benjamin, a Hebrew of Hebrews; in regard to the law, a Pharisee; as for zeal, persecuting the church; as for legalistic righteousness, faultless" (Phil. 3:4–6).

4. The Greek manuscripts differ on the precise word order of *pros heauton*. Should this phrase be construed with the verb *to stand* or the verb *to pray*? The translation may either be "stood apart by himself and prayed" or "stood up and prayed to himself." The translators of the NIV have taken the second choice but with the following modification. They have understood the preposition *pros* in the sense of "about," although in the accompanying footnote they give the translation "to." *The Modern Language Bible* (New Berkeley) reads: "The Pharisee stood up and said this prayer for himself."

5. Lev. 16:29–31; 23:27–32; Num. 39:7; Jer. 36:6.

6. *SB*, II:241–44; *SB*, IV: 1, 77–114; J. Behm, *TDNT*, IV:924–35.

7. *SB*, II:244–46; Jeremias, *Parables*, p. 140. God told the farmer, "Be sure to set aside a tenth of all that your fields produce each year" (Deut. 14:22).

8. Berakoth 28b, Zeraim, *The Babylonian Talmud*, p. 172.

9. Jeremias, *Parables*, p. 143.

10. Consult the study on the verb *hilaskomai* by F. Büchsel, *TDNT*, III:316. *The Modern Language Bible* (New Berkeley) provides a literal translation of the Greek text, "God, be merciful to me, the sinner" (Luke 18:13).

11. Manson, *Sayings*, p. 312.

12. Mánek, *Frucht*, p. 113; Linnemann, *Parables*, p. 61.

13. Jeremias, *Parables*, p. 144.

14. F. F. Bruce, "Justification in Non-Pauline Writings of the New Testament," *EQ* 24 (1952): 68.

Chapter 39: Pounds

1. Matt. 11:5, 6; Luke 7:22.

2. Josephus, *War*, 1:668; *Antiquities*, 17:194.

3. Josephus, *War*, 2:80; *Antiquities*, 17:300.

4. Joseph took Jesus and Mary to Nazareth and not to Bethlehem because Archelaus was reigning *(basileuei)* in Judea, Matt. 2:22. In Mark 6:14, 22, 26, Herod Antipas is called king. M. Zerwick, "Die Parabel vom Thronanwärter," *Bib* 40 (1959): 662.

5. Josephus, *War*, 2:111; *Antiquities*, 17:339.

6. Considering the fluctuations of monetary values, translators express equivalencies in terms of a period of labor performed by a workingman.

7. Exod. 22:25; Lev. 25:35–37; Deut. 23:19, 20; Neh. 5:7; Ps. 15:5; Prov. 28:8; Ezek. 18:8, 13, 17; 22:12.

8. Derrett, *Law in the New Testament*, p. 23, indicates that charging high interest rates was not unheard of in the ancient world. By way of example, he refers to lending rates that Cato Elder charged.

9. Some scholars have conjectured that the word *cities* has entered the text because of a misunderstanding of the Aramaic word for talents. In Aramaic the two expressions are quite similar: cities is *kᵉrakin* and talents is *kakᵉrin*. E. Nestle suggested a possible misreading of the text in an article published in the *Theologische Literaturzeitung*, no. 22, 1895. M. Black, *Aramaic Approach*, p. 2, defends Nestle's suggestion, even though Dalman, *Words of Jesus*, p. 67, had pointed out that in the parallel of Matt. 25:21, 23, the servants are not given talents but are placed over many things. Luke has the word *cities* to express the general concept of many things. Moreover, a king entering his kingdom could endow servants with authority over cities, which a master (Matthew 25) could not do.

10. Luke uses the masculine definite article with *heteros* (another) in the sense of "different." Plummer, *St. Luke*, p. 441.

11. Morris, *Luke*, p. 275.

12. G. Harder, *TDNT*, VI:547, 554.

13. Textually it is debatable whether this verse is part of the parable or whether copyists inserted it into the text from a marginal note. Moreover, those witnesses (for example, D, W, 565 and some of the Latin, Syriac, and Coptic versions) that omit the verse may have done so because of the parallel in Matt. 25:28, 29 (which does not have it) or for stylistic reasons to provide a closer link between Luke 19:24 and 26. On the basis of external and internal evidence, however, it seems best to retain verse 25. Metzger, *Textual Commentary*, p. 144.

14. Derrett, *Law in the New Testament*, p. 28.

15. Whether the speaker in Luke 19:26 is the king or Jesus depends on the interpretation of the preceding verse. Plummer, *St. Luke*, p. 443. Because of the authoritative phrase "I tell you," the words seem to reflect a comment made by Jesus. Marshall, *Luke*, p. 708.

16. In similar form the saying occurs in Matt. 13:12; 25:29; Mark 4:25; and Luke 8:18.

17. Derrett, *Law in the New Testament*, p. 30.

18. F. D. Weinert, "The Parable of the Throne Claimant (Luke 19:12, 14–15a, 27) Reconsidered," *CBQ* 39 (1977): 505–14.

19. Ridderbos, *Coming of the Kingdom*, p. 515, comments that "it is hardly possible to explain" the parable of the pounds "in any other way than as a reference to Jesus' departure from earth to heaven, and to the vocation of the disciples on earth."

20. Plummer, *St. Luke*, p. 444.

21. Zerwick, "Thronanwärter," p. 667.

22. Compare L. Guy, "The Interplay of the Present and Future in the Kingdom of God (Luke 19:11–44)," *Tyn Bul* 48 (1997): 124–25.

Conclusion

1. 2 Sam. 12:1–4. Other examples are the parable of the woman from Tekoa (2 Sam. 14:4–7) and Jehoash's message to Amaziah (2 Kings 14:9).

2. Hunter, *Parables*, p. 15.

3. T. W. Manson, *The Teaching of Jesus* (Cambridge: Cambridge University Press, 1951), p. 69, counts a total of sixty-five parables. A. M. Hunter, *Interpreting the Parables* (Philadelphia: Westminster, 1960), p. 11, holds the number to "about 60."

4. J. Jeremias, *Unknown Sayings of Jesus* (London: SPCK, 1958), p. 2.

5. Jeremias, *Parables*, pp. 84–85, says that "it is impossible to avoid the conclusion that the interpretation of the parable of the tares is the work of Matthew himself." He comes to this conclusion on the basis of linguistic considerations.

6. Jülicher, *Gleichnisreden*, 2:385–406, considers the parable of the vineyard and the tenants a creation of the early church. Likewise, R. Bultmann, *The History of the Synoptic Tradition* (New York: Harper & Row, 1963), p. 177.

7. Marshall, *Eschatology and the Parables*, p. 11.

8. M. D. Goulder, "Characteristics of the Parables in the Several Gospels," *JTS* 19 (1968): 52.

9. Morris, *Luke*, p. 40.

10. Goulder, "Characteristics of the Parables," p. 55.

11. B. Gerhardsson, "The Seven Parables in Matthew XIII," *NTDS* 19 (1972–1973): 18.

12. Marshall, *Luke*, p. 401.

13. G. E. Ladd, "The Sitz im Leben of the Parables of Matthew 13: The Soils," in *Studia Evangelica*, ed. F. L. Cross (Berlin, 1964), 2:204.

14. Goulder, "Characteristics of the Parables," p. 56, wants to include the parable of the sower but can only do so by turning to its interpretation in succeeding verses. However, the parable itself shows no contrast.

15. A. Wikenhauser, *New Testament Introduction* (New York: Herder and Herder, 1965), p. 217.

16. Rom. 12:12; Eph. 6:18; Phil. 4:6; Col. 4:2; 1 Thess. 5:17.

17. P. T. O'Brien, "Prayer in Luke-Acts," *TB* 24 (1973): 118.

18. Ridderbos, *Coming of the Kingdom*, p. 132.

19. Linnemann, *Parables*, p. 35, in spite of all the evidence, asserts, "There can be found only a few, if any, parables, which Jesus directed explicitly to his disciples: most are spoken to his opponents, to men who took offense at his behaviour or were indignant at his sayings."

20. Jeremias, *Parables*, p. 41, allows for the assumption of Jesus repeating his parables to more than one audience. At the same time he intimates that both Matthew and Luke contradict themselves when they represent sayings of Jesus as addressed to the crowd in the one instance and to the disciples in the other. This judgment appears rather inappropriate in the light of the repetitive oral teaching of Jesus.

Select Bibliography

COMMENTARIES

Albright, W. F., and Mann, C. S. *Matthew*. New York: Doubleday, 1971.

Allen, W. C. *The Gospel according to St. Matthew (ICC)*. Edinburgh: T. & T. Clark, 1922.

Bock, D. L. *Luke, BECNT* 3ᴮ. Grand Rapids: Baker, 1996.

Calvin, J. *Harmony of the Evangelists*. 3 vols. Grand Rapids: Eerdmans, 1949.

Ellis, E. E. *The Gospel of Luke*. Longdon: Nelson, 1996.

Fitzmyer, J. A. *The Gospel according to Luke (X–XXIV), AB*, 2 vols. New York: Doubleday, 1985.

Godet, F. *Commentary on St. Luke's Gospel*. 2 vols. Edinburgh: T. & T. Clark, 1870.

Green, H. B. *The Gospel according to Matthew*. London: University Press, 1975.

Hendriksen, W. *The Gospel of Luke*. Grand Rapids: Baker, 1978.

———. *The Gospel of Mark*. Grand Rapids: Baker, 1975.

———. *The Gospel of Matthew*. Grand Rapids: Baker, 1973.

Lane, W. L. *The Gospel according to Mark*. Grand Rapids: Eerdmans, 1974.

Lenski, R. H. C. *Interpretation of St. Luke's Gospel*. Columbus: Wartburg, 1946.

———. *Interpretation of St. Mark's Gospel*. Columbus: Augsburg, 1946.

———. *Interpretation of St. Matthew's Gospel*. Columbus: Lutheran Book Concern, 1943.

McNeile, A. H. *The Gospel according to St. Matthew*. London: Macmillan, 1915.

Marshall, I. H. *The Gospel of Luke*. Grand Rapids: Eerdmans, 1978.

Morison, J. *A Practical Commentary on the Gospel according to St. Matthew*. Boston: Bartlett, 1884.

Morris, L. *The Gospel according to Luke*. Grand Rapids: Eerdmans, 1974.

Plummer, A. *Exegetical Commentary on the Gospel according to St. Matthew*. Grand Rapids: Eerdmans, 1956.

———. *The Gospel of Luke (ICC)*. New York: C. Scribner's Sons, 1902.

Swete, H. B. *The Gospel according to St. Mark*. London: Macmillan, 1908.

Van Bruggen, J. *Lucas: Het Evangelie als voorgeschiedenis*. Kampen: Kok, 1996.

STUDIES

Armstrong, E. A. *The Gospel Parables*. New York: Sheed & Ward, 1969.

Bailey, K. E. *Finding the Lost: Cultural Keys to Luke 15*. St. Louis: Concordia, 1992.

———. *Poet and Peasant*. Grand Rapids: Eerdmans, 1976.

———. *Through Peasant Eyes*. Grand Rapids: Eerdmans, 1980.

Bishop, E. F. F. *Jesus of Palestine*. London, 1955.

Blomberg, C. L. *Interpreting the Parables*. Downers Grove, Ill.: InterVarsity, 1990.

Bouquet, A. C. *Everyday Life in New Testament Times*. New York: Scribner, 1954.

Bray, G. *Biblical Interpretation: Past and Present*. Downers Grove, Ill. and Leicester: Inter-Varsity, 1996.

Brouwer, A. M. *De Gelijkenissen*. Leiden: Brill, 1946.

Bruce, A. B. *The Parabolic Teaching of Christ*. New York: A. C. Armstrong, 1908.

Buttrick, D. *Speaking Parables*. Louisville: Westminster/John Knox, 2000.

Crossan, J. D. *In Parables: The Challenge of the Historical Jesus*. New York: Harper & Row, 1973.

Daniel-Rops, H. *Daily Life in the Time of Jesus*. New York: Hawthorn, 1962.

Derrett, J. D. M. *Law in the New Testament*. London: Longman and Todd, 1970.

———. *Studies in the New Testament*. 2 vols. Leiden: Brill, 1977–1978.

Dodd, C. H. *The Parables of the Kingdom*. London: Nesbit, 1935.

Findlay, J. A. *Jesus and His Parables*. London: Epworth, 1951.

Gerhardsson, B. *The Good Samaritan—The Good Shepherd?* Lund, Copenhagen: Gleerup, 1958.

Gundry, R. H. *The Use of the Old Testament in St. Matthew's Gospel*. Leiden: Brill, 1967.

Hunter, A. M. *Interpreting the Parables*. Philadelphia: Westminster, 1960.

———. *The Parables Then and Now*. Philadelphia: Westminster, 1971.

Ireland, D. J. *Stewardship and the Kingdom of God: An Historical, Exegetical, and Contextual Study of the Parable of the Unjust Steward in Luke 16:1–13*. NovT Supp 70. Leiden: Brill, 1992.

Jeremias, J. *Parables of Jesus*. New York: Scribner, 1963.

Jülicher, A. *Die Gleichnisreden Jesu*. 2 vols. Tübingen: Buchgesellschaft, 1963.

Kingsbury, J. D. *The Parables of Jesus in Matthew 13*. Richmond: John Knox, 1969.

Levison, N. *The Parables: Their Background and Local Setting*. Edinburgh: Clark, 1926.

Linnemann, E. *Parables of Jesus*. London: SPCK, 1966.

Longenecker, R. N., ed. *The Challenge of Jesus' Parables*. Grand Rapids: Eerdmans, 2000.

McArthur, H. K., and R. M. Johnston, *They Also Taught in Parables: Rabbinic Parables from the First Centuries of the Christian Era*. Grand Rapids: Zondervan, Academie Books, 1990.

Mánek, J. *Und Brachte Frucht*. Stuttgart: Calwer, 1977.

Manson, T. W. *The Sayings of Jesus*. London: SCM, 1950.

Marshall, I. H. *Eschatology and the Parables*. London: Tyndale, 1963.

Michaelis, W. *Die Gleichnisse Jesu*. Hamburg: Furche-Verlag, 1956.

Oesterley, W. O. E. *The Gospel Parables in the Light of Their Jewish Background*. New York: Macmillan, 1936.

Ridderbos, H. N. *The Coming of the Kingdom.* Philadelphia: Presbyterian & Reformed, 1962.

———. *Studies in Scripture and Its Authority.* St. Catharines: Paideia, 1978.

Schippers, R. *Gelijkenissen van Jezus.* Kampen: J. H. Kok, 1962.

Scott, B. B. *Hear Then the Parable: A Commentary on the Parables of Jesus.* Minneapolis: Fortress, 1989.

Seagren, D. *The Parables.* Wheaton: Tyndale House, 1978.

Sider, J. W. *Interpreting the Parables.* Grand Rapids: Zondervan, 1995.

Smith, B. T. D. *The Parables of the Synoptic Gospels.* Cambridge, England: SPCK, 1937.

Stein, R. H. *An Introduction to the Parables of Jesus.* Philadelphia: Westminster, 1981.

Thielicke, H. *The Waiting Father.* New York: Harper, 1959.

Via, D. O. *The Parables.* Philadelphia: Fortress, 1967.

Wallace, R. S. *Many Things in Parables.* Grand Rapids: Eerdmans, 1963.

Wilkinson, J. *Jerusalem as Jesus Knew It.* London: Thames and Hudson, 1978.

Tools

Bauer, W.; Arndt, W. F.; Gingrich, F. W.; Danker, F. *A Greek-English Lexicon of the New Testament.* Chicago: University of Chicago Press, 1978.

Berkhof, L. *Principles of Biblical Interpretation.* Grand Rapids: Baker, 1964.

Black, M. *An Aramaic Approach to the Gospels and Acts.* Oxford: Clarendon, 1967.

Brown, C., ed. *New International Dictionary of New Testament Theology.* 3 vols. Grand Rapids: Zondervan, 1975–1978.

Charles, R. H. *Apocrypha and Pseudepigrapha of the Old Testament in English.* 2 vols. Oxford: Clarendon, 1977.

Epstein, I., ed. *The Babylonian Talmud.* 18 vols. (Soncino ed.). London: Soncino, 1948–1952.

Josephus, Flavius. The Loeb Classical Library edition. London and New York: Heinemann and Putnam, 1966–1976.

Kittel, G., and Friedrich, G., eds. *Theological Dictionary of the New Testament.* Translated by G. W. Bromiley. 9 vols. Grand Rapids: Eerdmans, 1964–1976.

Liddell, H. G., and Scott, R. *A Greek-English Lexicon.* Oxford: Clarendon, 1968.

Metzger, B. M. *A Textual Commentary on the Greek New Testament.* 2d ed. Stuttgart: Deutsche Bibelgesellschaft, 1994.

Mickelsen, A. B. *Interpreting the Bible.* Grand Rapids: Eerdmans, 1963.

Robertson, A. T. *A Grammar of the Greek New Testament.* New York: Hodder and Stoughton, George H. Doran, 1915.

Schürer, E. *A History of the Jewish People in the Time of Jesus Christ,* Division II, vol. I. Edinburgh: T. & T. Clark, 1885.

Strack, H. L., and Billerbeck, P. *Kommentar zum Neuen Testament aus Talmud und Midrasch.* 5 vols. München: Beck, 1922–1928.

Simon J. Kistemaker (Ph.D., Free University, Amsterdam) is emeritus professor of New Testament at Reformed Theological Seminary in Orlando, Florida. He is the author of numerous commentaries in Baker's New Testament Commentary Series, including the recently released volume on Revelation.